From Oslo to Iraq and the Roadmap

Edward W. Said

Foreword by Tony Judt
Afterword by Wadie E. Said

BLOOMSBURY

First published in Great Britain 2004
This paperback edition published 2005

Copyright © 2004 by the Estate of Edward W. Said
Foreword copyright © 2004 by Tony Judt
Afterword copyright © 2004 by Wadie E. Said

All chapters originally appeared in essay form in *Al-Ahram*,
Al-Hayat, or *The London Review of Books*

Maps by the Foundation for Middle East Peace and Jan de Jong

The moral right of the author has been asserted

A CIP catalogue record for this book
is available from the British Library

Bloomsbury Publishing Plc, 38 Soho Square, London W1D 3HB

ISBN 0 7475 7662 9
9780747576624

10 9 8 7 6 5 4 3 2 1

All papers used by Bloomsbury Publishing are natural,
recyclable products made from wood grown in well-managed forests.
The manufacturing processes conform to the
environmental regulations of the country of origin.

Printed by Clays Ltd, St Ives plc

www.bloomsbury.com/edwardsaid

CONTENTS

Contents

PART THREE   Israel, Iraq, and the United States

When Edward Said died in September 2003, after a decade-long battle against leukemia, he was probably the best-known intellectual in the world. *Orientalism*, his controversial account of the appropriation of the East in modern European thought and literature, has spawned an academic subdiscipline in its own right: a quarter of a century after its first publication it continues to generate irritation, veneration, and imitation. Even if its author had done nothing else, confining himself to teaching at Columbia University in New York—where he was employed from 1963 until his death—he would still have been one of the most influential scholars of the late twentieth century.

But he did not confine himself. From 1967, and with mounting urgency and passion as the years passed, Edward Said was also an eloquent, ubiquitous commentator on the crisis in the Middle East and an advocate for the cause of the Palestinians. This moral and political engagement was not really a displacement of Said's intellectual attention—his critique of the West's failure to understand Palestinian humiliation closely echoes, after all, his reading of nineteenth-century scholarship and fiction in *Orientalism* and subsequent books (notably *Culture and Imperialism*, published in 1993). But it transformed the professor of comparative literature at Columbia into a very public intellectual, adored or execrated with equal intensity by many millions of readers.

This was an ironic fate for a man who fitted almost none of the moulds to which his admirers and enemies so confidently assigned him. Edward Said lived all his life at a tangent to the various causes with which he was associated. The involuntary "spokesman" for the overwhelmingly Moslem Arabs of Palestine was an Episcopalian Christian, born in 1935 to a Baptist from Nazareth. The uncompromising critic of imperial condescension was educated in some of the last of the colonial schools that had trained the indigenous elite of the European Empires;

for many years he was more at ease in English and French than in Arabic and an outstanding exemplar of a Western education with which he could never fully identify.

Edward Said was the idolized hero of a generation of cultural relativists in universities from Berkeley to Bombay, for whom "orientalism" underwrote everything from career-building exercises in "post-colonial" obscurantism ("writing the other") to denunciations of "Western Culture" in the academic curriculum. But Said himself had no time for such nonsense. Radical anti-foundationalism, the notion that everything is just a linguistic effect, struck him as shallow and "facile": human rights, as he observed on more than one occasion, "are not cultural or grammatical things, and when violated they are as real as anything we can encounter."[1]

As for the popular account of his thought which has Edward Said reading (Western) writers as mere by-products of colonial privilege, he was quite explicit: "I do not believe that authors are mechanistically determined by ideology, class, or economic history." Indeed, when it came to the business of reading and writing Said was an unabashedly traditional humanist, "despite the scornful dismissal of the term by sophisticated post-modern critics."[2] If there was anything that depressed him about younger literary scholars it was their over familiarity with "theory" at the expense of the art of close textual reading. Moreover, he enjoyed intellectual disagreement, seeing the toleration of dissent and even discord within the scholarly community as the necessary condition for the latter's survival—my own expressed doubts about the core thesis of *Orientalism* were no impediment to our friendship. This was a stance that many of his admirers from afar, for whom academic freedom is at best a contingent value, were at a loss to comprehend.

This same, deeply felt humanistic impulse put Edward Said at odds with another occasional tic of engaged intellectuals, the enthusiastic endorsement of violence—usually at a safe distance and always at someone else's expense. The "Professor of Terror," as his enemies were wont to

1. See Edward Said, *Humanism and Democratic Criticism* (New York: Columbia University Press, 2004), pp. 10, 136.
2. See Edward Said, *Culture and Imperialism* (New York: Vintage Books, 1994), p. xxii; Edward Said, *Orientalism*, "Preface to the Twenty-fifth Anniversary Edition" (New York: Vintage Books, 1994), p. xxiii.

characterize Said, was in fact a consistent critic of political violence in all its forms. Unlike Jean-Paul Sartre, a comparably influential intellectual for the previous generation, Said had some firsthand experience of physical force—his university office was vandalized and sacked, and both he and his family received death threats. But whereas Sartre did not hesitate to advocate political murder as both efficacious and cleansing, Said never identified with terrorism, however much he sympathized with the motives and sentiments that drove it. The weak, he wrote, should use means that render their oppressors uncomfortable—something that indiscriminate murder of civilians can never achieve.[3]

The reason for this was not that Edward Said was placid or a pacifist, much less someone lacking in strong commitments. Notwithstanding his professional success, his passion for music (he was an accomplished pianist, a close friend and sometime collaborator of Daniel Barenboim), and his gift for friendship, he was in certain ways a deeply angry man—as the essays in this book frequently suggest. But despite his identification with the Palestinian cause and his inexhaustible efforts to promote and explain it, Said quite lacked the sort of un-interrogated affiliation to a country or an idea that allows the activist or the ideologue to subsume any means to a single end.

Instead he was, as I suggested, always at a slight tangent to his affinities. In this age of displaced persons he was not even a typical exile, since most men and women forced to leave their country in our time have a place to which they can look back (or forward): a remembered—more often mis-remembered—homeland that anchors the transported individual or community in time if not in space. Palestinians don't even have this. There never was a formally-constituted Palestine, and Palestinian identity thus lacks that conventional anterior reference.

---

3. In his 1961 preface to the French edition of Frantz Fanon's *The Wretched of the Earth*, Sartre described the violence of anticolonial revolutions as "man recreating himself . . . to shoot down a European is to kill two birds with one stone, to destroy an oppressor and the man he oppresses at the same time: there remain a dead man and a free man; the survivor, for the first time, feels a *national* soil under his foot." Jean-Paul Sartre, preface to *The Wretched of the Earth* by Frantz Fanon (New York: Grove Press, 1968), pp. 21–22. Contrast Said, whose models for Palestinian resistance are Gandhi's India, King's civil rights movement, and Nelson Mandela (see "The Tragedy Deepens," December 2000, in the present volume).

In consequence, as Said tellingly observed just a few months before his death, "I still have not been able to understand what it means to love a country." That, of course, is the characteristic condition of the rootless cosmopolitan. It is not very comfortable or safe to be without a country to love; it can bring down upon your head the anxious hostility of those for whom such rootlessness suggests a corrosive independence of spirit. But it *is* liberating: the world you look out upon may not be as reassuring as the vista enjoyed by patriots and nationalists, but you see further. As Said wrote in 1993, "I have no patience with the position that 'we' should only or mainly be concerned with what is 'ours.' "[4]

This is the authentic voice of the independent critic, speaking the truth to power . . . and supplying a dissenting voice in conflicts with authority: as Said wrote in *Al-Ahram* in May 2001, "whether Israeli intellectuals have failed or not in their mission is not for us to decide. What concerns us is the shabby state of discourse and analysis in the Arab world." It is also the voice of the free-standing "New York intellectual," a species now fast approaching extinction—thanks in large measure to the same Middle Eastern conflict in which so many have opted to take up sides and identify with "us" and "ours."[5] Edward Said, as the reader of these essays will discover, was by no means a conventional "spokesman" for one party in that conflict.

The Munich daily *Die Süddeutscher Zeitung* headed its obituary of Said: *Der Unbequeme*, "the Uncomfortable Man." But if anything his lasting achievement was to make *others* uncomfortable. For the Palestinians Edward Said was an under-appreciated and frequently irritating Cassandra, berating their leaders for incompetence—and worse. To his critics Said was a lightning rod, attracting fear and vituperation. Implausibly, this witty and cultivated man was cast as the very devil: the corporeal incarnation of every threat—real or imagined—to Israel and Jews alike. To an American Jewish community suffused with symbols of victimhood he was a provocatively articulate remembrancer of Israel's very own vic-

---

4. See "Israel, Iraq and the United States," *Al-Ahram* October 10–16, 2002, in the present volume; Said, *Culture and Imperialism*, p. xxv.

5. To its lasting credit, Columbia University withstood considerable internal and public pressure to censure or even remove Said because of his public interventions on the Palestinian behalf.

tims. And by his mere presence here in New York, Edward Said was an ironic, cosmopolitan, *Arab* reminder of the parochialism of his critics.

The essays in this book cover the period December 2000 through July 2003. They thus take us from end of the Oslo decade, the onset of the second intifada and the final breakdown of the "peace process," through the Israeli re-occupation of the West Bank and Gaza, the massacres of September 11, 2001, the American retaliation in Afghanistan and the long run-up to the U.S. attack on Iraq—a distinctly turbulent and murderous thirty-two months. During this time Edward Said wrote copiously and urgently about the alarming state of affairs in the Middle East, contributing at least one article a month, often more, despite his worsening medical condition (to which there is no reference in these writings until August 2002, and then only a casual, passing allusion).

All but one of the pieces collected here were contributed to an Arab-language outlet, the Cairo newspaper *Al-Ahram*. These writings are thus an opportunity for Edward Said's Western readers to see what he had to say to an Arab audience. What they show is that Said in his final years was consistently pursuing three themes: the urgent need to tell the world (above all Americans) the truth about Israel's treatment of the Palestinians; the parallel urgency of getting Palestinians and other Arabs to recognize and accept the reality of Israel and engage with Israelis, especially the Israeli opposition; and the duty to speak openly about the failings of Arab leadership.

Indeed, Said was above all concerned with addressing and excoriating his fellow Arabs. It is the ruling Arab regimes, especially that of the Palestinian Liberation Organization, who come in for the strongest criticism here: for their cupidity, their corruption, their malevolence and incredulity. This may seem almost unfair—it is, after all, the United States that has effective power, and Israel that was and is wreaking havoc among Edward Said's fellow Palestinians—but Said seems to have felt it important to tell the truth to and about his *own* people, rather than risk indulging "the fawning elasticity with regard to one's own side that has disfigured the history of intellectuals since time immemorial" (December 2000).

In the course of these essays Said recounts checklists of Israeli abuses (see e.g., "Palestinians Under Siege" in December 2000; "Slow Death: Punishment by Detail" in August 2002; or "A Monument to Hypocrisy" in February 2003), a grim, depressing reminder of how Ariel Sharon's government is squeezing the lifeblood from the quarantined Palestinian communities: abuses against civilians that were once regarded as criminal acts even in wartime are now accepted behavior by a government ostensibly at peace. But in Edward Said's account these abuses are not the accidental, unfortunate by-product of the return to power of a belligerent, irredentist general, but rather the predictable—and in Said's case, predicted—consequence of the Palestinians' engagement in the late, unlamented "peace process" itself.

For those of us who welcomed the Oslo process and watched hopefully as it developed over the course of the nineties, Said's disenchanted critique is depressing. But in retrospect it is difficult to deny that he got it right and we were wrong. As imagined by the Israeli peace party and welcomed by many others—Palestinians included—the Oslo process was supposed to build confidence and trust between the two sides. Contentious issues—the governance of Jerusalem, the right of return for Palestinian refugees, the problem of the Jewish settlements—would be dealt with "later," in "final status negotiations." Meanwhile the PLO would gain experience and credibility in the administration of autonomous Palestinian territory, and Israelis would live in peace. Eventually, two states—one Jewish, one Palestinian—would live in stable proximity, their security underwritten by the international community.

This was the premise behind the Declaration of Principles signed on the White House Lawn in September 1993. But the whole thing was deeply flawed. As Said reminds us, there were not two "sides" to these negotiations: there was Israel, an established modern state with an awesome military apparatus (by some estimates the fourth strongest in the world today), occupying land and people seized thirty years earlier in war. And there were the Palestinians, a dispersed, displaced, disinherited community with neither an army nor a territory of its own. There was an occupier and there were the occupied. In Said's view, the only leverage that the Palestinians had was their annoying *facticity*: they were there, they wouldn't go away, and they wouldn't let the Israelis forget what they had done to them.

Having nothing to give up, the Palestinians had nothing to negotiate. To "deal" with the occupier, after all, is to surrender—or collaborate. That is why Said described the 1993 Declaration as "a Palestinian Versailles"[6] and why he resigned in anticipation from the Palestinian National Council. If the Israelis needed something from the Palestinians, Said reasoned, then the things that the Palestinians wanted—full sovereignty, a return to 1967 frontiers, the "right of return," a share of Jerusalem—should be on the table at the outset, not at some undetermined final stage. And then there was the question of Israel's "good faith."

When the initial Declaration was signed in 1993 there were just 32,750 Jewish housing units in settlements on the West Bank and in Gaza. By October 2001 there were 53,121—a 62 percent increase, with more to come. From 1992 to 1996, under the Labor governments of Yitzhak Rabin and Shimon Peres, the settler population of the West Bank grew by 48 percent, that of Gaza by 61 percent. To put it no stronger, this steady Israeli takeover of Palestinian land and resources hardly conformed to the spirit of the Oslo Declaration, whose Article 31 (Clause 7) explicitly states that "Neither side shall initiate or take any step that will change the status of the West Bank and the Gaza Strip pending the outcome of the permanent status negotiations."

Meanwhile, even as the PLO was authorized to administer the remaining Palestinian districts, Israel was constructing a network of "Jewish" roads crisscrossing those same regions and giving settlers and other Israelis exclusive access to far-flung housing units (and scarce aquifers) protected by permanent military installations.[7] The whole exercise was driven forward partly by an anachronistic Israeli conflation of land with security; partly by a post-1967 irredentist eschatology (with the Old Testament invoked as a sort of real estate contract with a partisan God); and partly by longstanding Zionist enthusiasm for territorial enlargement as an end in itself. From the Palestinian point of view the effect was to make the Oslo process an agonizing exercise in slow strangulation, with Gaza

6. Edward Said, *The Politics of Dispossession: The Struggle for Palestinian Self-Determination 1969–1994* (New York: Vintage Books, 1995), p. xxxiv.
7. This had the paradoxical consequence of segregating Jews and Arabs even as they became ever more economically interdependent: Israelis relying on cheap Palestinian labor, Palestinians dependent upon Israel for jobs and access to markets.

in particular transformed into a virtual prison under Palestinian warders, the Israeli army standing guard just outside the perimeter fence.

And then, in the year 2000, came the long-postponed "permanent status negotiations" themselves: first at Camp David and then, desperately, at Taba in the Sinai. Edward Said, of course, had no time for the conventional American view that President Clinton and Prime Minister Ehud Barak virtually gave away the farm and that even then the ungrateful PLO and its leader Yasir Arafat refused the gift. This is not because Said had any sympathy for Arafat but because the original Camp David offer was—as Tanya Reinhart described it in the Israeli daily *Yediot Aharanot* on July 8, 2000—so palpably a "fraud." The Palestinians were to get 50 percent of their own land, chopped into separate and often noncontiguous cantons; Israel was to annex 10 percent of the land; and the remaining 40 percent was to be left "undecided"—but under indefinite Israeli rule.

Five months later, at Taba, the Palestinians were offered an improved territorial deal, certainly the best they could ever have hoped for from an Israeli government. But the resulting Palestinian state would still have been utterly dependent on Israel and vulnerable to its whims; the grievances of Palestinian refugees were never fully addressed; and on the contentious issue of sovereignty over Jerusalem the Israelis would not budge. Indeed, even the last-minute Israeli concessions were still encumbered with what Said nicely terms "conditions and qualifications and entailments (like one of the endlessly deferred and physically unobtainable estates in a Jane Austen novel) . . ."

Meanwhile Barak had continued to expand the population of the very settlements that his own negotiators recognized as a major impediment to agreement. Even if the PLO leaders had wanted to sell the Taba agreements to their constituents, they might have had difficulty doing so: the second intifada that burst out following Sharon's meticulously timed visit to the Temple Mount has been a disaster for the Palestinians, but it was born out of years—the Oslo years—of frustration and humiliation. On these grounds, as well as for reasons of his own, Arafat instructed the Palestinians not to sign.

Taba, and especially Camp David, were the bitter fruits of Oslo, and in Edward Said's view the PLO's error in engaging the process in the first place was well illustrated by its inevitable rejection of the outcome, retroactively discrediting the whole strategy of negotiations. In a June 2002 article, Said is scathingly unforgiving of the PLO apparatchiks and their leader, who for a while did rather well out of the power they exercised as the "Vichy-like" governors of occupied Palestine under Israel's benign oversight. They were and are "a byword for brutality, autocracy and unimaginable corruption" ("Palestinian Elections Now," *Al-Ahram,* June 13–19, 2002).

In other contributions to the same newspaper Said writes that Arafat and his circle "have made our situation worse, much worse." "Palestinians (and by extension other Arabs) have been traduced and hopelessly misled by their leaders," who have neither high principles nor practical, pragmatic strategies. "It has been years since Arafat represented his people, their sufferings and cause, and like his other Arab counterparts, he hangs on like a much too-ripe fruit without real purpose or position" ("Arab Disunity and Factionalism," *Al-Ahram,* August 15–21, 2002).

What, then, is to be done? If the Palestinian leadership is corrupt and incompetent; if Israeli governments won't even keep faith with their own stated commitments, much less the desires of their interlocutors; if there is so much fear and loathing on all sides, how should the two-state solution be implemented, now that Israelis, Palestinians and the international community—even the Americans—all at last accept it in principle? Here, once again, Edward Said was at odds with almost everyone.

In 1980, when he first publicly pressed for a two-state solution, Said was attacked and abused from all sides, not least by Arafat's own Al Fateh movement. Then, in 1988, the Palestinian National Council belatedly conceded that the best possible outcome was indeed the division of Palestine into two states—one Israeli, one Palestinian—echoing Said's insistence that there was no alternative to reciprocal territorial self-determination for Jews and Arabs alike.[8] But as the years went by, with half of the occupied territories expropriated; with the Palestinian community in shambles and the putative Palestinian territory a blighted landscape of isolated enclaves, flattened olive groves and ruined houses,

---

8. See e.g., Edward Said, "Who Would Speak for Palestinians," *New York Times,* May 24, 1985.

where humiliated adults were fast losing the initiative to angry, alienated adolescents, Said drew the increasingly irresistible conclusion.

Israel was never going to quit the West Bank, at least not in any way that would leave it in a coherent, governable condition. What kind of a state could the West Bank and Gaza ever constitute? Who but a criminal mafia would ever *want* to take on the task of "governing" it? The "Palestine" of PLO imaginings was a fantasy—and a rather unappealing one at that. For good or ill there was only going to be one real state in the lands of historic Palestine: Israel. This was not utopia; it was merely hard-headed pragmatism shorn of illusion. The genuinely realistic approach lay in accepting this fact and thinking seriously about how to make the best of it. "Much more important than having a state is the kind of state it is."[9] For the last decade of his life Edward Said was an unbending advocate of a single, secular state for Israelis and Palestinians.

What grounds did Edward Said have for his faith in a single-state solution, a non-exclusive, secular, democratic alternative to the present impasse? In the first place, the status quo is awful and getting worse: two peoples, each sustained by its exclusive victim narrative, competing indefinitely across the dead bodies of their children for the same tiny piece of land. One of them is an armed state, the other a stateless people, but otherwise they are depressingly similar: what, after all, is the Palestinian national story if not a reproachful mirror to Zionism, a tale of expulsion, diaspora, resurrection, and return? There is no way to divide the disputed "homeland" to mutual satisfaction and benefit. Little good can come of *two* such statelets, mutually resentful, each with an influential domestic constituency committed to the destruction and absorption of its neighbor.

In the second place, something fundamental has changed in the Palestinian condition. For four decades millions of Palestinian Arabs—in Israel, in the occupied territories, in refugee camps across the Arab world and in exile everywhere—had been all but invisible. Their very existence was long denied by Israeli politicians; their memory of expulsion had been removed from the official record and passed unmentioned in history books; the record of their homes, their villages, and their land was expunged from the very soil itself. That, as Said, noted, was why he kept

9. Said, *The Politics of Dispossession*, p. xliii.

on telling the same story: "There seems to be nothing in the world that sustains it; unless you go on telling it, it will just drop and disappear." And yet "it is very hard to espouse for five decades, a continually losing cause." It was as though Palestinians had no existence except when someone committed a terrorist atrocity—at which point that is *all* they were, their provenance uncertain, their violence inexplicable. [10]

That is why the "right of return" had so central a place in all Palestinian demands—not because any serious person supposed that Israel could take "back" millions of refugees and their descendants, but from the deeply felt need for *acknowledgement*: a recognition that the initial expulsion took place, that a primordial wrong was committed. That is what so annoyed Said about Oslo: it seemed to excuse or forgive the Israelis for the occupation and everything else. But "Israel cannot be excused and allowed to walk away from the table with not even a *rhetorical demand* [my emphasis] that it needs to atone for what it did." ("What Price Oslo?" *Al-Ahram*, March 14–20, 2002). Attention must be paid.

But attention, of course, *is* now being paid. An overwhelming majority of world opinion outside of the United States sees the Palestinian tragedy today much as the Palestinians themselves see it. They are the natives of Israel, an indigenous community excluded from nationhood in its own homeland: dispossessed and expelled, illegally expropriated, confined to "Bantustans," denied many fundamental rights and exposed on a daily basis to injustice and violence. Today there is no longer the slightest pretence by well-informed Israelis that the Arabs left in 1948 of their own free will or at the behest of foreign despots, as we were once taught. Benny Morris, one of the leading Israeli scholars on the subject, recently reminded readers of the Israeli daily newspaper *Ha'aretz* that Israeli soldiers did not merely expel Palestinians in 1948–49, in an early, incomplete attempt at ethnic cleansing; they committed war crimes along the way, including the rape and murder of women and children.[11]

---

10. Said, *The Politics of Dispossession*, pp. xviii, 118. For the quite remarkable thoroughness with which Israeli archeologists and bureaucrats "cleansed" Israel of all evidence of its Palestinian past, see Meron Benvenisti, *Sacred Landscape: The Buried History of the Holy Land since 1948* (Berkeley: University of California Press, 2000).

11. Benny Morris, interviewed in *Ha'aretz*, January 8, 2004.

Of course Morris notoriously sees nothing wrong in this record—he treats it as the collateral damage that accompanies state building.[12] But this brings us to the third ground for thinking Said may be right about the chances for a single state. Just as the Palestinian cause has begun to find favor in public opinion, and is gaining the moral upper hand, so Israel's international standing has precipitately collapsed. For many years the insuperable problem for Palestinians was that they were being expelled, colonized, occupied, and generally mistreated not by French colons or Dutch Afrikaners but, in Edward Said's words, by "the Jewish citizens of Israel, remnants of the Nazi Holocaust, with a tragic history of genocide and persecution."

The victim of victims is in an impossible situation—not made any better, as Said pointed out, by the Arab propensity to squeeze out from under the shadow of the Holocaust by minimizing or even denying it.[13] But when it comes to mistreating others even victims don't get a free pass for ever. The charge that Poles often persecuted Jews before, during, and after World War II can no longer be satisfactorily deflected by invoking Hitler's three million Polish victims. *Mutatis mutandis*, the same now applies to Israel. Until the military victory of 1967, and even for some years afterwards, the dominant international image of Israel was the one presented by its left-Zionist founders and their many admirers in Europe and elsewhere: a courageous little country surrounded by enemies, where the desert had been made to bloom and the indigenous population airbrushed from the picture.

Following the invasion of Lebanon, and with gathering intensity since the first intifada of the late 1980s, the public impression of Israel has steadily darkened. Today it presents a ghastly image: a place where sneering eighteen-year-olds with M16 carbines taunt helpless old men ("security measures"); where bulldozers regularly flatten whole apartment blocks ("collective punishment"); where helicopters fire rockets into residential streets ("targeted assassination"); where subsidized settlers frolic in grass-fringed swimming pools, oblivious of Arab children a few meters

---

12. "I don't think that the expulsions of 1948 were war crimes. You can't make an omelet without breaking eggs." *Ha'aretz*, January 8, 2004.

13. See Said, *The Politics of Dispossession*, p. xviii; and "Barenboim and the Wagner Taboo," *Al-Ahram*, August 16–22, 2001.

away who fester and rot in the worst slums on the planet; and where retired generals and cabinet ministers speak openly of bottling up the Palestinians "like drugged roaches in a bottle" (Rafael Eytan) and cleansing the land of its Arab cancer.[14]

Israel is utterly dependant on the United States for money, arms, and diplomatic support. One or two states share common enemies with Israel; a handful of countries buy its weapons; a few others are its de facto accomplices in ignoring international treaties and secretly manufacturing nuclear weapons. But outside Washington, Israel has no *friends*— at the United Nations it cannot even count on the support of America's staunchest allies. Despite the political and diplomatic incompetence of the PLO (well documented in Said's writings); despite the manifest shortcomings of the Arab world at large—"lingering outside the main march of humanity";[15] despite Israel's own sophisticated efforts to publicize its case, the Jewish state today is widely regarded as a—*the*—leading threat to world peace. After thirty-seven years of military occupation, Israel has gained nothing in security; it has lost everything in domestic civility and international respectability; and it has forfeited the moral high ground forever.

The newfound acknowledgement of the Palestinians' claims and the steady discrediting of the Zionist project (not least among many profoundly troubled Israelis) might seem to make it harder rather than easier to envisage Jews and Arabs living harmoniously in a single state. And just as a minority of Palestinians may always resent their Jewish neighbors, there is a risk that some Israelis will never, as it were, forgive the Palestinians for what the Israelis have done to them. But as Said understood, the Palestinians' aggrieved sense of neglect and the Israelis' insistence on the moral rectitude of their case were twin impediments to a resolution of their common dilemma. Neither side could, as it were, "see" the other. As

14. Already in 1975 the head of the housing department of Israel's Interior Ministry was reporting to Prime Minister Yitzhak Rabin that Israel's *own* Arabs were a "cancer in the Jewish body that has to be curbed and contained." See Ilan Pappe, *A History of Modern Palestine: One Land, Two Peoples* (New York: Cambridge University Press, 2004), p. 227. Thirty years on, only the metaphor has changed: "Something like a cage has to be built for them [Palestinians]. There is no choice—there is a wild animal there that has to be locked up." Benny Morris, *Ha'aretz*, January 8, 2004.

15. Said, *The Politics of Dispossession*, p. 371.

Orwell observed in his "Notes on Nationalism," "If one harbors any-where in one's mind a nationalistic loyalty or hatred, certain facts, though in a sense known to be true, are inadmissible."

Today, in spite of everything, there is actually a better appreciation by some people on both sides of where—quite literally—the other is coming from. This, I think, arises from a growing awareness that Jews and Arabs occupy the same space and will continue to do so for the foreseeable future. Their fates are hopelessly entangled. Fence or no fence, the terri-tory now ruled by Israel can only be "cleansed" of its Arab (or its Jewish) residents by an act of force that the international community could not countenance. As Said notes, "historic Palestine" is now a lost cause—but so, for the same reasons, is "historic Israel." Somehow or other, a single institutional entity capable of accommodating and respecting both com-munities will have to emerge, though when and in what form is still obscure.

The real impediment to new thinking in the Middle East, in Edward Said's view, was not Arafat, or Sharon, nor even the suicide bombers or the ultras of the settlements. It was—and is—the United States. The one place where official Israeli propaganda has succeeded beyond measure, and where Palestinian propaganda has utterly failed, is in America. American Jews (rather like Arab politicians) live in "extraordinary self-isolation in fantasy and myth" ("Crisis for American Jews," May 2002). Many Israelis are terribly aware of what occupation of the West Bank has done to their own society (if somewhat less sensitive to its effect on oth-ers): "Rule over another nation corrupts and distorts Israel's qualities, tears the nation apart, and shatters society" (Haim Guri).[16] But most Americans, including virtually every American politician, have no sense of any of this.

That is why Edward Said insists in these essays upon the need for Palestinians to bring their case to the American public rather than just, as he puts it, imploring the American president to "give" them a state. American public opinion matters, and Said despaired of the uninformed anti-Americanism of Arab intellectuals and students: "It is not acceptable to sit in Beirut or Cairo meeting halls and denounce American imperial-

---

16. Quoted in Tom Segev, *Elvis in Jerusalem* (New York: Metropolitan Books, 2002), p. 125.

ism (or Zionist colonialism for that matter) without a whit of under-standing that these are complex societies not always truly represented by their governments' stupid or cruel policies." But as an American he was frustrated above all at his *own* country's political myopia: only America can break the murderous deadlock in the Middle East, but "what the U.S. refuses to see clearly it can hardly hope to remedy."[17]

Whether the United States will awaken to its responsibilities and opportunities remains unclear. In view of the green light given to Ariel Sharon by President Bush in April 2004 to retain occupied land on the West Bank and ignore international laws and boundaries, there is little ground for optimism. In any event, we in the United States must engage a debate about Israel and the Palestinians that many people would prefer to avoid, even at the cost of isolating America—with Israel—from the rest of the world. In order to be effective, this debate has to happen in America itself, and it must be conducted by Americans. That is why Edward Said was so singularly important. Over three decades, virtually single-handed, he wedged open a conversation in America about Israel, Palestine, and the Palestinians. In so doing he performed an inestimable public service at considerable personal risk. His death opens a yawning void in American public life. He is irreplaceable.

Tony Judt
March 2004

17. Edward Said, "Suicidal Ignorance," *Al-Ahram*, November 15–21, 2001, in the present volume; and "Blind Imperial Arrogance," *Los Angeles Times*, July 20, 2003.

PART ONE

The Second Intifada Begins, Clinton's Failure

CHAPTER ONE

Palestinians Under Siege

Since September 29, 2000, the day after Ariel Sharon, guarded by about a thousand Israeli police and/or soldiers, visited Jerusalem's Haram al-Sharif (the Noble Sanctuary) in a gesture designed explicitly to assert his right as an Israeli to visit the Muslim holy place, a conflagration has erupted that continues as I write in mid-November. Sharon himself is unrepentant, blaming the Palestinian Authority for "deliberate incitement" against Israel "as a strong democracy" whose "Jewish and democratic character" the Palestinians wish to change. He says that he went there "to inspect and ascertain that freedom of worship and free access to the Temple Mount is granted to everyone," although he mentions neither the huge swarm of guards he took with him nor that the area was sealed off before, during, and after his visit, which scarcely assures freedom of access (*Wall Street Journal*, October 4, 2000). He also neglects to say that on the twenty-ninth the Israeli army shot eight Palestinians dead, or that Israel unilaterally annexed East Jerusalem in June 1967 and that it is therefore under military occupation, which according to international law its natives are entitled to resist by any means possible: it was this truth that triggered the new intifada. Besides, the Temple Mount is supposed by archaeologists to lie beneath two of the oldest and greatest Muslim shrines in the world going back a millennium and a half, a convergence of religious topoi that it would take more than a heavy-booted visit by a notoriously brutal and right-wing Israeli general with Palestinian blood on his hands from, among other massacres that began during the 1950s, Sabra, Shatila, Qibya, and Gaza, to sort out.

The Union of Palestinian Medical Relief Committees says that as of November 7, 170 people have been killed, 6,000 wounded: this does not include 14 Israeli deaths (8 of them soldiers) and a slightly larger number of wounded. (A few days later the figure for the dead climbed to over 200.) The earlier figures come from the Israeli organization B'tselem. The

Palestinian deaths include at least 22 boys under the age of fifteen and, says B'tselem, 13 Palestinian citizens of Israel who were killed by the Israeli police in demonstrations inside Israel. Both Amnesty International and Human Rights Watch have issued reports sternly upbraiding Israel for the disproportionate use of force against civilians and, according to Phil Reeves in the *Independent* (November 12, 2000), Amnesty has published another report condemning Israel for harassment, torture, and illegal arrests of Arab children in Israel and Jerusalem. Gideon Levy in *Ha'aretz* (November 12) notes with alarm that most of the handful of Arab Knesset members have been punished for their vociferous objections to Israel's policy toward Palestinians; some have been relieved of committee assignments, others are facing trial, still others are undergoing police interrogation, all this, he concludes, as part of "the process of demonization and delegitimization being conducted against the Palestinians," inside Israel as well as in the Occupied Territories.

Normal life (the phrase is somewhat oxymoronic) for Palestinians living in the occupied West Bank and in the Gaza Strip has disappeared. Even those three hundred or so privileged Palestinians with peace process–designated VIP status have lost that status, and like the rest of the approximately 3 million people who endure the double burden of life under the Palestinian Authority and the Israeli occupation regime—to say nothing of the brutality of thousands of Israeli settlers, some of whom turn into the rampaging vigilantes terrorizing Palestinian villages and large towns like Hebron—they are subject to the closures, encirclements, and barricaded roads that impede all movement for them. Yasir Arafat himself is not immune from the indignity of having to ask permission to leave or enter the West Bank or Gaza, where his airport is opened and closed summarily by the Israelis and his headquarters have been bombed punitively by Israeli missiles fired from helicopter gunships. As for the flow of goods into and out of the territories, to say nothing of workers, ordinary travelers, tourists, students, the aged, and the sick: they have been immobilized or, to put it more concretely, imprisoned. According to the UN Special Coordinator's Office in the Occupied Territories, Palestinian trade with Israel accounts for 79.8 percent of total trade transactions; Jordan, which is next, accounts for 2.39 percent, a very low figure directly ascribable to Israel's control of the entire Palestine-Jordan frontier (in addition of course to the Syrian, Lebanese, and Egyptian borders). With Israel's closure, therefore, the Palestinian economy has lost three times the amount of money taken in from donor sources during the first six months of 2000; the losses average $19.5 million per day (*Al-Hayat,* November 9, 2000). For an impoverished and colonized population dependent on the Israeli economy—thanks to the economic agreements signed by the PLO under the Oslo accords—this is a severe hardship.

What hasn't slowed down is the rate of Israeli settlement-building, which under the supposedly pro-peace regime of Ehud Barak has increased by 96 percent over the past few years, according to the authoritative Report on Israeli Settlement in the Occupied Territories (RISOT). It adds, "1,924 settlement units have been started" since Barak took office in July 1999. This figure does not take into account the enormous and ongoing program of road-building, the constant expropriation of land that that requires, in addition to systematic deforestation, ravaging, and despoiling of Palestinian agricultural land undertaken both by the army and by the settlers. The Gaza-based Palestinian Committee on Human Rights has meticulously documented the "sweepings" of olive groves and vegetable farms by the Israeli army (or, as it prefers to be known, Israeli Defense Force) near the Rafah border, for example, and on either side of the Gush Katif settlement block, which is part of the 20 percent of Gaza still occupied illegally by a few thousand settlers, who can water their lawns and fill their swimming pools while the million Palestinian inhabitants of the Strip (80 percent of them refugees from former Palestine) live in a parched water-free zone. In fact, Israel controls all the water supply of the Occupied Territories, uses 80 percent of it for the personal use of its Jewish citizens, rationing the rest for the Palestinian population: this issue was never seriously negotiated during the Oslo peace process.

What of the much-vaunted peace process itself? What have been its accomplishments, and why, if indeed it was a peace process, has the loss and the miserable condition of Palestinian life become so much greater than before the Oslo accords were signed in September 1993? And why is it, as William Orme Jr. of the *New York Times* noted on November 5, that "the Palestinian landscape is now decorated with the ruins of projects that were predicated on peaceful integration"? And what does it mean to speak of peace if Israeli troops and settlements still exist in such large numbers? Again, according to RISOT, 110,000 Jews lived in illegal settlements in Gaza and the West Bank before Oslo; the number has increased to 195,000 in 2000, a figure that doesn't include the over 150,000 Jews who have been added as residents to annexed (also illegally) Arab East Jerusalem. Has the world been deluded, or has the overwhelmingly preponderant rhetoric of "peace" been in essence a gigantic fraud?

The answer to these questions has been there all along, although either buried in reams of documents signed by the two parties under American auspices, and therefore basically unread except for the small handful of people who negotiated them, or simply ignored by the media and the governments whose job it now appears was to press on with disastrous information, investment, and enforcement policies regardless of what horrors were taking place on the ground. A few people, myself included, have tried faithfully to chronicle what has been taking place from the initial Palestinian surrender at Oslo until the present, but in comparison with the mainstream media and the governments, not to mention huge funding agencies like the World Bank, the European Union, and many private foundations, Ford principally, who have played along with the deception, our voices have had a negligible effect except, sadly, to prophesy what is now taking place. Such complicity and cruelty on such a scale would require the talents of a Swift to dissect.

In any case, the disturbances of the past few weeks have not been confined to Palestine and Israel. Not since 1967 has the Arab and Islamic world been as rocked by demonstrations and displays of anti-American and anti-Israeli sentiment as now. Angry street demonstrations are a daily occurrence in Cairo, Damascus, Casablanca, Tunis, Beirut, Baghdad, and Kuwait; literally millions of people have expressed their support of the Al-Aqsa Intifada, as it has been dubbed, as well as their outrage at the cringing submissiveness of their governments. The Arab summit in Cairo in October 2000 produced the usual ringing denunciations of Israel and a few more dollars for Arafat's Authority, but even the diplomatic minimum—the recall of ambassadors—was not enacted. On the day after the summit, the American-educated Abdullah of Jordan, whose knowledge of the Arabic language is reported to have progressed to the secondary school level, flew off to Washington to sign a trade agreement with the

United States, Israel's chief supporter. Hosni Mubarak of Egypt is too dependent on the $2 billion in annual U.S. aid for him so much as to demur at U.S. policy. Like the others, he needs the United States to protect him from his people far too much for him to oppose Clinton and his peacemaking team of former Israeli lobby officials. Meanwhile the sense of Arab anger, humiliation, and frustration continues to build up, whether because the regimes are so undemocratic and unpopular or because all the basic elements of human life—employment, income, nutrition, health, education, infrastructure, transportation, environment—have so fallen beneath tolerable limits that only appeals to Islam and generalized expressions of outrage will do, instead of a sense of citizenship and participatory democracy. This bodes ill for the future, the Arabs' as well as Israel's.

Popular wisdom in policy and foreign affairs circles during the last quarter century has had it that Palestine as a cause is essentially dead, that pan-Arabism is a mirage, and that the handful of mostly discredited and unpopular leaders of the Arab countries have seen the light, accepted Israel and the United States as partners, and in the process of shedding their Arab nationalism have settled for a modernizing, pragmatic, deregulated, and privatized globalization, whose early prophet was Anwar al-Sadat and whose influential drummer boy has been the *New York Times* columnist and Middle East expert Thomas Friedman. When this important commentator happened in late October to find himself trapped in Ramallah, besieged and bombed by the Israeli army, he suddenly woke up for the first time, in more than seven years of columns praising the Oslo peace process, to the fact that "Israeli propaganda that the Palestinians mostly rule themselves in the West Bank is fatuous nonsense. Sure, the Palestinians control their own towns, but the Israelis control all the roads connecting these towns and therefore all their movements. Israeli confiscation of Palestinian land for more settlements is going on to this day—seven years into Oslo." He concludes that only "a Palestinian state in Gaza and the West Bank" can bring peace, but of course he neglects to say anything about what kind of state it would be, and about ending military occupation, which the Oslo documents rather precisely also said nothing about (*New York Times*, October 31, 2000). Why he never discussed this in the hundreds of columns he wrote since September 1993, and why even now he doesn't say that Oslo's cumulative logic has been to produce today's bloody results, defies common sense but is typical of the racism and hypocrisy of discourse on the subject.

In the meantime the Panglossian optimism of those who took it upon themselves to make sure that Palestinian misery was kept out of the news seems to have disappeared in a cloud of dust, including and above all the "peace" on which the United States and Israel have worked so hard to consolidate in their own narrow interests. Moreover, the old frameworks that survived the cold war have slowly crumbled as the Arab leaderships have aged, without viable successors in sight. Egypt's Mubarak has refused even to appoint a vice-president, Arafat has no clear successor, and as in the case either of Iraq's and Syria's "democratic socialist" Ba'ath republics or Jordan's kingdom, the rulers' sons have taken or will take over with the merest fig leaf of legitimacy to cover their dynastic autocracy.

A turning point has been reached, however, and for this the Palestinian intifada is a significant marker. For not only is it an anticolonial rebellion of the kind that has been seen periodically in Setif, Sharpeville, Soweto, and elsewhere, it is also part of the general malaise against the new economic order that brought us the events of Seattle and Prague. And for most of the world's Muslims, its costly human sacrifices belong in the same columns as Sarajevo, Mogadishu, Baghdad under U.S.-led sanctions, and Chechnya. What must be clear to every ruler, including Bill Clinton and Ehud Barak, is that the period of stability guaranteed under the Israeli-U.S.–local Arab regimes' dominance is now genuinely threatened by vast popular forces of uncertain magnitude, unknown direction, unclear vision. Business as usual, which had long meant increasing the distance between citizen and a controlling power felt to be either alien or a minority of some sort in order to enhance the fortunes of a tiny group of people, has been brought to a standstill for the time being. A rough beast whose hour has come around at last is struggling to be born in a shape that cannot now be accurately forecast. But that it will somehow belong to the unofficial culture of the dispossessed, the silenced, and the scorned, deferred or buried for several decades, seems like a strong likelihood, and that it will bear in itself the distortions of years of past official policy seems equally strong.

Ironically enough, it has been the actual geographical map of the peace process that most dramatically shows the kinds of distortions that have been building up while the measured discourse of peace and bilateral negotiations have systematically disguised the realities. Just as ironically, though, in literally none of the many dozens of news reports and television stories broadcast since the present crisis began has there been a map shown to indicate where and why the conflict has taken the exact form in which it has been unfolding. I think it is correct to say that most people hearing phrases such as "the parties are negotiating," and "let's get back to the negotiating table," and "you are my peace partner" have assumed that there is parity between Palestinians and Israelis who, thanks to the brave souls from each side who met secretly in Oslo, have been finally settling the questions that "divide" them, as if each side had a side, a piece of land, a territory from which to face the other. This is a seriously, indeed mischievously misleading mental picture, designed whether through inadvertence or continued propagandistic repetition to disguise the bizarre disproportion between the sides.

That this skewed picture is kept in place as a result of human effort, consider the following: citing an Anti-Defamation League survey of editorials published in the mainstream U.S. press, *Ha'aretz* on October 25 said that there was "a pattern of support for Israel [that] expressed sympathy for its plight," with nineteen newspapers expressing support for Israel in 67 editorials, seventeen giving "balanced analysis," and only nine "voicing criticism against Israeli leaders (particularly Ariel Sharon), whom they accused of responsibility for the conflagration." Fairness and Accuracy in Media (FAIR) on November 3 noted that the three major networks broadcast 99 stories about the intifada between September 28 and November 2, yet only four of the 99 mentioned the "occupied territories." The same report said that phrases such as "Israel . . . again feeling isolated and under siege," "Israeli soldiers under daily attack," and in a place where soldiers were forced back, "Israelis have surrendered territory to Palestinian violence," and "the ever-widening eruptions of violence in Israel" are threaded through the commentary, obscuring the facts of occupation and military imbalance. (The Israeli Defense Force has been using tanks, American- and British-supplied Cobra and Apache attack helicopters, missiles, mortars, and heavy machine guns, none of which the Palestinians possess.

Moreover, the American newspaper of record, the *New York Times*, has run only one op-ed piece written by a Palestinian or Arab individual (and he happens to be a supporter of Oslo) in a literal blizzard of editorial comment basically supporting the U.S. and Israeli positions; the *Wall Street Journal* has not even done that, nor has the *Washington Post*. On November 12 the most-watched television program *60 Minutes* broadcast a segment effectively designed to let the Israeli army "prove" that the killing of twelve-year-old Muhammad al-Durrah, who became the icon of Palestinian suffering during the intifada, was mounted theatrically by the Palestinian Authority; this included planting the boy's father before Israeli guns, and even the French TV crew that filmed the forty-minute episode recording the horrifying event, in such a way as to prove an ideological point.

Granted that the U.S. media and, by extension, U.S. popular opinion are the choice battlefield, and granted that the media situation in Europe reveals a more balanced picture: it is nonetheless true, I believe, that the real geographical bases of the current bloody events have been deliberately obscured in this most geographical of contests. No one can be expected to follow or, more important, retain a cumulatively accurate picture of the positively Kafkaesque provisions on the ground of the mostly secret negotiations between Israel and a disorganized, premodern, and tragically incompetent Palestinian team, dictatorially under Arafat's thumb. In two books—*Peace and Its Discontents* (1996) and *The End of the Peace Process* (2000)—I have followed these in some detail, but it may be useful here to summarize them with maps—maps, I should add, that have long been available but that, to the best of my knowledge, have never accompanied the news reports and television pictures proliferating in the world's media. Forgotten, because marginalized by Israel and especially by the United States, have been the relevant UN Security Council Resolutions 242 and 338, which stipulate unequivocally that land acquired by Israel through the war of 1967 must be given back in return for peace. The Oslo peace process began by trampling all over those resolutions, practically consigning them to the rubbish bin.

Nowhere has this egregious tampering with accepted international conventions been so crucial as during the aftermath of the failed Camp David summit that took place last July. Since that time it has been popular wisdom that, as Clinton and Barak have tirelessly but falsely claimed, the Palestinians were the ones to blame, not the Israelis, whose opening position has always been that the 1967 territories were not going to be returned. The U.S. press, for example, has gone on relentlessly about Israel's "generous" offer, and that Barak was willing to concede part of East Jerusalem and anywhere between 90 and 94 percent of the West Bank to the Palestinians. Yet no commentary in the United States and Europe has even tried to establish what precisely was "offered" or what the territory was in the West Bank that he was offering 90 percent of. All of that in fact was chimerical nonsense, as Tanya Reinhart showed in an article that appeared on July 13 in Israel's largest daily, *Yediot Aharonot,* entitled "The Camp David Fraud": she says that the Palestinians were offered 50 percent in separated cantons, 10 percent was to be annexed by Israel, and no less than 40 percent was to be left "under debate," to use the euphemism for continued Israeli control. For if you annex 20 percent, refuse (as he did) to dismantle or stop settlements, refuse over and over again to return to the 1967 lines and give back East Jerusalem, then decide to keep whole areas like the Jordan Valley and so completely encircle the Palestinian territories as to let them have no borders with any state except Israel, in addition to retaining the notorious "bypassing" roads and the adjacent areas, the 90 percent is quickly reduced to something like 50 or 60 percent, the greater part of which being projected for sometime in the very distant future, given that even the last Israeli redeployment, agreed to at the Wye River Plantation meetings of 1998 and reconfirmed at Sharm el Sheikh in 1999, has still not occurred. (It bears repeating that Israel is still the only state in the world with no officially declared borders.) And when we see what part that 50 to 60 percent constitutes of the former Palestine from which Palestinians were driven in 1948 and that is now Israel, we suddenly realize that it isn't 90 percent but about 12 percent that is really the area being "conceded." Even "conceded" is the wrong word, since these were territories taken by conquest and hence were only very partially being *returned,* an altogether different matter.

To begin with, let us recall some facts. In 1948 Israel took over what was historical or Mandatory Palestine (destroying and depopulating 531 Arab villages in the process. Two-thirds of the population were driven out: they are the 4 million refugees of today) except for the West Bank and Gaza, which went to Jordan and Egypt respectively. Both were subsequently lost to Israel in 1967, which controls them to this day except for a few areas under a highly qualified and circumscribed Palestinian autonomy, in effect an economically dependênt colonial zone for the Israeli economy, its size and contours decided unilaterally by Israel during the period of the interim accords according to the Oslo process. Few people realize that even under the Oslo process the Palestinian areas that have this autonomy or self-rule do not have sovereignty, which is not to be decided until the final status negotiations settle the matter. In short, Israel took 78 percent of Palestine in 1948, the remaining 22 percent in 1967. It is only the 22 percent that is in question now, even excluding West Jerusalem (of whose 19,325 dunams Jews owned 4,830, Arabs 11,190; state land was 3,305 dunams. The sources for this are in an indispensable book edited by Salim Tamari, *Jerusalem 1948: The Arab Neighborhoods and Their Fate in the War,* published in 1999 in Jerusalem by the Institute Jerusalem Studies and the Badil Resource Center), all of which Arafat conceded in advance to Israel at Camp David.

But what land has in fact been returned by Israel so far? Would that it could be described in a straightforward way because it cannot—by design. This is part of Oslo's malign genius, that even Israel's "concessions" were so heavily encumbered with conditions and qualifications and entailments (like one of the endlessly deferred and physically unobtainable estates in a Jane Austen novel) that they could not be enjoyed by the Palestinians in any way resembling self-determination; on the other hand, they could be described as a kind of concession, thus making it possible for everyone (including the Palestinian leadership) to say that actual territory was under (mostly) Palestinian control. The device itself was to redivide and subdivide an already divided Palestinian territory into three subzones, Areas A, B, and C, in ways entirely devised and controlled by the Israeli side since, I have pointed out for several years, the Palestinians until only quite recently had neither any maps of their own nor, among the negotiating team, any individuals who were familiar enough with the actual geography to contest decisions or to provide alternative plans. One result of the latter situation was the bizarre arrangement for subdividing Hebron after the Ibrahimi mosque massacre of twenty-nine Palestinians by Dr. Baruch Goldstein that took place in February 1994. Map One here shows how the core of the Arab town (120,000), 20 percent of it in fact, is under the control of about four hundred Jewish settlers about 0.03 percent of the total protected by the Israeli army!

MAP ONE

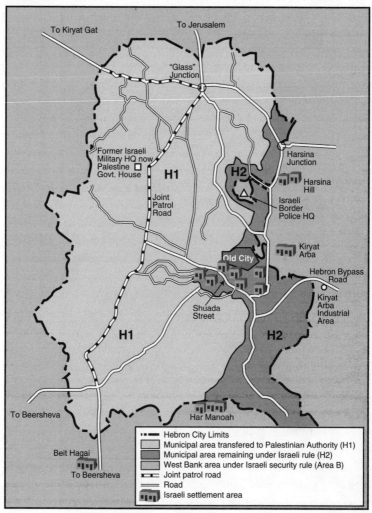

To Kiryat Gat

To Jerusalem

"Glass"
Junction

Former Israeli
Military HQ now
Palestine □
Govt. House

H1

H2

Harsina
Junction

Harsina
Hill

Joint
Patrol
Road

Israeli
Border
Police HQ

Old City

Kiryat
Arba

Hebron Bypass
Road

Kiryat
Arba
Industrial
Area

Shuada
Street

H1

H2

To Beersheva

Har Manoah

Hebron City Limits
Municipal area transferred to Palestinian Authority (H1)
Municipal area remaining under Israeli rule (H2)
West Bank area under Israeli security rule (Area B)
Joint patrol road
Road
Israeli settlement area

Beit Hagai

To Beersheva

Foundation for Middle East Peace

Map Two shows the first of what was to be a series of Israeli pullbacks that were made in widely separated, noncontiguous areas. Gaza is separated from Jericho by miles and miles of Israeli-held land, but both belong to Area A, which, in the West Bank, was limited to 1.1 percent of the whole, not a slice at all. Area A in Gaza is much larger mainly because

MAP TWO

Transfer to (full) Palestinian
Self rule
(Cairo - Agreement -1994)

WEST BANK

Full Pal.
Selfrule
A - 1.1%

Israeli Security
and Civil Control
C - 89.9%

West Bank

GAZA STRIP
Full Pal.
Selfrule
A - 65%

Jericho

ISRAEL

East
Jerusalem

Gaza

Cairo Agreement 1994   *Map © Jan de Jong*

Gaza, with its arid land and overpopulated and rebellious masses, was always considered a net liability for the Israeli occupation, which was happy—except for the choice agricultural land at its heart, the Gush Katif settlements, retained until now by Israel along with the harbor, the borders, and the entrances and exits—to be rid of it.

Maps Two, Three, and Four (which are what was presented by Israel as an optimal withdrawal map at the Camp David summit, though

MAP THREE

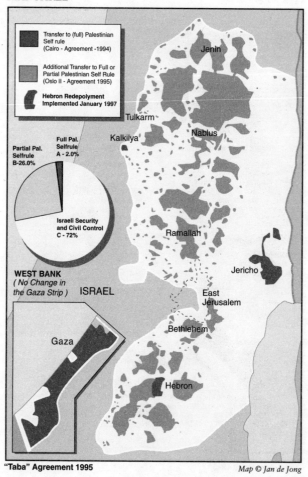

Transfer to (full) Palestinian
Self rule
(Cairo - Agreement -1994)

Additional Transfer to Full or
Partial Palestinian Self Rule
(Oslo II - Agreement 1995)

Hebrew Redepolyment
Implemented January 1997

Jenin

Tulkarm

Kalkilya

Nablus

Partial Pal.
Selfrule
B-26.0%

Full Pal.
Selfrule
A - 2.0%

Israeli Security
and Civil Control
C - 72%

Ramallah

Jericho

WEST BANK
*(No Change in
the Gaza Strip)* ISRAEL

East
Jerusalem

Bethlehem

Gaza

Hebron

"Taba" Agreement 1995 *Map © Jan de Jong*

announced in May) show the snail's pace and the parsimony by which
Israel allowed the hapless Palestinian Authority to take over large population centers (Area A), and at the same time allowed the Authority in
Area B to help police the main village areas, near where settlements were
being built all the time. But even then Israel held all the real security in its
hands (despite the joint patrols between Palestinian and Israeli officers),
and in Area C it kept about 60 percent of the territory for itself, there to

15

MAP FOUR

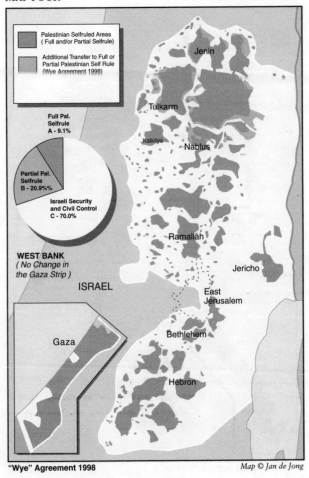

Palestinian Selfruled Areas
(Full and/or Partial Selfrule)

Additional Transfer to Full or
Partial Palestinian Self Rule
(Wye Agreement 1998)

Full Pal.
Selfrule
A - 9.1%

Partial Pal.
Selfrule
B - 20.9%%

Israeli Security
and Civil Control
C - 70.0%

WEST BANK
*(No Change in
the Gaza Strip)*

ISRAEL

Gaza

Jenin

Tulkarm

Kalkilya

Nablus

Ramallah

Jericho

East
Jerusalem

Bethlehem

Hebron

"Wye" Agreement 1998   *Map © Jan de Jong*

build more settlements, open up more roads, and establish military areas, all of which—in Jeff Halper's words—were intended to set up a matrix of control from which the Palestinians would never be free. (Along with the work of the Dutch geographer Jan de Jong, Jeff Halper has written the most impressive studies of Israeli territorial planning during the Oslo process, and these, of course, have appeared in journals with a very small circulation. Thus, for instance, his study of the trans-Israel highway in

MAP FIVE

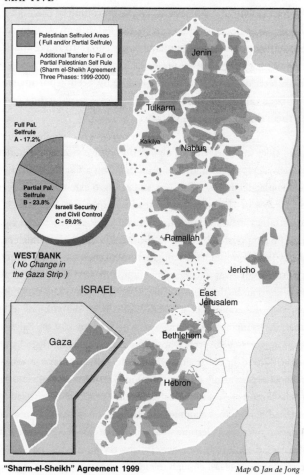

Legend:
- Palestinian Selfruled Areas (Full and/or Partial Selfrule)
- Additional Transfer to Full or Partial Palestinian Self Rule (Sharm el-Sheikh Agreement Three Phases: 1999-2000)

Full Pal. Selfrule A - 17.2%

Partial Pal. Selfrule B - 23.8%

Israeli Security and Civil Control C - 59.0%

WEST BANK (No Change in the Gaza Strip)

ISRAEL

Gaza

Jenin

Tulkarm

Kalkilya

Nablus

Ramallah

Jericho

East Jerusalem

Bethlehem

Hebron

"Sharm-el-Sheikh" Agreement 1999   *Map © Jan de Jong*

"The Road to Apartheid" (*News From Within,* May 2000) and his "The 94 Percent Solution: A Matrix of Control" (*Middle East Report* 216, Fall 2000).

But the point of these various zones, as a quick look at any of the maps reveals, is that the various parts of Area A are not only separated from one another but are surrounded by Area B and, more important, Area C. In other words, the closures and encirclements that have turned the Palestinian areas into besieged spots on the map (and that are the core of Barak's racist policy of "separation") have been long in the making and, worst of all, have been conspired in by the Palestinian Authority, which has signed all the relevant documents since 1994. To make matters still worse, as Amira Hass, the courageous *Ha'aretz* correspondent in the Palestinian territories who has single-handedly been reporting things as they have been taking place (rather than as Israeli propaganda was trying to make them seem), wrote on October 18:

> The two sides [in 1993] agreed on a period of five years for completion of the new deployment and the negotiations on a final agreement. The Palestinian leadership agreed again and again to extend its trial period, in the shadow of Hamas terrorist attacks and the Israeli elections. The "peace strategy" and the tactic of gradualism adopted by the leadership were at first supported by most of the Palestinian public, which craves normalcy [and, I would have thought, the real ending of the occupation, which, to repeat, was nowhere mentioned in any of the Oslo documents]. The Fatah (the main faction of the PLO) was the backbone of support for the concept of gradual release from the yoke of military occupation. Its members were the ones who kept track of the Palestinian opposition, arrested suspects whose names were given to them by Israel [summarily tried in secret and without defense attorneys in the State Security Courts, warmly endorsed by Vice President Al Gore and President Bill Clinton as part of their support for "peace"], imprisoned those who signed manifestoes claiming that Israel did not intend to rescind its domination over the Palestinian nation. The personal advantage gained by some of these Fatah members [in the regime of VIP passes that I referred to above] is not enough to explain their support of the process: for a long time they really and truly believed that this was the way to independence.

But, she goes on to say, even these men were members of "the Palestinian nation," and they had wives, children, and siblings who suffered the results of Israeli occupation and were quite entitled to ask whether support for the peace process did not also mean support for the occupation. She concludes:

More than seven years have gone by, and Israeli security has administrative control of 61.2 percent of the West Bank and about 20 percent of the Gaza Strip (Area C), and security control over another 26.8 percent of the West Bank (Area B).

This control is what has enabled Israel to double the number of settlers in 10 years, to enlarge the settlements, to continue its discriminatory policy of cutting back water quotas for three million Palestinians [remember that the main aquifers for Israel's water supply are on the West Bank], to prevent Palestinian development in most of the area of the West Bank, and to seal an entire nation [minus the 4 or 4.5 million refugees who are categorically denied their right of return to their homes even as any Jew anywhere still has absolute and unrestricted right of "return" at any time] into restricted areas, imprisoned in a network of bypass roads meant for Jews only. During these days of strict internal restriction of movement in the West Bank [and in and out of Gaza], one can see how carefully each road was planned: So that 200,000 Jews [plus the 150,000 in Jerusalem] have freedom of movement, about three million Palestinians are locked into their Bantustans until they submit to Israeli demands.

More details can be added. The Palestinian Authority is locked into this astonishingly ingenious, if in the long run utterly stupid, arrangement via security committees made up of the Mossad, the CIA, and the Palestinian security services, of whom there are at least fifteen (some say nineteen) components. By way of compensation, Israel and high-ranking members of the Authority operate lucrative monopolies on building materials, tobacco, oil, and so on, the profits of which are deposited in Israeli banks. Not only are Palestinians subject to harassments from Israeli troops, but they have also watched their own men participating in this abuse of their rights along with hated alien agencies. These largely secret security committees also have a mandate to survey books, media, public statements, and general rhetoric on the Palestinian side, to rule on what constitutes "incitement" against Israel, and then to get it deleted or circumscribed. Palestinians of course have no such right against American or Israeli incitements. As for the slowness of the pace of this unfolding process, which rather resembles one of the hugely complicated devices for remorselessly wearing down the individual's patience in Kafka or Borges, the argument offered by the United States and Israel is that Israel's security is being safeguarded; never have I heard anything said about Palestinian security. Clearly then we must conclude, as Zionist discourse has always stipulated, that the very existence of Palestinians, no matter how circumscribed, confined, and stripped of power, constitutes a racial, religious threat to Israel's security. All the more remarkable that, in the midst of such amazing unanimity at the height of the present crisis, an Israeli anthropologist, Danny Rabinowitz, spoke bravely of Israel's "original sin" in destroying Palestine in 1948, which with few exceptions Israelis have chosen either to deny or to forget completely (*Ha'aretz,* October 15).

If the West Bank's geography has been altered to Israel's advantage, small wonder that Jerusalem's has been so completely changed. Annexed in 1967, East Jerusalem added seventy square kilometers to Israel's area; another 54 were filched from the West Bank and added to the metropolitan area ruled for so long by Western liberal darling Mayor Teddy Kollek, who with his deputy Meron Benvenisti was personally responsible for the demolition of several hundred Palestinian homes of Haret al-Maghariba that were cleared away for the immense plaza in front of the Wailing Wall. A rather more sobering portrait than the usual encomia to Kollek's golden era emerges from *Separate and Unequal: The Inside Story of Israeli Rule in East Jerusalem,* by Amir S. Cheshin, Bill Hutman, and Avi Melamed (Harvard University Press, 1999). In any event, since 1967 East Jerusalem has been systematically Judaized, its borders inflated, enormous housing projects built, new roads and bypasses constructed, so as to make it unmistakably and virtually unreturnable and, for the dwindling, discriminated-against, and harassed Arab population of the city, unlivable. As Deputy Mayor Avraham Kehila said in July 1993, "I want to make the Palestinians open their eyes to reality and understand that the unification of Jerusalem under Israeli sovereignty is irreversible." (See Map Five. A small footnote to how humanly foolish such policies are is that recent small-arms firing on the new Jerusalem settlement of Gilo from the neighboring Palestinian village of Beit Jala is unanimously reported in the media without mentioning that Gilo was built on confiscated land from Beit Jala. Even Palestinians are unlikely to forget their past so easily.)

The Camp David summit in July in effect broke down because Israel and the United States presented all the arrangements I have been discussing here, only slightly modified, as the basis for the final settlement of the Palestinian-Israeli conflict. Reparations were basically dismissed by the Israelis, and this after all the years of occupation since 1967, not to mention the catastrophe of 1948 and its aftermath. I have seen no mention in the Western media of a long report of what went on in Camp David written by Akram Haniyeh, editor of the Ramallah daily *Al-Ayyam*, and a Fateh loyalist who since his deportation by the Israelis in 1987 has been close to Arafat. This report makes it absolutely clear that from the Palestinian point of view Clinton simply reinforced the Israeli position, and that Barak wanted a quick conclusion to such grave matters as the refugee problem and Jerusalem, and a formal declaration from Arafat ending the conflict definitively, in order to save his career as prime minister. Haniyeh's well-written and gripping account of what took place is soon to appear in English translation in the Washington-based *Journal of Palestine Studies*. Painstakingly it shows that even the much-vaunted and "unprecedented" Israeli position on Jerusalem was tailored to the hard-line position of the Israeli right wing—in other words, that Israel would retain conclusive sovereignty over even the Al-Aqsa mosque. "The Israeli position," Haniyeh justly says, "was to reap everything, and at a cheap price: the Palestinian 'golden' signature, a final recognition, and the precious 'end of conflict' promise. All this, without a return of all the land, and without acknowledging full sovereignty and, most dangerous of all, without paying any price for the refugee issue" (87).

As Haniyeh's report makes very clear, the United States bears a heavy burden of responsibility, virtually equal to Israel's, for the terrible plight of the Palestinian people. Ever since 1967 it has disbursed over $200 billion in financial and military aid to Israel, without conditions of any sort, plus the blanket political support that allows Israel to get away with anything it wishes to do. Tony Blair's Britain, in foreign policy a puerile copycat of the United States, is scarcely less enthusiastic for Israel's murderous style, supplying the Jewish state with military hardware that goes directly to the West Bank and Gaza occupation forces to facilitate their killing. No state in the history of foreign aid has received anywhere nearly as much as Israel, and no state (aside from the United States itself) has defied

MAP SIX

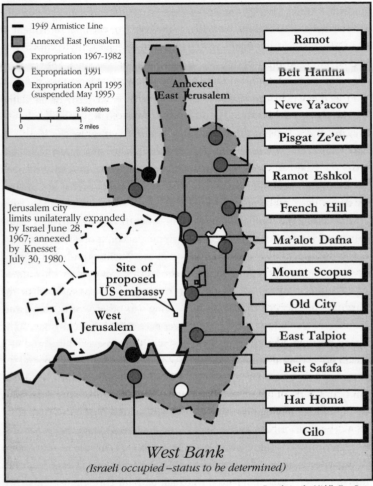

Legend:
- — 1949 Armistice Line
- Annexed East Jerusalem
- Expropriation 1967-1982
- Expropriation 1991
- Expropriation April 1995 (suspended May 1995)

0   2   3 kilometers
0   2 miles

Annexed East Jerusalem

Jerusalem city limits unilaterally expanded by Israel June 28, 1967; annexed by Knesset July 30, 1980.

Site of proposed US embassy

West Jerusalem

Ramot
Beit Hanina
Neve Ya'acov
Pisgat Ze'ev
Ramot Eshkol
French Hill
Ma'alot Dafna
Mount Scopus
Old City
East Talpiot
Beit Safafa
Har Homa
Gilo

West Bank
(Israeli occupied –status to be determined)

East Jerusalem: Land Expropriations, 1967–1995   *Foundation for Middle East Peace*

the international community on so many issues for so long. Even the most minor of U.S. machine politicians believes it necessary to do public obeisance to Israel, and so menacing has the Israeli lobby's stranglehold on political discourse become that only a handful of those intellectuals who take advanced positions on race, human rights, globalization, and U.S.

imperialism will venture even one word of criticism about Israel's dreadful human rights policy. In the weeks of atrocities against Palestinians that have been shown on American TV, there has been no protest from the intellectual or political community, even though the merest child is aware that the United States is in fact paying for those helicopters, missiles, and tanks that kill Palestinian stone-throwers with impunity. As for the policy hacks in charge of the "peace process"—every one of them like Dennis Ross and Martin Indyk a former employee of the Israeli lobby—they continue to press the Palestinians for more concessions, flexibility, and ending of "violence," even as Israel escalates its state terrorism against Palestinian civilians. Were Al Gore to become president, this policy would, if it is at all possible, turn even more pro-Israeli, so committed is the man to Israel and so close is he to Israel's leading pro-rejectionist and anti-Arab racist in the United States, Martin Peretz, owner of *The New Republic*.

Caught between his own track record of having already signed seven years of peace process agreements with Israel and the prospect of signing what was obviously meant to be the last one, Yasir Arafat balked, as much because he might have awakened to the enormity of what he had already signed away (I would like to think that his nightmares are made up of unending rides on the bypassing roads in Area C) as because he was aware how much popularity he had lost. Never mind the corruption, the despotism, the spiraling unemployment now up to 25 percent, the sheer poverty of most of his people: it was enough for him as a Muslim to realize finally that having been kept alive by Israel and the United States, he would be thrown back to his people without the Haram and without a real state, or even a prospect of viable statehood. That was Israel's design from the beginning, which neither Peace Now nor the Likud had any trouble living with. The young Palestinians who throw stones and fire slingshots at Israeli Merkavas and Cobras have clearly had enough and, despite Arafat's feeble efforts to control them, have bravely taken to the streets on their own.

It is time to conclude on two relatively hopeful points. One is that despite the media stranglehold in the United States and (to a lesser extent) in Europe and the heavily censored Arab world, there is now a fantastic amount of alternative information available on the Internet. Cyberactivists and hackers have opened a vast new reservoir of material that any-one with a minimum amount of literacy can easily tap into. What Israel has depended on in the past—either the ignorance or laziness of journalists or, on the other hand, their complicity with the misinformation of concealment and distortion—is handily countered by reports not only from journalists like Robert Fisk, David Hirst, John Pilger, and Phil Reeves in the English press (there aren't any equivalents in the U.S. establishment media) but from extracts from the Israeli and Europe-based Arab press, the research of individual scholars, and information gleaned from archives, international and UN organizations, and activist NGO collectives in Palestine, Israel, Europe, Australia, and North America. In this as in so many other instances, reliable information is the greatest enemy of oppression and secret injustice. That so many clichés and myths are stripped of their efficacy is a great encouragement but can never be, alas, a substitute for political leadership of the kind both Israelis and Palestinians so desperately now need.

My last point is an attempt to work a way out of what is so stunning an aspect of the Zionist-Palestinian conflict, which is the almost total opposition between the mainstream Israeli and Palestinian points of view. We were dispossessed and uprooted in 1948, they think they won independence justly. We recall that the land we left and the territories we are trying to liberate from military occupation are all part of our national patrimony; they think it is theirs by biblical fiat and diasporic affiliation. Today by any conceivable standards we are the victims of the violence; they think they are. There is simply no agreed-upon common ground, no common narrative, no possible area for genuine reconciliation. Our claims exclude each other. Even the notion of a common life shared (unwillingly it is true) in the same small piece of land is unthinkable. Both peoples think of separation, perhaps even of isolating and forgetting the other.

The pressure is greater on the Israelis, whose military actions and unwise peace strategy derive from a huge preponderance of power on their side, and the blindness to the consequences of what they are doing now, laying up years and years of resentment and hatred that every Muslim and Arab feels is justified. Ten years from now there will be demographic parity between Arabs and Jews in historical Palestine: what then?

Can the tanks, barricades, and house demolitions continue as before? So then what if a group of universally respected historians and intellectuals, half Palestinian, the other half Israeli, held a series of meetings to try to agree where a modicum of truth in this conflict actually lies, to see whether the known sources can guide both of them to an agreed-upon body of facts—who took what from whom, who did what to whom, and so on—which in turn might more equitably reveal a way out of the present impasse? It is too early perhaps for a Truth and Reconciliation Commission, but something like a Historical Truth and Political Justice Committee would be more appropriate.

It is clear to everyone on the ground, I think, that the old Oslo framework, which has done so much damage, is no longer at all workable (a recent Bir Zeit poll shows that only 3 percent of the Palestinian population want to return to the old negotiations) and that the Palestinian negotiating team led by Arafat can no longer hold the center, much less the nation. Everyone, I think, feels that enough is enough: the occupation has gone on too long, the peace talks have dragged on with too little improvement, the goal, if it was to have been independence, hasn't been clear (thank Rabin, Peres, and their Palestinian counterparts for that particular failure), and the suffering of ordinary people, whether because of Israeli practices or the Authority's crude incompetence, greed, and brutality, has gone further than can be endured. So the way seems to lie via stone-throwing in the streets, which is yet another futile road with its own tragic suffering. The only hope is to keep trying to rely on reason and the idea of coexistence between two peoples in one land. For now, though, the Palestinians are in desperate need of protection and guidance, which—true to its horrendous policy of always siding with and militarily supplying those who are responsible for atrocities (e.g., Indonesia, Turkey, Israel, Colombia, etc.)—the United States, along with Israel, opposes. The international community must be marshaled into some action, but that seems like a distant prospect for now.

The task actually belongs therefore to citizens and intellectuals who uphold real principles of truth and justice, not that fawning elasticity with regard to one's own side that has disfigured the history of intellectuals since time immemorial. Otherwise, as Barak plans for punishing, containing, and stifling the Palestinians in ever more punitive bombings of civilians, and tighter and tighter sieges and closures, the future looks calamitous and cannot, as he and his American mentors suppose, bring the Palestinians to heel. When will the Israelis realize—as some already have—that a sustained racist brutality against Arabs, in a Middle East where Israel is surrounded by 300 million Arabs and 1.2 billion Muslims, will bring the Jewish state neither normalcy nor security?

N.B. *I should like to thank the following for their work and support: Shifra Stern, Ali Abunimah, Andrew Rubin, Mustafa Barghuti, Ibrahim Abu-Lughod, Linda Butler, Sara Roy, Raji Sourani, Noam Chomsky, Jeffrey Aronson.*

London Review of Books, December 14, 2000

CHAPTER TWO

The Tragedy Deepens

No one really knows whether the Al-Aqsa Intifada temporarily subsided because Yasir Arafat expressed his public disapproval of it on November 17, 2000, or whether the lull was only a short-lived one that was generated out of fatigue or a search for new positions. Despite the enormous cost in lives and property to Palestinians, however, the essential problems remain, and the Israelis continue their blind and finally stupid assault on Palestinians with the strangulation, economic blockade, and bombings of cities and towns continuing without respite.

Every Arab leader who welcomed Barak's election in 1999 should now be asked to repeat his declaration so that their hollowness can be demonstrated again and again. I find official Arab attitudes virtually incomprehensible, having spent most of my life trying to decipher them according to the laws of reason and elementary common sense. Did they seriously believe that Barak was the savior of the peace process, and if so, weren't they aware that to save the peace process was nothing less than to prolong the Palestinian agony? Did they think that he was any different from the great "war hero" who has devoted his entire career to killing Arabs, and if he was, why did it take them so long to find out that he wasn't? Does subservience to the United States require so much subservience, so many acrobatics, such a complicated twisting and turning, and so profound a prostration? How long and for what do they cling to a repressive, basically rejectionist status quo with neither the will nor the capacity to wage war or to live in peace, simply to please a distant and arrogant superpower that has shown them and their people so much contempt, inhumanity, and utter, unspeakable cruelty?

Can they not do anything more substantial than what they are doing when Israel is using helicopter gunships to kill Palestinian civilians and destroy their homes, while the United States supplies Israel with the largest-ever order of attack helicopters during the past ten years and Israel has added $500 million to its budget for settlements? Not one word of official protest against U.S. policy that has brought such catastrophe to our people. It is this timorousness that allows U.S. policy-makers, of whom the unregretted Dennis Ross—single-handedly the mediocre individual who has done more to advance Israel's interest than anyone—is but one, to say that the Arabs trust the United States and its policies and remain close friends and allies of the United States. Surely the time has come to speak frankly of a hypocrisy and brutality without parallel, instead of standing silently by cap in hand as more and more Palestinians are killed with arms paid for by U.S. taxpayers.

But the core of the tragedy is what is happening to the victims themselves, the Palestinian people. Here one must speak and think rationally, not letting emotion and the passions of the moment sway the mind too much. My general impression is that Palestinians everywhere feel the absence of real leadership, a voice or an authority that can speak both of the present and of the future with some sense of vision, some articulation of a coherent, inclusive goal beyond the usual platitudes that repeat what is obviously designed to postpone decisions and visions with mere rhetoric. No one has any doubt that Palestinians are struggling against military occupation and have been doing so for thirty-three years. But there are 4 million refugees struggling against exile, in addition to the 1 million Palestinian citizens of Israel who have been living under a regime of racial and religious discrimination that has too long been hidden under fatuous labels like "Israeli democracy." One of the many problems with Oslo has been that Palestinian negotiators focused exclusively on the occupation to the neglect of the other two dimensions. But it should finally be clear that in all three instances it is Zionism that we fight against, and until we have a leadership that can formulate an integrated strategy on all three fronts, we do not have leadership. The tragedy is that as the intifada goes on, lives are tragically lost every day, in a political setting or framework that deepens the differences between Palestinians instead of bringing them closer together. We need a new vision, a new voice, a new truth.

Isn't it now clear that old slogans like "a Palestinian state" and "Jerusalem our capital" have brought us to this impasse? Shouldn't we expect a real leader to speak to all Palestinians honestly, fearlessly, without duplicity or winks at the United States and Israel, and to chart a course forward that links together opposition to occupation, to exile, and to racial discrimination? Why continue to delude people with the empty hope that "struggle," a word that seems to mean that others should do the dying, will get the Arab world generally and the Palestinians particularly what all have so long wanted? It is nothing short of alarming that after more than half a century of blustering, of expending blood and treasure, of militarizing, or abrogating democracy and the most elementary requirements of citizenship in the Arab world, we find ourselves facing the same enemy, the same defeats, the same tactical shifts and hypocritical about-faces with the same tired arsenal of threats, promises, slogans, and clichés, all of which have been proved more or less worthless and have produced the same failures from 1967 to Amman to October 1973 to Beirut to Oslo.

No one can deny that Palestine is an exception to nearly all the colonial issues of the past two hundred years: it is exceptional but not removed from history. Human history is full of similar, if not absolutely the same, instances, and what has surprised me, as someone living at a distance from the Middle East but close to it in all sorts of ways, is how insulated from the rest of the world we keep ourselves. Whereas, I believe, a great deal can be learned from the history of other oppressed peoples in the Americas, Africa, Asia, and even Europe. Why do we resist comparing ourselves, say, with the South African blacks, or with the American Indians, or with the Vietnamese? By comparing, I don't mean mechanically or slavishly but rather creatively and imaginatively.

The late Eqbal Ahmad, who was certainly one of the two or three most brilliant analysts of contemporary history and politics that I ever knew, always drew attention to the fact that successful liberation movements were successful precisely because they employed creative ideas, original ideas, imaginative ideas, whereas less successful movements (like ours, alas) had a pronounced tendency to use formulas and an uninspired repetition of past slogans and past patterns of behavior. Take as a primary instance the idea of armed struggle. For decades we have relied in our minds on ideas about guns and killing, ideas that from the 1930s until today have brought us plentiful martyrs but have had little real effect either on Zionism or on our own ideas about what to do next. In our case, the fighting is done by a small brave number of people pitted against hopeless odds: stones against helicopter gunships, Merkava tanks, missiles. Yet a quick look at other movements—say, the Indian

29

nationalist movement, the South African liberation movement, the American civil rights movement—tells us first of all that only a mass movement employing tactics and strategy that maximizes the popular element ever makes any difference on the occupier and/or oppressor. Second, only a mass movement that has been politicized and imbued with a vision of participating directly in a future of its own making, only such a movement has a historical chance of liberating itself from oppression or military occupation. The future, like the past, is built by human beings. They, and not some distant mediator or savior, provide the agency for change.

It is clear to me, for example, that the immediate task in Palestine is to establish the goal of ridding ourselves of the occupation, using imaginative means of struggle. That would necessarily involve large numbers of Palestinians intervening directly in the settlement process, blocking roads, preventing building materials from entering—in other words, isolating the settlements instead of allowing them, containing a far smaller number of people, to isolate and surround Palestinians, which is what occurs today. It is still true, for instance, that the laborers who build the Israeli settlements on a daily basis are in fact Palestinians: this should give some fairly simple idea of how deeply misled, misguided, undermobilized, and unpoliticized the Palestinian people are today. After thirty-three years of building Israeli settlements, Palestinian workers should immediately be provided by the Authority with alternative employment. Can't a few dollars be spared from the millions spent on useless security and unproductive bureaucracy? This is of course a failing of the leadership, but in the end it is also those individuals who know better—professionals, intellectuals, teachers, doctors, and so on—who have the power of expression and the means to do so who have still not put enough pressure on the leadership to make it responsive to the situation.

And there at once is the greatest tragedy of all: a people is giving passionately of itself, losing the flower of its youth and all its energies in a valiant confrontation with a sadistic and implacably cruel enemy who has no compunction about choking Palestinians to death, and still Mr. Arafat is silent. He has not truly and honestly addressed his people since the crisis began, not even a ten-minute broadcast to give it strength, to explain his policies, to tell the people where we are, how we got here, and where, after all this bloodshed and suffering, where we are going. Not one minute of time spent telling the truth to his own people, even as he tours the world from France to China meeting with presidents and prime ministers to no avail whatever. Is his heart made of stone, is his conscience completely anesthetized? I find this astoundingly incomprehensible, and this after thirty years of leading us from one catastrophe and ill-considered adventure to another, without respite and without even a whispered "Thank you for bearing with me and my appalling, bumbling mistakes and miscalculations for so long!" I for one am fed up with his attitude of contempt for his people, and for his stony autocratic imperturbability, his inability either to listen or to take other people seriously, his unending ambiguities, secrecy, and blindingly irrational lurches from one patron to another, all the while leaving his long-suffering people to fend for themselves. Lead, Mr. Arafat, lead your people, and if you can't or don't want to, please say so truthfully. But what you have been doing since Oslo began has been to mislead, to dodge, to make secret deals that have profited a few of the many corrupt politicians who surround you but have made our general situation worse, much worse.

The Al-Aqsa Intifada is an intifada against Oslo and against the people who constructed it, not only Dennis Ross and Ehud Barak but a small irresponsible coterie of Palestinian officials. These people should now have the decency to stand before their people, admit their mistakes, and ask (if they can get it) for popular support if they have a plan. If there isn't one (as I suspect), they should then have the elementary courtesy at least to say so. Only by doing this can there be anything more than tragedy at the end of the road. Palestinian officials signed the agreement to partition Hebron, they signed many other agreements without getting prior assurances that the settlements would end (and at least not be increased) and that all signs of military occupation would be effaced. They must now explain publicly what they thought they were doing and why they did it. Then they must let us express our views on their actions and their future. And for once they must listen and try to put the general interest before their own, despite the millions of dollars they have either squandered or squirreled away in Paris apartments and valuable real estate and lucrative business deals with Israel. Enough is enough.

Al-Ahram, December 7–13, 2000
Al-Hayat, December 12, 2000

CHAPTER THREE

American Elections: System or Farce?

For over a month, the entire world has been transfixed by the spectacle of an unresolved U.S. presidential election (2000), as George W. Bush and Al Gore employ battalions of lawyers to fight out a very close election in the Florida and U.S. Supreme Courts. What first emerged from the sound and fury of the struggle (awarded finally to Bush by a very right-wing Supreme Court) is that the United States is less a society of laws than a society of lawyers. This is the most litigious country on earth, where if you have enough money and power you can do virtually anything, even win an election when it is clear that you have lost it. Over $3 billion were spent on the campaign, enough to rebuild and run an entire school system in a medium-size American town. What was at stake, as Ralph Nader pointed out in his finally disappointing campaign, was a system of spoils and patronage. For each of the two candidates, one the son of a former president, the other the son of a former senator, the prospect of the presidency was mainly about power, power that could keep literally thousands, perhaps even millions, of people prosperous as appointees, employees, lobbyists, as well as millions more in industry, the military, the bureaucracy, and the universities, all of whom would benefit in one case, lose out relatively speaking in the other. Thus with the change to a Republican administration in Washington there will be a return to the city of the old Reagan and Bush crowd, led by Dick Cheney and James Baker, who seem as if they have only been biding their time and playing golf while Bill Clinton and his crowd were running the world. The transfer in sheer wealth and prestige should not be underestimated.

But to return to the law and lawyers: after years of sending U.S. observers to supervise Third World elections on the assumption that America leads the world in democratic process, I am surprised that the Congo's Laurent Kabila and Zimbabwe's Robert Mugabe didn't make the suggestion that some of their people be sent to the United States to survey and help to manipulate our elections here. What was revealed in the unendingly broadcast news from Florida was that U.S. elections are a frighteningly antiquated, inequitable, and undemocratic hodgepodge of rules and regulations designed to keep out the poor and disadvantaged in maximum numbers. More important, the American ideological system—which came dangerously close to breaking down completely—once again saved the day, papering over and then removing from awareness the fundamentally junglelike struggle of all against all that is the underlying reality when it comes to the power and money of the ultimate prize.

And Florida's inequities were only Florida's. Had the recounts begun in Iowa, New Mexico, Wisconsin, and Maryland, the whole edifice might indeed have crumbled, revealing it to be a very poorly held together paper castle designed, in the final analysis, to keep people from thinking too deeply and too critically. What does it mean, therefore, for one candidate to have won the popular vote, and the other to have won the election as the result of a decision by a nine-member Supreme Court staffed by five right-wing Republicans voting in favor of their party, with the other four of them mounting a lusterless defense of principle and equity? That certainly cannot be called democracy. Nor is this all. What I had never known concretely before was that there is no uniform federal election code that guarantees the same rights and the same voting apparatus to each citizen. In Florida, for instance, the state has ruled that no one who was ever charged with a felony is allowed to vote. This means that about half a million people, most of them poor and black, were denied the right to vote for the president. In addition, each county in the state has its own kind of voting machine and style of voting: this runs the gamut from sophisticated machines to primitive, hand-manipulated pieces of paper. Discrepancies of every kind are therefore certain.

Plus one more thing. Particularly in southern states, where the federal civil rights and voting statutes are not well enforced, there were many reports of blacks (families or individuals) who were prevented from voting by white policemen. All sorts of trumped-up charges were manufactured against them, from driving without a valid license to failure to register. Since the Democratic Party attracts the vote of indigent and/or minority voters who are under the impression that the Democrats are more progressive than Republicans, this meant that Gore lost large numbers of prospective voters to Bush. This in addition to the 90,000 people in Florida who voted for Ralph Nader.

As if this weren't enough to make clear that George W. Bush had absolutely no real chance of becoming president except as a result of the physical and political irregularities of the election as administered in one very unprogressive state, Florida, whose governor is Jeb Bush, George's brother, there is also the undemocratic electoral college system, which is a legacy of oligarchy and slavery. How it has endured for so long is inexplicable. The system was originally designed in the eighteenth century to protect property and race, so that a popular election might take place, only to be reratified (or not) by a small group of designated electors who would be seen as confirming (or not) the election results. It is this group that Bush gained to his advantage, even though the popular vote (one person–one vote) had gone against him.

Is this unusual? Yes and no. It is true that only one other election in American history made it possible for someone to lose the popular vote and another to become president, but it is also true that the whole system functions essentially as a system of control rather than of democratic participation. We shall never know how many abuses took place in the past. Two percent of the U.S. population owns 80 percent of the wealth, and to continue maintaining this disproportionality, the majority has either to be kept under control ideologically or to be kept out of the system, preferably both. No more than 35 to 40 percent of eligible citizens vote, because they sense, correctly, that their vote does not mean what it should. What counts is that wealthy candidates can manipulate both the mechanisms of voting and/or the media (preferably both) and guarantee the absence of change that has kept the United States a country of the very rich supported by a middle class that aspires, or believes that it can aspire, to the American "dream." And it is the survival of this dream, with its underlying belief in the need to perpetuate the system, that has kept this country so extraordinarily anachronistic by comparison with other industrial democracies. No wonder then that the United States has effectively dismantled most of the attributes of the welfare state (absence of health insurance, Social Security and labor unions under constant attack, a badly funded educational system, unceasing complaints about "government spending" on welfare even as the defense budget exceeds

$350 billion, the largest ever in history, and extraordinarily punitive prison and police systems). The market rules over everything without regard for the justice and security to which each citizen should be entitled.

I do not want to be misunderstood as saying that everyone in the United States is brainwashed. Far from it. What I do want to point out is that (a) the system favors the rich and powerful (one of the reasons why Bush won was that he spent far more money than anyone) and in effect works to preserve their ascendancy through a multiplicity of means, including the electoral college and ideological systems, at the same time that the whole world is filled with the rhetoric of American democracy and freedom, most of it misleadingly propagandistic; (b) in reality there is a constant struggle in America that the disadvantaged, including women, racial minorities, and underpaid workers like teachers and nurses, try to wage against the system, with varying degrees of success, but that at present is mostly a discouraging struggle as the effects of the "free" market undermine labor in favor of the largest employers, who are coddled by the government through favorable tax laws, loopholes in Social Security payments, and unfair labor practices.

To me, the ideological system is the most interesting case of all. Not having come to this country until most of my secondary schooling was over, I was first struck and have continued to be fascinated by how the powerful presence of violence and conflict in this society is routinely masked and covered up with a more overwhelming rhetoric and an unending stream of pacifying thought, stressing the country's unity, the perfection in it of democratic practice and theory, the animating and always benign influence of the Constitution (which, although a secular document reflecting the wealthy, white, slaveholding, Anglophilic men who wrote it, is treated with the reverence accorded to scripture by any good fundamentalist anywhere), the complete fulfillment of public idealism, and the utter benignness of everything about America, always the most exceptional country that ever existed. I suspect that all this is ingrained in schoolchildren, so that by the age of twelve or thirteen—barring the birth of a critical sense in the individual—most mature Americans tend to believe all this, or at least have little opportunity in the public domain to voice different sentiments.

Certainly it is absolutely true that in the mainstream discourse is heavily policed: alternative or radical or dissenting voices are either kept out completely or sent to the margins, where they have no chance at all of gaining acceptance. So it was with the elections during the past month. No sooner did the Supreme Court make its scandalous decision than the commentators began to put the spin out that American democracy has been restored, national unity established, and so on and on ad nauseam. As if the flaws in the system were forgettable accidents and therefore not worth dwelling on.

And this brings me to my final point, which is the contempt for history and for rational understanding that underlies the ideological chorus in every one of its individual manifestations. The subtle question is whether the willing manufacture of consent is worse or better than censorship by coercion. Back of the purification of reality that ideological consent requires is the idea that knowledge of history, the critical history that articulates the whole truth and violence of American politics, is to be opposed at all costs as basically disrupting what Michel Foucault and others have called governability. The moment a large number of people challenge not just an aspect of the system like a presidential election but the whole thing, a red light goes on in the boardrooms of America where the real decisions are made.

Remember that CNN, Time Warner, Disney, NBC, Fox News, and the rest are part of the same ideological system, serve the same clientele, and are owned by the same relatively tiny group of people whose interest is to keep things as they are. Memory is an inhibition, a possible threat to their hegemony, just as it is very dangerous for a critic to keep making connections between supposedly un- or nonpolitical institutions like the Supreme Court and the Constitution, and on the other hand, base commercial interests. It can't have been a mere accident that Supreme Court Justice Antonin Scalia is a well-known right-wing Republican and a central figure in the majority opinion in favor of George W. Bush (and hence against a complete recount) and who also has two sons working as lawyers in the very same law firm that represented Bush. Or that Justice Clarence Thomas, also part of the conservative majority for Bush on the Court, has a wife who worked for a right-wing Washington think tank doing studies of people who were being considered for the Bush cabinet.

Chief Justice William Rehnquist, also a Bush supporter, was once a well-known election officer blocking possible antagonists from voting during the election of 1964 in Arizona. One can immediately see that the system is to be kept functioning no matter how difficult the task or numerous the obstacles. Whether Gore would have been a better president than Bush is a question to be answered with these constants in mind. Those who voted for Nader believe that only an outsider to the system, a candidate who spoke about making real democracy the issue, would have made a genuine difference.

Al-Ahram, December 21–27, 2000
Al-Hayat, December 2000

CHAPTER FOUR

Trying Again and Again

The last-ditch American effort to make Yasir Arafat terminate his own people's sovereign existence bears the heavy imprint not only of the U.S. Israeli lobby but also of Bill Clinton's political style. To say of Clinton's bridging proposals, as they have been euphemistically called, that they are a sort of fast-food peace is to scant and even underestimate their malevolent sloppiness. What in their all-purpose catchiness, their antihistorical bullying, and the egotistical urgency of their manner they most resemble is Clinton at his desk, one hand holding the telephone to his ear, the other clutching at the pizza slice he munches away at, even as his various staffers, funders, fixers, cronies, and golf-playing buddies mill around him giving (and getting) favors, loans, grants, deals, mortgages, and gossip.

This is then scarcely a fitting end for a struggle that has cost hundreds of thousands of lives and untold treasure for well over a century. Put forward in a language that (speaking as a teacher of how language is used and abused) fairly reeks of a dismissive silliness combined with vagueness, Clinton proposes what in effect is a warmed-over Israeli intention to perpetuate control over Palestinian lives and land for the foreseeable future. The underlying premise is that Israel needs protection from Palestinians, not the other way around. And there's the flaw in the whole thing: that Israel is not only forgiven its thirty-three-year-old occupation, its fifty-two-year-old oppression and dispossession of the entire Palestinian people, its countless brutalizations and dehumanizations of the Palestinians individually and collectively, but is rewarded with such things as annexation of the West Bank land, a long (and doubtless inexpensive) lease of the Jordan Valley, and the terminal annexation of most of East Jerusalem, plus early warning stations on Palestinian territories, plus control of all Palestinian borders (which are only to be with Israel, not with any other state), plus all the roads and water supply, plus the cancellation of all refugee rights of return and compensation except as Israel sees fit. As for the famous land swap by which Israel magnanimously gives up a little bit of the Negev Desert for the choicest bits of the West Bank, Clinton overlooks the fact that that particular Negev area earmarked by Israel just happens also to have been used by it as a toxic waste dump! Besides, given the peculiar divisions cutting up East Jerusalem—all of which is illegally annexed land anyway—and the three (instead of four) cantons into which the West Bank territory ceded conditionally by Israel will be divided, all of what has been described as an American breakthrough proposal pretty much dissolves. What the Palestinians are left with are material sacrifices that make Israeli "concessions" look like child's play.

The sacrifices demanded by Clinton are of course a cancellation of the Palestinian right of return for refugees and, just as great, a Palestinian declaration of the end of the conflict with Israel. First of all, the right of return for refugees (the right to a secure life in a place of one's choice) is a right guaranteed not just by UN resolutions but by the Charter of the United Nations and the Universal Declaration of Human Rights. Clinton's formula for getting around this little problem reveals the man's approach to the world: "I believe we need to adopt a formulation on the right of return that will make clear that there is no specific right of return to Israel itself but does not negate the aspiration of the Palestinian people to return to the area." To which area? Iraq, Jordan, and Syria, for example, can easily be described as belonging to "the area." Who does Clinton think he is fooling? So then why purposely and transparently try to confuse Palestinians with the phrase "the area" if what is actually meant is not allowing them a right to return to the country from which they were in fact driven?

As Clinton well knows (he is a lawyer by training), there can be no negotiation at all when it comes to human rights; according to the very laws that the United States pretends to uphold when it bombs some defenseless country like Sudan or post–Gulf War Iraq, no one can therefore either modify or negate any of the major human rights. Moreover it is impossible, for example, to uphold rights against discrimination or against the right to work in some cases and not in others. Basic human rights are not elements of a menu, to be chosen or rejected at will: they are meant to have the stability of universal acceptance, especially by charter members of the United Nations. Granted, the implementation of rights is always a major problem, but that has nothing to do with the fact that as rights they exist whether or not they are implemented, and therefore cannot be abrogated, modified, or, as Clinton seems to think, reformulated.

Similarly, the right to choose one's place of residence as a refugee: that too is inalienable and nonnegotiable. Neither Arafat nor Clinton nor certainly Barak has any right at all to tamper with the right, nor to attempt by crude bamboozling to "reformulate" it in a way that suits Israel or renounces it in any way. Why must Israel always be an exception, and why must Palestinians always be required to accept things that no people has ever been asked to accept before? It seems to me indecent for Clinton to have gone to war, dragging all of NATO with him and destroying Serbia in the process, on behalf of the Kosovo Albanian right of return, and then ask Palestinians to renounce theirs.

A second point here is to recall that Israel, which continues with unremitting obduracy to deny any responsibility for Palestinian dispossession, maintains an unchallenged Law of Return for any Jew anywhere. How it can continue to do so and with a kind of ruffianly churlishness refuse even to discuss a similar Palestinian right defies logic, to say nothing of elementary fairness. There is also the matter of compensation, not only for the enormous losses of 1948 but for the thirty-three years of spoliation and exploitation that have come with the ever-present military occupation. Bill Clinton wants all that dropped, as if by not mentioning a word about reparations, the whole subject would disappear. It seems condescending to tell Palestinians that Israel will mutter a few words about understanding or even recognizing their suffering and get off without a single mention of responsibility. Who is that typically 1950s-style propaganda formula supposed to placate? Israel, or the Jewish Agency?

But Arafat did indeed come to Washington in response to Clinton's summoning, and because he is who he is, Arafat will probably not refuse or accept outright. He will waffle, and maneuver, and come and go, will conditionally accept, as more Palestinians will have sacrificed their lives and, almost as important, their livelihoods for naught.

Over the past weeks I have tried in every way available to me to get Arafat for once in his long domination of Palestinian affairs to address his people honestly, directly, in a straightforward way. But he persists in silence. And his advisers and associates also flutter around, powerless to influence him or to come up with anything by way of alternatives. Yet again I want to say, we need a new kind of leadership, one that can mobilize and inspire the whole Palestinian nation; we have had enough of flying visits in and out of Cairo, Rabat, and Washington, enough of lies and misleading rhetoric, enough of corruption and rank incompetence, enough of carrying on at the people's expense, enough of servility before the Americans, enough of stupid decisions, enough of criminal incompetence and uncertainty. It is clear that no matter what happens now, the Palestinians will be blamed: unabashed Zionist prophets like Thomas Friedman of the *New York Times,* who has not one word of criticism for Israeli brutality and keeps demanding that Arabs recognize his "organic" connection as a Jew to Palestine without ever acknowledging that that right was implemented in conquest and wholesale Palestinian dispossession, will upbraid Palestinians for wrecking the peace and continue broadcasting his half-truths in the American media, but all to no avail. Whether he and his associates like it or not, Israel can have peace only when the Palestinian right is first acknowledged to have been violated, and when there is apology and remorse where there is now arrogance and rhetorical bluster.

Our first duty as Palestinians is to close this Oslo chapter as expeditiously as possible and return to our main task, which is to provide ourselves with a strategy of liberation that is clear in its goals and well defined in its practice. For this we must at some point have the partnership of like-minded Israelis and diaspora Jews who understand that you cannot have occupation and dispossession as well as peace with the Palestinian people. South African apartheid was defeated only because blacks as well as whites fought it. That the PLO has long thought that it could make peace with Israel and somehow tolerate occupation is only one of its numerous strategic as well as tactical mistakes. A new generation is arising now that no longer respects the old taboos and will not tolerate the lamentable "flexibility" that has given Palestinian liberation the status of a question mark rather than a beacon of hope.

There are two contradictory realities on the ground on which Clinton's Washington talks will founder. One is that the energies released by the intifada are not easily containable in any available form for the foreseeable future: Palestinian protest at what Oslo has wrought is a protest against all aspects of the status quo. The second reality is that whether we like it or not, historical Palestine is now a binational reality suffering the devastation of apartheid. That must end and an era of freedom for Arabs and Jews must soon begin. It falls to us to try now to provide the signposts for a new era. Otherwise it is easy to foresee years more of fruitless and costly struggle.

Al-Ahram, January 11–17, 2001
Al-Hayat, January 11, 2001

CHAPTER FIVE

Where Is Israel Going?

The story is told of the celebrated writer Guy de Maupassant who, shortly after the Eiffel Tower was built in mid-nineteenth-century Paris, would go around the city complaining endlessly about how much he disliked the great structure. And yet he would nevertheless unfailingly go to the Tower's restaurant for lunch every single day. When his attention was drawn to the paradox in his behavior, Maupassant coolly answered, "I go there because being inside it is the only place in Paris where you don't actually have to look at or even see the Tower."

My general impression is that for most Israelis, their country is invisible. Being in it means a certain blindness or inability to see what it is and what it has been happening to it and, just as remarkably, an unwillingness to understand what it has meant for others in the world and especially in the Middle East. By the time these lines appear in print, the Israeli elections will have taken place, and perhaps, as has been supposed for several weeks now, Ariel Sharon will have become prime minister. Just as happened in the months before and immediately after Ehud Barak's election, a great deal of U.S. media attention has been focused on Sharon in various attempts to make him seem like a plausible, or at least a less bizarre and outrageous, candidate. I do not think that anyone outside Israel is really convinced, but it is stunningly odd that a majority of Israelis would consider turning to the unregenerate old killer of Palestinians after four months under Ehud Barak of uselessly spilling Palestinian blood and collectively punishing several million Arab residents of the West Bank, Gaza, and Israel proper, without anything having been achieved. According to the polls, Israelis have opted for a man who will bring them more rather than less violence, which it must be added at once makes Israel's own future relations with the Palestinians, the Arab states, and the Muslim world even less likely to be peaceful and less free of difficulty. The question is how people could contemplate so obviously counterproductive a choice unless they simply had no idea what the world thought of them to begin with, no idea that such destruction and such cruelty would earn further alienation and dislike and, hence, insecurity.

Flirting with Sharon now is therefore a turning further inward, a resolute dismissal of the outside world in favor of the old and thoroughly discredited policy of bashing Arabs that has made Israel a more and more isolated and discredited country than it has ever been. Of course, life goes on within it just as it does everywhere else, and in all sorts of ways, it should be obvious that most Israelis are normal people who want to live normal lives, bring up their families, prosper in their work, and carry on without fear of catastrophe or war. Yet as a people, their collective history has been very much an unwelcome part of modern Arab history and, for Palestinians in particular, an almost unmitigated disaster. There is nothing quite like this equal and opposite relationship anywhere else in the world, and in fact, I have yet to meet a Palestinian to whom even the most benign aspect of Israel's existence has not simultaneously also meant something quite concretely negative for Palestine and Palestinians. It is difficult to look at an Israeli landscape, for instance, without also seeing the obliterated Palestinian farm or village that it has replaced; hard to hear of someone immigrating to Israel from Romania or Russia without also feeling the anguish of an exiled Palestinian prevented from returning home.

And so it has gone for over fifty years, life in one community has meant frustration and suffering in the other, measure for measure, tit for tat, inexorably and remorselessly. No Palestinian needs reminding that every Israeli triumph has been a symmetrical Palestinian loss.

Even after 1967, when Israelis and Palestinians were thrown together demographically more than ever before, the distance and difference between the two worlds deepened and widened in spite of the total proximity between them. Military occupation never made for understanding, and so the post-Oslo years provided for little enough mutuality, except where the relatively small and privileged group of security people and the negotiators were concerned. But what I have found most puzzling is the extent to which so many Israelis seem to have been disappointed and angered by the Al-Aqsa Intifada, as if the unceasing rate of settlement activity, the frequent closures, the expropriations, the thousands of humiliations, punishments, and arbitrary difficulties created for Palestinians by Israelis while the two were supposed to be negotiating a peace with each other were all negligible, as if Israel's magnanimity in "allowing" little bits of Palestinian autonomy were enough to wipe the slate clean and should have made the entire people grateful to Israel for its concessions. Rather than trying to connect the Israeli policy of military occupation with the intifada as cause and effect, many Israelis now seem to want Sharon to take over and, as one of them said to a journalist, "deal with the Arabs," as if "the Arabs" were so many flies or a swarm of annoying bees.

What seems never to have occurred even to Israeli peaceniks is that the incredibly slow and tortured pace of Israeli steps in ceding territory here and there, plus the thousands of conditions and the many, many hours that went into negotiating all the unimaginably complicated conditions that Israel attached to every little step it took, such as moving some troops from one side of the West Bank to the other, plus the constant building of new settlements, plus the new subdivisions and roads that cut up Gaza and the West Bank more and more, plus the frequent closures, the continued use of torture, the settler violence in places like Hebron, plus the fact that under Barak no territory at all was given up, as if all this—which made matters worse, not better—were something that the pro-peace camp in Israel had not absorbed or understood. Even though it must be said that Palestinians have behaved as all colonized peoples in history have behaved toward the colonizer: they rebelled in protest. What is so difficult or obscure about that, and why do so evidently well endowed a people as the Israelis resist understanding the most elementary aspects of human behavior?

But consider that if one allows for a moment that all those things being done to Palestinians as part of a peace process were supposed to be making things better—yes, better—then one must have the strangest possible sense of oneself, the weirdest imaginable psychology. What does this inverted sense of cause and effect reveal about the person? What does it suggest to believe that punishment and sadism will actually improve relationships between people? A recent article by Amira Hass in *Ha'aretz* (January 28, 2001) describes in excruciating detail what it means for all Palestinians today to use the roads, and how miserable, frightening, and absolutely hateful the experience is for everyone, young, old, male, or female, just because Israel has set out to make it that way for the whole people. This is pure punitive sadism: it serves no security or long-range purpose except to make life a hell for all Palestinians who spend most of their time on the roads in the normal course of their lives, enduring endless delays, detours, searches, humiliations, and interrogations and, much of the time, failing to reach their destinations just because of Israeli caprice. How can that possibly help anyone, and how can anyone, except someone so hopelessly out of touch with reality, believe otherwise?

I can quite easily imagine that Israelis who are in favor of such procedures are, when it comes to all other aspects of life, quite like other people. It is only when and where Arabs are concerned that things are believed to be different. Not once, to my knowledge, did an Israeli leader stop and say, for example, we have wronged these people, we have driven them out of their homes, we have destroyed their society and dispossessed them, let us at least remember that and try to make things easier for them now. Never during the long and tortuous negotiating sessions of the peace process was it so much as whispered to the press that an Israeli official had said something magnanimous or had intimated that he felt some twinge of conscience for what had been done in the name of Israel to an entire people. All we heard was that every inch of land that was discussed was released to Palestinians with thousands of conditions attached, that an already-divided Palestine was subdivided three, four, and more times in order to keep it just out of Palestinian reach, so that Palestinians would have more hurdles to jump over and more years to wait before they could reach anything like a viable state of autonomy. And still the hundreds of political prisoners were kept in their cells, and still Israel's Palestinian citizens were kept in their impoverished villages, their substandard schools and municipalities, unable to buy or lease land for religious and ethnic reasons just so that Israel could maintain a Jewish majority in lordly style, so that Israeli Jews could bully and oppress another people without having to think about them or even see too much of them.

You don't have to have the gifts either of Aristotle or of De Gaulle to realize that Israel's policy of official blindness is never going to bring victory, any more than Sharon's policy in Lebanon was a success, or Barak's "peace" policy was going to bring peace or end the Al-Aqsa Intifada. Like

Maupassant in the Eiffel Tower restaurant, an Israel led by a hawkish general is going deeper and deeper into a place from which it can neither escape nor win the battle. Far from *really* withdrawing into itself, it is making certain on the contrary that it will remain connected to the Arab world in the worst way via its army, settlers, conquerors, and ranting ideologues, while its citizens, its artists, its ordinary people are paralyzed by visions of escape and a clean slate that have no more chance of realization now than they ever did. Fanciful ideas of Israeli power today as embodied in the people who like Sharon are at best a postponement, and a bloody one at that, of the inevitable realization that apartheid can work only if *two* peoples accept the notion of separation with inferiority that the strong imposes on the weak. But since that is not the case (and has never happened in history), it will always be unlikely that people will cheerfully accept their enslavement. Why are Israelis en masse fooling themselves into thinking that it will work in so small an area and so historically saturated a geography as Palestine's?

So long as they believe in the miracle of an Israel separated from its circumstances and environment—a bizarre notion that Sharon's election campaign has encouraged—Israeli Jews resemble members of a cult rather than citizens of a modern secular state. And in some ways, it is true that Israel's early history as a pioneering new state was that of a utopian cult, sustained by people much of whose energy was in shutting out their surroundings while they lived the fantasy of a heroic and pure enterprise. How damaging and how tragic this collective delusion has been is more evident with the passing of each day, and which the coming to power of so anachronistic and ill-suited a figure as the discredited Sharon brings to a garish, bizarre new light. How long will the awakening take, and how much more pain will have to be felt, before the opening of eyes is fully accomplished?

Al-Ahram, February 8–14, 2001
Al-Hayat, March 2, 2001

CHAPTER SIX

The Only Alternative

I first visited South Africa in May 1991: a dark, wet, wintry period, when apartheid still ruled, although the African National Congress (ANC) and Nelson Mandela had been freed. Ten years later I returned, this time to summer, in a democratic country in which apartheid has been defeated, the ANC is in power, and a vigorous, contentious civil society is engaged in trying to complete the task of bringing equality and social justice to this still divided and economically troubled country. But the liberation struggle that ended apartheid and instituted the first demo cratically elected government on April 27, 1994, remains one of the great human achievements in recorded history. Despite the problems of the present, South Africa is an inspiring place to visit and think about, partly because for Arabs, it has a lot to teach about struggle, originality, and perseverance.

I came here this time as a participant in a conference on values in education, organized by the Ministry of Education. Qader Asmal, the minister of education, is an old and admired friend whom I met many years ago when he was in exile in Ireland. I shall say more about him in my next article. But as a member of the cabinet, a longtime ANC activist, and a successful lawyer and academic, he was able to persuade Nelson Mandela (now eighty-three, in frail health, and officially retired from public life) to address the conference on the first evening. What Mandela said then made a deep impression on me, as much because of Mandela's enormous stature and profoundly affecting charisma as for the well-crafted words he uttered. Also a lawyer by training, Mandela is an especially eloquent man who, in spite of thousands of ritual occasions and speeches, always seems to have something gripping to say.

This time it was two phrases about the past that struck me in a fine speech about education, a speech that drew unflattering attention to the depressed present state of the country's majority, "languishing in abject conditions of material and social deprivation." Hence, he reminded the audience, "our struggle is not over," even though—here was the first phrase—the campaign against apartheid "was one of the great moral struggles" that "captured the world's imagination." The second phrase was in his description of the antiapartheid campaign not simply as a movement to end racial discrimination but also as a means "for all of us to assert our common humanity." Implied in the words "all of us" is that all of the races of South Africa, including the pro-apartheid whites, were envisaged as participating in a struggle whose goal finally was coexistence, tolerance, and "the realization of humane values."

The first phrase struck me cruelly: why has the Palestinian struggle not (yet) captured the world's imagination and why, even more to the point, does it not appear as a great moral struggle that, as Mandela said about the South African experience, receives "almost universal support . . . from virtually all political persuasions and parties"?

True, we have received a great deal of general support, and yes, ours is a moral struggle of epic proportions. The conflict between Zionism and the Palestinian people is admittedly more complex than the battle against apartheid, even if in both cases one people paid and the other is still paying a very heavy price in dispossession, ethnic cleansing, military occupation, and massive social injustice. The Jews are a people with a tragic history of persecution and genocide. Bound by their ancient faith to the land of Palestine, their "return" to a homeland promised them by British imperialism was perceived by much of the world (but especially by a Christian West responsible for the worst excesses of anti-Semitism) as a heroic and justified restitution for what they suffered. Yet for years and years few paid attention to the *conquest* of Palestine by Jewish forces, or to the Arab people already there who endured its exorbitant cost in the destruction of their society, the expulsion of the majority, and the hideous system of laws—a virtual apartheid—that still discriminates against them inside Israel and in the Occupied Territories. Palestinians were the silent victims of a gross injustice, quickly shuffled offstage by a triumphalist chorus of how amazing Israel was.

After the reemergence of a genuine Palestinian liberation movement in the late 1960s, the formerly colonized peoples of Asia, Africa, and Latin America adopted the Palestinian struggle, but in the main the strategic balance was vastly in Israel's favor; it has been backed unconditionally by the United States ($5 billion in annual aid), and in the West the media, the liberal intelligentsia, and most governments have been on Israel's side. For reasons too well known to go into here, the official Arab environment was either overtly hostile or lukewarm in its mostly verbal and financial support.

Because, however, the shifting strategic goals of the Palestine Liberation Organization (PLO) were always clouded by useless terrorist actions and were never addressed or articulated eloquently, and because the preponderance of cultural discourse in the West was either unknown to or misunderstood by Palestinian policy-makers and intellectuals, we have never been able to claim the moral high ground effectively. Israeli information could always both appeal to (and exploit) the Holocaust as well as the unstudied and politically untimely acts of Palestinian terror, thereby neutralizing or obscuring our message, such as it was. We never concentrated as a people on cultural struggle in the West (which the ANC early on had realized was the key to undermining apartheid), and we simply did not highlight in a humane, consistent way the immense depredations and discriminations directed at us by Israel. Most television viewers today have no idea about Israel's racist land policies, or its spoliations, tortures, and systematic deprivation of the Palestinians just because they are *not Jews*. As a black South African reporter wrote in one of the local newspapers here while on a visit to Gaza, apartheid was never as vicious and as inhumane as Zionism: ethnic cleansing, daily humiliations, collective punishment on a vast scale, land appropriation, etc., etc.

But even these facts, were they known better as a weapon in the battle over values between Zionism and the Palestinians, would not have been enough. What we never concentrated on enough was that to counteract Zionist exclusivism, we would have to provide a solution to the conflict that, in Mandela's second phrase, would assert our common humanity as Jews and Arabs. Most of us still cannot accept the idea that Israeli Jews are here to stay, that they will not go away, any more than Palestinians will go away. This is understandably very hard for Palestinians to accept, since they are still in the process of losing their land and being persecuted on a daily basis. But with our irresponsible and unreflective suggestion in what we have said—that they will be forced to leave (like the Crusaders)—

we did not focus enough on ending the military occupation as a moral imperative or on providing a form for their security and self-determinism that did not abrogate ours. This, and not the preposterous hope that a volatile American president would give us a state, ought to have been the basis of a mass campaign everywhere. Two people in one land. Or, equality for all. Or, one person–one vote. Or, a common humanity asserted in a binational state.

I know we are the victims of a terrible conquest, a vicious military occupation, a Zionist lobby that has consistently lied in order to turn us either into nonpeople or into terrorists—but what is the real alternative to what I've been suggesting? A military campaign? A dream. More Oslo negotiations? Clearly not. More loss of life by our valiant young people, whose leader gives them no help or direction? A pity, but no. Reliance on the Arab states who have reneged even on their promise to provide emergency assistance now? Come on, be serious.

Israeli Jews and Palestinian Arabs are locked in Sartre's vision of hell, that of "other people." There is no escape. Separation can't work in so tiny a land, any more than apartheid did. Israeli military and economic power insulates Israelis from having to face reality. This is the meaning of Sharon's election, an antediluvian war criminal summoned out of the mists of time to do what: put the Arabs in their place? Hopeless. Therefore it is up to us to provide the answer that power and paranoia cannot. It isn't enough to speak generally of peace. One must provide the concrete grounds for it, and those can only come from moral vision, and neither from "pragmatism" nor "practicality." If we are all to live—this is our imperative—we must capture the imagination not just of our people but of our oppressors. And we have to abide by humane democratic values.

Is the current Palestinian leadership listening? Can it suggest anything better than this, given its abysmal record in a "peace process" that has led to the present horrors?

Al-Ahram, March 1–7, 2001
Al-Hayat, March 2, 2001

CHAPTER SEVEN

Freud, Zionism, and Vienna

This is a parable worth a few lines here, although it derives from a rather peculiar personal experience of mine that has attracted unusual, if undeserved, media and public attention. Ordinarily, I don't use myself as an example, but because this one has been so misrepresented and also because it might illuminate the context of the Palestinian-Zionist struggle it took place in, I have permitted myself to use it. In late June and early July 2000, I made a personal family visit to Lebanon, where I also gave two public lectures. Like most Arabs, my family and I were very interested to visit South Lebanon to see the recently evacuated "security zone" militarily occupied by Israel for twenty-two years, from which troops of the Jewish state were unceremoniously expelled by the Lebanese resistance. Our visit took place on July 3, during which day-long excursion we spent time in the notorious Khiam prison, built by the Israelis in 1987, in which eight thousand people were tortured and detained in dreadful, bestial conditions. Right after that we drove to the border post, also abandoned by Israeli troops, now a deserted area except for Lebanese visitors who come there in large numbers to throw stones of celebration across the still heavily fortified border. No Israelis, neither military nor civilians, were in sight.

During our ten-minute stop I was photographed there without my knowledge pitching a tiny pebble in competition with some of the younger men present, none of whom of course had any particular target in sight. The area was empty for miles and miles. Two days later my picture appeared in newspapers in Israel and all over the West. I was described as a rock-throwing terrorist, a man of violence, and so on and so on, in the familiar chorus of defamation and falsehood known to anyone who has incurred the hostility of Zionist propaganda.

Two ironies stand out. One is that although I have written at least eight books on Palestine and have always advocated resistance to Zionist occupation, I have never argued for anything but peaceful coexistence between us and the Jews of Israel once Israel's military repression and dispossession of Palestinians has stopped. My writings have circulated all over the world in at least thirty-five languages, so my positions are scarcely unknown and my message is very clear. But having found it useless to refute the facts and arguments I have presented and, more important, having been unable to prevent my work from reaching larger and larger audiences, the Zionist movement has resorted to shabbier and shabbier techniques to try to stop me. Two years ago they hired an obscure Israeli-American lawyer to "research" the first ten years of my life and "prove" that even though I was born in Jerusalem, I was never really there; this was supposed to show that I was a liar who had misrepresented my right to return, even though—and this is the stupidity and triviality of the argument—the invidious Israeli Law of Return allows any Jew anywhere the "right" to come to Israel and live, whether or not they have even set foot in Israel before.

Besides, so crude and inaccurate were this lawyer's methods of investigation that many people whom he interviewed wrote in and contradicted what he said; none of the journals, except one, that he approached for publication accepted his article because of its misrepresentations and distortions. Not only was this campaign an effort to discredit me personally (the editor of the journal that published it said openly that he had printed the silly rubbish produced by this hired gun simply because he wanted to discredit me personally precisely because I have a lot of readers), but quite amazingly it was meant to show that all Palestinians are liars and cannot be believed in their assertions about a right to return.

Fast upon the heels of this orchestrated effort there came the business of the stone-throwing. And here is the second irony. Despite Israel's twenty-two-year devastation of South Lebanon, its destruction of entire villages, the killing of hundreds of civilians, its use of mercenary soldiers to plunder and punish, its deplorable use of the most inhuman methods of torture and imprisonment in Khiam and elsewhere—despite all that, Israeli propaganda, aided and abetted by a corrupt Western media, chose to focus on a harmless act of mine, blowing it up to monstrously absurd proportions that suggested that I was a violent fanatic interested in killing Jews. The context was left out, as were the circumstances—that I simply threw a pebble, that no Israeli was anywhere present, that no physical injury or harm was threatened to anyone. More bizarrely still, a whole, again orchestrated campaign was mounted to try to get me dismissed from the university where I have taught for thirty-eight years. Articles in the press, commentary, letters of abuse, and death threats were all used to intimidate or silence me, including those by colleagues of mine who suddenly discovered their allegiance to the state of Israel. The comedy of it all, the total lack of logic that tried to connect a trivial incident in South Lebanon to my life and works, was to no avail, however. Colleagues rallied to my side, as did many members of the public. Most important, the university administration magnificently defended my right to my opinions and actions, and noted that the campaign against me wasn't at all about my having thrown a stone (an act rightly characterized as protected speech) but about my political positions and activity that resisted Israel's policy of occupation and repression.

The latest episode in all this Zionist pressure is in some ways the saddest and most shameful. In late July 2000 I was contacted by the director of the Freud Institute and Museum in Vienna to ask if I would accept an invitation to deliver the annual Freud lecture there in May 2001. I said yes and on August 21 received an official letter from the Institute's director inviting me to do so in the name of the board. I promptly accepted, having written about Freud and having for many years been a great admirer of his work and life. (Incidentally, it should be noted that Freud was an early anti-Zionist but later modified his view when Nazi persecutions of European Jews made a Jewish state seem like a possible solution to widespread and lethal anti-Semitism. But I believe that his position vis-à-vis Zionism was always an ambivalent one.)

The topic I proposed for my lecture was "Freud and the Non-European" in which I intended to argue that although Freud's work was for and about Europe, his interest in ancient civilizations like those of Egypt, Palestine, Greece, and Africa was an indication of the universalism of his vision and the humane scope of his work. Moreover, I believed that his thought deserved to be appreciated for its antiprovincialism, quite unlike that of his contemporaries, who denigrated non-European cultures as lesser or inferior.

Then without warning on February 8, 2001, I was informed by the

Institute's chairman, a Viennese sociologist by the name of Schülein, that the board had decided to cancel my lecture because, he said, of the political situation in the Middle East "and the consequences of it." No other explanation was given. It was a most unprofessional and lamentable gesture, very much in contradiction with the spirit and the letter of Freud's work. In over thirty years of lecturing all over the world, this had never happened to me, and I immediately responded by asking Schülein in a one-sentence letter to explain to me how a lecture on Freud in Vienna had anything to do with "the political condition in the Middle East." I have of course received no answer.

To make matters worse, the *New York Times* published a story on March 10 about the episode, along with a grotesquely enlarged version of the famous photograph in South Lebanon last July, an event that had taken place well before the Freud people invited me in late August. When Schülein was interviewed by the *Times,* he had the gall to bring up the photo and say what he never had the courage to say to me, that *it* (as well as my criticism of Israel's occupation) was the reason for the cancellation, given, he added, that it might offend Viennese Jewish sensitivities in the context of Jörg Haider's presence, the Holocaust, and the history of Austrian anti-Semitism. That a respectable academic should say such rubbish beggars the imagination, but that he should do so even as Israel is besieging and killing Palestinians mercilessly on a daily basis—that is indecent.

What in their appalling pusillanimity the Freudian gang did not say publicly was that the real reason for the unseemly cancellation of my lecture was that it was the price they paid to their donors in Israel and the United States. An exhibition of Freud's papers mounted by the Institute has already been in Vienna and New York; now the hope is that it will be put on in Israel. The potential funders seem to have said that they would pay for the exhibition in Tel Aviv only if my lecture were canceled. The spineless Vienna board caved in, and my lecture was canceled accordingly, not because I advocate violence and hatred, but because I do not!

I said at the time that Freud was hounded out of Vienna by the Nazis and the majority of the Austrian people. Today those same paragons of courage and intellectual principle ban a Palestinian from lecturing. So low has this particularly unpleasant brand of Zionism sunk that it cannot justify itself by open debate and genuine dialogue. It uses the shadowy mafia tactics of threat and extortion to exact silence and compliance. So desperately does it seek acceptance that it reveals itself in Israel and through its supporters elsewhere, alas, to be in favor of effacing the Palestinian voice entirely, whether by choking Palestinian villages like Bir Zeit, or by shutting down discussion and criticism wherever it can find collaborators and cowards to carry out its reprehensible demands. No wonder that in such a climate Ariel Sharon is Israel's leader.

But in the end these thuggish tactics backfire, since not everyone is afraid and not every voice can be silenced. After fifty years of Zionist censorship and misrepresentation, the Palestinians continue their struggle. And everywhere, despite poor media coverage, despite the venality of institutions like the Freud Institute, despite the cowardice of intellectuals who put their consciences to sleep, people speak up for justice and peace. Immediately after Vienna canceled my invitation, the London Freud Museum invited me to deliver the lecture I was to have given in Vienna. (After being driven from Vienna in 1938, Freud spent the last year of his life in London.) Two Austrian institutions, the Institute for the Human Sciences and the Austrian Society for Literature, invited me to lecture in Vienna at a date of my choosing. A group of distinguished psychiatrists and psychoanalytic critics (including Mustafa Safouan) wrote a letter to the Freud Institute protesting the cancellation. Many others have been shocked at such naked bullying and have said so in public. Meanwhile, Palestinian resistance continues everywhere.

I still believe it is our role as a people seeking peace with justice to provide an alternative vision to Zionism's, a vision based on equality and inclusion rather than on apartheid and exclusion. Each episode such as the one I have described here augments my conviction that neither Israelis nor Palestinians have any alternative to sharing a land that both claim. I also believe that the Al-Aqsa Intifada must be directed toward that end, even though political and cultural resistance to Israel's reprehensible occupation policies of siege, humiliation, starvation, and collective punishment must be vigorously resisted. The Israeli military causes immense damage to Palestinians day after day: more innocent people are killed, their land destroyed or confiscated, their houses bombed and demolished, their movements circumscribed or stopped entirely. Thousands of civilians cannot find work, go to school, or receive medical treatment as a result of these Israeli actions. Such arrogance and suicidal rage against the Palestinians will bring no results except more suffering and more hatred, which is why in the end Sharon has always failed and resorted to useless murder and pillage. For our own sakes, we must rise above Zionism's bankruptcy and continue to articulate our own message of peace with justice. If the way seems difficult, it cannot be abandoned. When any of us is stopped, ten others can take his or her place. That is the genuine hallmark of our struggle, and neither censorship nor base complicity with it can prevent its success.

Al-Ahram, March 15–21, 2001
Al-Hayat, March 16, 2001

CHAPTER EIGHT

Time to Turn to the Other Front

Until the intifada is understood in the West as a civilian uprising against colonial oppression, the Palestinians have no chance of obtaining equality and justice.

During the past several weeks, the Israeli government has vigorously pursued policies on two fronts, one on the ground, the other abroad. The first is vintage Sharon or, for that matter, vintage Israeli military. The idea is to hit Palestinians in every way possible, making their lives unbearable and so confined and strangulated as to make them feel that they can no longer endure remaining there. The rationale for this, as the Palestinian scholar Nur Masalha has studied it in three important books, is that Zionism has always wanted more land and fewer Arabs; from Ben-Gurion to Rabin, Begin, Shamir, Netanyahu, Barak, and now Sharon, there is an unbroken ideological continuity in which the Palestinian people is seen as an absence to be desired and fought for.

This is so obvious and, at the same time, so carefully obscured from the international (and even regional) public's view as to require only some additional remarks here. The core idea is that if Jews have all the rights to "the land of Israel," then any non-Jewish people there are entitled to no rights at all. It is as simple as that, and as ideologically unanimous. No Israeli leader or party has ever considered the Palestinian people as a nation or even as a national minority (after the ethnic cleansing of 1948). Culturally, historically, humanly, Zionism considers Palestinians as lesser or inferior. Even Shimon Peres, who occasionally seems to speak a humane language, cannot bring himself ever to consider the Palestinians as worthy of equality. Jews must remain a majority, own all the land, define the laws for Jews and non-Jews alike, guarantee immigration and repatriation for Jews alone. And though all sorts of inconsistencies and contradictions exist (e.g., why should there be democracy, as it is called, for one people and not for another in a "democratic" state?), Israel pursues its policies—

ethnocentric, exclusivist, intolerant—regardless. No other state on earth except Israel could have maintained so odiously discriminatory a policy against a native people only on religious and ethnic grounds, a policy that forbids native people to own or keep land or to exist free of military repression, but for its amazing international reputation as a liberal, admirable, and advanced country.

This brings me to the second front of Israeli policy, which must be seen therefore through a double lens. Even as it besieges Palestinian towns using medieval techniques like ditches and total military blockades, it can do so with the aura of a besieged victim of dangerous, exterminationist violence. Israeli soldiers (called a "defense force") bomb Palestinian homes with helicopter gunships, advanced missiles, and tank barrages; Israeli soldiers kill 400 civilians, cause 12,000 casualties, bring economic life down to a 50 percent poverty level and 45 percent unemployment; Israeli bulldozers destroy 44,000 Palestinian trees, demolish houses, create fortifications that make movement impossible; Israeli planners build more settlements and settlement roads—all this while maintaining the image of a poor, defenseless, and terribly threatened people. How? By a concerted international, especially American, public relations campaign, as cynical as it is effective.

Last week (March 2001) alone Sharon, Peres, and Avraham Burg (Knesset speaker) were in the United States to consolidate the Israeli image as righteously fighting off terrorist violence. The three of them circulated through one influential public platform after another, gaining support and sympathy for Israel's policies every minute. In addition, the media announced that the Israeli government had hired two public relations firms to continue promoting its policies through advertisements, concerted lobbying efforts, and Washington congressional liaisons. News of the Palestinian intifada has gradually disappeared from the media. After all, how long can "violence," which seems to be directed neither at long-standing injustice (such as military occupation and collective punishment) nor at a particular policy (such as Israel's adamant refusal to regard Palestinian claims as having any merit whatever), keep hold of reporters whose every deviation from an accepted pro-Israeli editorial policy is punished? It's not only that reporters have no great story to report (such as a ready narrative of Palestinian liberation), it is also that

Israel has never been firmly indicted for years and years of massive human rights abuses against the entire Palestinian population.

Senator George Mitchell's commission of inquiry as well as Mary Robinson's similar set of human rights experts, comprising a distinguished group that includes Richard Falk of Princeton, will doubtless come to similar conclusions. I have read the Robinson report, and it is unequivocally damning of Israel's cruelty and disproportionate military response to what is in effect an anticolonial civilian uprising. But one can be certain that few people will see or be affected by these excellent reports. Israel's public relations machine, in the United States especially, will make certain of that.

Such propaganda campaigns in the United States are far more effective there than they are in the United Kingdom, for instance. Robert Fisk, the excellent Middle East reporter for the *Independent,* has complained of attacks on him and his paper by the British Israeli lobby, but he continues to write fearlessly. And when the Canadian media tycoon Conrad Black tried to stop or censor criticism of Israel in the *Daily Telegraph* or the *Spectator,* both of which he owns, a chorus of his own writers and others, like Ian Gilmour, were able to respond to him *in his own* papers.

This could not happen in the United States, where leading newspapers and journalists for the most part simply do not permit pro-Palestinian editorial comment at all. The *New York Times* has had only two or three columns like that, as against dozens of "neutral" or pro-Israel commentaries. A similar pattern obtains in every major U.S. newspaper. Thus the average reader is inundated with dozens upon dozens of articles about "violence," as if that violence were somehow equal to, or worse than, Israel's attacks with helicopters, tanks, and missiles. If it is sadly true that one Israeli death appears to be worth many Palestinian deaths on the ground, then it is also true that for all their actual suffering and daily humiliation, Palestinians in the media seem scarcely more human than the cockroaches and terrorists to which they have been compared.

The simple fact of the matter is that the Palestinian intifada is unprotected and ineffective so long as it does not appear to be a struggle for liberation in the West. The United States is Israel's strongest supporter at $5 billion a year, and the one thing that Israelis have long understood is the direct value of their propaganda, which in no uncertain terms allows them to do *anything at all* and still retain an image of serene justice and confident right. As a people, we Palestinians have to do what the South African antiapartheid movement did, that is, gain legitimacy in Europe and especially in the United States, and consequently delegitimize the apartheid regime. The whole principle of Israeli colonialism must be similarly discredited in order for any progress in Palestinian self-determination to be made.

This task can no longer be postponed. During the 1982 siege of Beirut by Sharon's armies, a substantial group of Palestinian businessmen and intellectuals met in London. The idea was to help alleviate Palestinian suffering and also to set up an information campaign in the United States: Palestinian resistance on the ground and the Palestinian image were seen as two equal fronts. But over time the second effort was totally abandoned, for reasons I still cannot completely understand. You don't have to be Aristotle to connect the propaganda framework turning Palestinians into ugly, fanatical terrorists with the ease with which Israel, performing horrendous crimes of war on a daily basis, manages to maintain itself as a plucky little state fighting off extermination, and maintaining unconditional U.S. support paid in full by an uncomprehending American taxpayer.

This is an intolerable situation, and until the Palestinian struggle resolutely focuses on the battle to represent itself as a narrative surviving valiantly against Israeli colonialism, we have no chance at all of gaining our rights as a people. Every stone cast symbolically in support of equality and justice must therefore be interpreted as such and not misrepresented as either violence or a blind rejection of peace. Palestinian information must change the framework, must take responsibility for it, and must do so immediately. There has to be a unified collective goal.

In a globalized world, in which politics and information are virtually equivalent, Palestinians can no longer afford to shirk a task that, alas, the leadership is simply incapable of comprehending. It must be done if the loss of life and property is to be stopped, and if liberation, not unending servitude to Israel, is the real goal. The irony is that truth and justice are on the Palestinian side, but until Palestinians themselves make that readily apparent—to the world in general, to themselves, to Israelis and Americans in particular—neither truth nor justice can prevail. For a people that has already endured a century's injustice, surely a proper politics of information is quite possible. What is needed is a redirected and refocused *will* to victory over military occupation and ethnically and religiously based dispossession.

Al-Ahram, March 29–April 4, 2001
Al-Hayat, April 4, 2001

CHAPTER NINE

These Are the Realities

Now in its seventh month [April 2001], the intifada has reached the most cruel and, for Palestinians, the most suffocating stage. Israel's leaders are clearly determined to do what they have always done, which is to make life impossible for this unjustly suffering people, and Sharon knows no limits to what he is willing to do, all of it in the name of a "principle" accepted by the United States, which is to refuse to do anything while "violence" continues. This therefore seems to entitle Sharon to lay siege to an entire population of 3 million people, even as he and Shimon Peres, surely the most dishonest and hypocritical of the lot of them, go around the world complaining of Palestinian terrorism. So let us not waste any time wondering how it is that they get away with such despicable tactics. The fact is that they do and will continue to do so for the foreseeable future.

Having said and admitted that, however, we have no reason to accept the consequences passively. Let us therefore look calmly at the situation from a tactical and a strategic point of view. This is what we find:

1. The Palestinian leadership that signed on to Oslo and the ruinous principle of U.S. tutelage, as well as all sorts of miserable concessions (including an ongoing settlement drive), is simply incapable of doing anything more than it is now doing, which is to attack Israel verbally and signal to it under the table that it is willing to return to the old (and useless) negotiations in more or less exactly the same way. Beyond that, it has little power and less credibility. Arafat's sheer genius at surviving has carried him as far as he can go, and even though the end of the line must be obvious to him, he has no intention of letting go. The illusion that he is Palestine and Palestine him stubbornly persists; so long as he is alive he will go on believing that, no matter what happens. The further difficulty is that all of his theoretical successors are lesser men and are likely to make matters worse.

2. U.S. policy is unaffected by the Palestinian plight, no matter how bad that is. Bush is as pro-Israeli as Clinton, and the Israeli lobby in the United States and Europe is as merciless in its lies and misinformation as it has always been, despite years of effort on the part of the Arabs to try to get close both to the U.S. administration and (surprisingly enough) to the Israeli lobby. And yet there is a great deal of untapped sympathy for the Palestinian cause in the United States and Europe, but there has never been any Palestinian campaign (among African Americans, Latino Americans, most of the churches that are not part of the fundamentalist churches of the South, the academic community, and even, as proved by a remarkable statement by several hundred rabbis supporting Palestinian rights in a paid advertisement in the *New York Times,* among Jewish Americans, many of whom are as aghast at Sharon and Barak as we are) to gain this constituency in a systematic way.

3. The Arab states are much less likely to be of more than marginal tactical help to the Palestinians than before. All of them have direct interests that tie them to U.S. policy; none of them has the capacity to be a strategic ally for the Palestinians, as the recent Amman summit proved conclusively. On the other hand, there is a wide gap separating rulers from ruled in the Arab world, and this is encouragement enough for the Palestinian cause, if it is directed toward emancipation and the end of occupation.

4. The Israelis will not stop their settlement policy nor their besieging of Palestinian life in general. Despite his bluster, Sharon is not a very intelligent or even competent man. He has relied on force and deception throughout his career, flirting with crime and terror most of the time, using it whenever he thought he could get away with it. We have never addressed the Israeli public—particularly those citizens disturbed by current developments, which in effect condemn Israel to unending strife— nor, unfortunately, do we now have anything to say, for example, to the hundreds of reservists who have refused military service during the intifada. There is a constituency inside Israel that we must find a way to engage, exactly as the ANC made it a point of policy to engage whites in the struggle against apartheid.

5. The Palestinian situation itself is remediable, since it is human beings who make history and not the other way around. There are enough young Palestinians all over the world and enough older ones who are

thoroughly and totally exasperated, dismayed, and sick to heart at a leadership that has gone from one disaster to another without ever being accountable, without ever telling the truth, and without ever being clear about its goals and aims (except for its own survival). As the late Eqbal Ahmad once said, the PLO has historically been very flexible strategically and extremely rigid tactically. In effect, this aphorism is exactly reflected in policy and performance since 1993. Arafat began by accepting UN Resolutions 242 and 338 as the basis of negotiations (strategic), then changed flexibly to accepting one strategic modification after another during the ensuing years; settlements were to be stopped, then they increased, and he accepted that, too. The same with Jerusalem, and the return of *all* territories. But Arafat never wavered in his tactics, which were to stay in the peace process and rely on the Americans no matter what happened. Strategically flexible, tactically rigid.

6. Therefore, we now need something that the situation demands but that all the actors resist: a real statement of goals and objectives. These have to include first and foremost the end of Israeli military occupation and the end of settlements. No other way can lead to peace and justice for Palestinians or for Israelis. There is no such thing as an "interim" peace (as Oslo had it all along, to the tremendous detriment of the Palestinian people). Nor are there some rights for Palestinians and not others. That is unacceptable nonsense. One set of laws and rights, one set of goals and objectives. On that basis a new Palestinian peace movement can be organized that *must include* Israeli and non-Israeli Jews, especially heroic individuals and groups like Rabbis for Human Rights and the movement led by Jeff Halper to end house demolitions.

7. What then are the objectives for that movement? First of all, an organized movement focused on Palestinian liberation and coexistence, in which everyone is part of a whole, instead of an idle spectator waiting for another Saladin or for orders to come down from above. There has to be concentration on the two other societies whose impact on Palestine is central. One is the United States, which provides Israel with the support without which the actual events taking place today in Palestine wouldn't be possible. After all, the U.S. taxpayer supplies Israel directly with $3 billion in aid, plus a constant resupply of weapons (like the helicopters now bombarding defenseless Palestinian towns and villages) that

amounts to a total of almost $5 billion. This aid must be stopped or radically modified. And second, Israeli society, which has gone on either passively endorsing racist policies against "inferior" Palestinians or has actively supported it by working in the army, Mossad, and Shin Bet to implement this humanly unacceptable and immoral policy. The wonder of it is that we have stood it for so long, as have many Israeli citizens who need to be involved in changing it.

8. Although every human rights declaration in the world today (including the UN Charter) gives a people the right to resist by any means when it is under military occupation, and the right for refugees to return to their homes, it is also the case that suicide bombings in Tel Aviv serve no purpose, political or ethical. They too are unacceptable. There's a huge difference between organized disobedience, or mass protest, on the one hand, and simply blowing up yourself and a few innocents, on the other. This difference has to be stated clearly and emphatically and engraved in any serious Palestinian program once and for all.

9. The other principles are fairly straightforward. Self-determination for both peoples. Equal rights for both. No occupation, no discrimination, no settlements. Everyone is included. Whatever negotiations are entered into must be on that basis, which must clearly be stated at the outset, and not left unsaid or implied as they were in the U.S.-sponsored Oslo process. The UN has to be the framework. In the meantime, it is up to us as Palestinians, Arabs, Jews, Americans, and Europeans to protect the unprotected and to end war crimes like collective punishment, bombing, and persecution, all of which Palestinians suffer from every day.

10. These are the realities today, at the heart of which is the enormous asymmetry, the tremendous disparity in power between Israel and the Palestinians. So we must capture the high moral ground immediately, by political means still at our disposal—the power to think, plan, write, and organize. This is true for Palestinians in Palestine, in Israel, in exile. No one is exempt from some obligation to our emancipation. It is sad that the present leadership seems totally incapable of understanding that and therefore must stand aside, which at some point it most certainly will.

Al-Ahram, April 19–25, 2001
Al-Hayat, April 17, 2001

CHAPTER TEN

Thinking About Israel

The word *Israel* has a quite unusual resonance in English, especially in the United States. To hear politicians repeat the familiar mantra about supporting Israel and keeping it strong is to realize that an actual country or state is not at issue, but rather an idea or talisman of some sort, one that far transcends the status of every other state or country in the world. A few weeks ago Senator Hillary Rodham Clinton publicly declared that she was donating $1,250 to Israeli settlers so that they could buy more gas masks and helmets, all this, she added solemnly, without a trace of irony or of the macabre humor that the situation deserved, as part of her commitment to keeping Israel strong and secure. Naturally enough—at least for those of us who live in the United States—this episode was reported as if it were an unremarkable, as opposed to a bizarre or preposterous, occurrence.

Newspapers like the *New York Times* and *Washington Post* are filled with columnists such as William Safire and Charles Krauthammer who in any other context would seem completely crazy. Both have taken to crowing over Sharon's tenure as head of Israel's government, not because he has shown a propensity to brute force and, on the whole, stupidly destructive actions, but because they argue with a completely straight face that he is the only figure capable of showing Palestinians the kind of disciplinary reasoning that will set them straight. He proposed magnanimously to give them 42 percent of the West Bank, or maybe a bit more, plus keeping all the settlements for Israel and ringing the Palestinian territories with permanent Israeli fences: this is reasonable and good as a way of solving the intifada. He said in an interview with the *Jerusalem Post* that after all, "we" have 1 million Arabs in Israel; why can't "they" (the Palestinians) tolerate a few hundred thousand Israeli settlers? And one more thing about Sharon's American defenders. What is fascinating is how they arrogate to themselves as Americans the right to tell Israel what it should be doing and thinking for its own good.

Israel has therefore been internalized as the private personal fantasy of every American supporter, or so the appearances seem to suggest. Yet American Jews have a special relationship that entitles them to perhaps a greater degree of involvement in telling Israel what it should be, in particular—and this is the most amazing feature of what I am discussing—on matters of security. No one bothers to note that Israeli citizens are the ones doing the fighting and planning, not long-distance diaspora Jews. It's all part of the domestication of Israel that keeps it away from history and the consequences of its actions. When you venture that Israel is laying up hatred and vindictiveness for itself in every Arab breast by virtue of its bombing and collective punishment, you are told in response that you are being anti-Semitic. Justice and wisdom don't enter into it, only what purports to be (in the case of Israel's Arab critics) an insensate, deeply ingrained hatred of Jews.

It is therefore little short of miraculous that despite its years of military occupation, Israel is never identified with colonialism or colonial practices. That seems to me the greatest failing of all, both of Palestinian information and discourse and even of Israeli dissent, when they undertake to be critical of Israeli government policy. There is an excellent analysis of "How Far Will Sharon Go?" in the current *New York Review of Books* (dated May 17, 2001) by Avishai Margalit, professor of philosophy at the Hebrew University, which is totally unlike American analyses of the situation in that (a) it minces no words about Israeli collective punishment against Palestinians; and (b) it doesn't attempt to dress up the situation with any fancy language about Israeli security, an appalling habit of intellectuals who feel the need to talk as if they are generals in order to take themselves seriously. My only criticism of Margalit is that he doesn't come straight out and call for the end of military occupation and for an Israeli acknowledgment of injustices done against the Palestinian people. That's what intellectuals are supposed to do, rather than go on about politics from the point of view of politicians. Be that as it may, what is very important about Margalit's writing here is that it demystifies Israel's aura, which has been slowly built up and carefully structured over the years so as to eliminate Palestinians from the picture altogether.

I think therefore that what any Palestinian peace effort must accomplish is first of all to connect Israel with its deeds, and to focus on ending those practices, rather than trying to make a deal with them or to have one brokered. One of the gravest flaws in Oslo was for the PLO leadership (i.e., Yasir Arafat) to have ignored what Israel had done as an occupying force, and even to have ignored the fact of occupation itself; one can't make a deal with occupation, which is like cancer in that it continues to expand, unless it is identified, surrounded, and then attacked. Israel's history proves it. For those who say that Israel must be accepted, the only sane response is to ask *which* Israel, since the country has never had internationally declared borders but continues to tinker endlessly with its own size. No other country since World War II has been in such a position, and there is no reason to let that go on indefinitely. Peace can only be made on the basis of full withdrawal and the end of occupation. These are concrete rather than general matters, which often divert us from our goal as a people seeking self-determination.

Whereas I can understand the Palestinian leadership's desire to do something *now* to try to end an obviously draining war of attrition, I also think it is grossly immoral and stupid simply to resume the Oslo negotiations as if nothing has happened. In September 1996 a mini-intifada broke out after Israel had provocatively opened a tunnel under the Al-Haram Al-Sharif, but that ended with many Palestinian deaths and nothing changed either on the ground or in the negotiations. Under Barak, as Margalit correctly notes, settlement-building increased along with every imaginable Palestinian difficulty. What is the point of the PLO continuing the unendurable sufferings of its people just for Mr. Arafat to be invited back to the White House? There is no point at all, but what surprises me is the Palestinian Authority's brazen attitude of simply continuing with its talk of resuming negotiations as if four hundred people had not died and thirteen thousand had never been wounded. Do these leaders have no dignity at all, no sense of propriety or even of their own history?

It would therefore seem that Israel's official callousness to the Palestinians has been internalized, not only by extreme American Zionists, the dreadful Ariel Sharon, and the Israeli political establishment, but also by the Palestinian leadership. In his April 27, 2001, *Jerusalem Post* interview, Sharon kept repeating that the intifada consists only of "terrorism" and therefore reduces all Palestinian action, except ending resistance and rearresting Islamic activists, to that and that only. For Arafat to negotiate peace with Sharon without removing the word "terrorism" from their vocabulary is tantamount to accepting the equation of the Palestinian struggle against occupation with terrorism, yet so far as I know, no concentrated effort is being made through information and addressing Israelis and Americans to restore reality to discourse. The logical assumption seems to be that Israel = military occupation = Palestinian resistance. So what must become central to Arab efforts now is to disrupt and even destroy the equation, not simply to put forward abstract arguments about the right of return for the Palestinian refugees.

Sharon's reentry into politics has brought with it a quite conscious effort on his part to shift the scene back to 1948, to attempt to restage Israel's conflict with the Palestinians as a battle for Israel's very survival. He seems to have had no difficulty in finding support for this atavistic, extremely regressive view among some (but obviously not all) Israelis, who have responded to the unstated idea that Jews can never live free of persecution and hostility. To an outsider, such a notion seems both improbable and untenable. For surely having established in many respects a powerful and successful state, Israeli Jews would seem now in an excellent position to be both confident and magnanimous in their attitude toward the victims they have so wrongfully treated. But now they continue to reenact the original situation in which they first dispossessed Palestinians, thereby reexperiencing the hostility and consternation that they themselves caused in others, feeling, however, that the trauma was theirs, not the Palestinians'. Sharon exploits this terrible syndrome, as dramatic an example of the neurosis Freud called the compulsion to repeat as one can find: one returns again and again to the scene of one's original trauma, allowing oneself to remain in the grip of a powerful neurotic fear without availing oneself of the solace either of reason or of reality.

Israeli policies therefore have to appear as they are, rather than as their propagandists wish them to seem. For this, we need the combined efforts of Israeli dissenters as well as Arab intellectuals and ordinary citizens. For not only have the corruptions of language and unexamined history infected the peace process fatally, but they seem to have entered the very thinking of leaders whose first responsibility is to the people they lead rather than to their enemies or their supposed patrons (in this case, the United States). The right lessons should be drawn from Colin Powell's remarks to Israel about its invasion of Gaza. He was basically condemning Palestinian resistance, then condemning the Israeli response to *that* as disproportionate; this is very far from the truth, of course, and it prolongs the distortions of perception that have crippled our arguments as an unjustly wronged people. If we are seen only as disrupters of Israel's presence—which, falsely portrayed as a beleaguered and victimized state, continues to be the image by which our resistance is judged—then we can only aspire to a mutilated solution and an even more ridiculously skewed kind of peace process. It would therefore seem to me that the first political task of any negotiations that stem from the intifada is to labor mightily to correct the initial error and restore Israel to its proper place as a mature colonial power collectively abusing an entire people against the laws both of war and of peace. Even the obdurate and hopelessly disorganized Palestinian leadership must be persuaded of this elementary reality before it goes on to do more damage than it has already.

In other words, as I argued in my last article, we must seize the moral high ground and press our case from there against the injustice of prolonged military occupation. Simply to make a temporary security agreement now is both futile and immoral. Besides, no such agreement can last, so long as Israeli settlements are still being constructed while Palestinians remain locked up in their collective prison. The only negotiations worth anything now must be about the terms of an Israeli withdrawal from *all* the territories occupied in 1967. Anything else is a waste of our time as a people.

Al-Ahram, May 3–9, 2001
Al-Hayat, May 14, 2001

CHAPTER ELEVEN

Defiance, Dignity, and the Rule of Dogma

During the discussion period that followed a lecture of mine at Oxford in 1998, I was stunned by a question put to me by a young woman, whom I later discovered to have been a Palestinian student working for her doctorate at the university. I had been speaking about the events of 1948, and how it seemed to me necessary not only to understand the connection between our history and Israel's but to study that other history as one concerning us as Arabs rather than avoiding or ignoring it totally as has been the case for such a long time. The young woman's question was to raise doubt about my views on the necessity of studying and learning about Israel. "Wouldn't that kind of attention paid to Israel," she said, "be a form of concession to it?" She was asking me if ignorant "nonnormalization" didn't constitute a better approach to a state that had for years made it a point of policy to stand in the way of and deny Palestinian self-determination, to say nothing of having caused Palestinian dispossession in the first place.

I must confess that the thought hadn't occurred to me, even during those long years when Israel was unthinkable in the Arab world and even when one had to use a euphemism like "the Zionist entity" to refer to it. After all, I found myself asking in return, two major Arab countries had made formal peace with Israel, the PLO had already recognized it and was pursuing a peace process with it, and several other Arab countries had trade and commercial relations with it. Arab intellectuals had made it a point of honor not to have any dealings with Israel, not to go there, not to meet with Israelis, and so on and so forth, but even they had been silent when, for instance, Egypt signed large deals selling natural gas to Israel and maintained diplomatic relations with the Jewish state during frequent periods of Israeli repression against the Palestinians. How could one possibly oppose analyzing and learning everything possible about a country whose presence in our midst for over fifty years had so influenced and shaped the life of every man, woman, and child in the Arab world?

In this young woman's understanding, therefore, the opposite of conceding was supposed to be defiance, the act of defying, resisting and refusing to bend under the will of a power that one perceived as unjust and unreasonable. That, I took it, was what she suggested we should be practicing toward Israel and not what I was trying to propose, which was a creative engagement with a culture and society that on all significant levels had behaved and (as the ongoing Israeli brutality against the Al-Aqsa Intifada shows) continues to behave with a policy of deliberate dehumanization toward Arabs in general and Palestinians in particular. In this the egregious Ariel Sharon is scarcely distinguishable from Barak, Rabin, and Ben-Gurion (leaving aside the truly vicious racism of many of Sharon's allies like Natan Scharansky, Avigdor Liberman, and Rabbi Ovadia Yousef). What I said in contrast was not only a matter of understanding *them* but also of understanding *ourselves* since our history was incomplete without consideration of Israel, what it represented in our lives, how it had done what it had, and so forth. Besides, I continue to believe as an educator that knowledge—any knowledge—is better than ignorance. There is simply no rational justification from an intellectual point of view for having a policy of ignorance, or using ignorance as a weapon in a struggle. Ignorance is ignorance, no more and no less. Always and in every case.

I remained puzzled, dissatisfied with my groping answer, and put off by the question, which has remained with me until the present. But once again it has appeared to challenge me unexpectedly. Let me explain. A short time ago it was revealed in the New York press that Hillary Rodham Clinton had been compelled by federal law to return $7,000 worth of jewelry given to her by Yasir Arafat; according to the same official U.S. government source, Madeline Albright, secretary of state during the second Clinton presidency, had received $17,000 worth of jewelry from the same generous donor. Suddenly it became possible to see the relationships between public and private attitudes in the Arab world and to understand the connection between the young student's defiant ideas about what she considered to be concessions to Israel on the one hand, and, on the other, the Palestinian leadership's abject and profligate generosity to American politicians who are in some measure directly responsible for the woes heaped upon the Palestinian people. Even as I write, American weapons of mass destruction, which are supplied in unlimited numbers to Israel, are being used illegally according to U.S. law to attack, kill, and maim unprotected Palestinian men, women, and children, to demolish their houses, raze their refugee camps, and make their lives basically unlivable. Yet for some years a policy of trying without reason or dignity to woo American leaders in the most vulgar way possible has been implemented, as if the personal pleasure and satisfaction of Hillary or Madeline, bought at the expense of Palestinian public money, were a form of policy rather than an indecent display of bribery of a sort. The grotesque assumption has been all along that countries like America and Israel are mirror images of Third World states in which, like Mobutu's Zaire, for instance, policy is made according to the ruler's whim or for his family's enrichment. What is missing here is any apprehension that these are complex, on the whole democratic, countries whose civil societies and their interests play a large, if not decisive, role in each country's behavior. But rather than address and try to change the mood or ideas of their civil societies, our leaders ignore them and concentrate instead on a quick fix: buttering up, flattering, or bribing the leader. Anyone who knows anything about either Israel or the United States will tell you that such tricks are absolutely useless; they may gain one a dinner or a scowling handshake from the late General Rabin in the White House, but little more than that.

The proof of what I am saying is plainly evident in the calamitous recent history of our dealings with the United States and Israel during the period since the Oslo accords were signed. Since the Palestinian leadership betrayed its people's trust and sacrifices by entering the Oslo process the way it did in the first place, and remaining in it as a weak and, alas, all-too-willing partner, it has at the same time maintained a public stance that can only be described as defiant—a defiance, one must immediately add, that is principally rhetorical and completely contradicted by official Palestinian behavior, which has remained (to say the least) mysteriously servile to the United States and to Israel. Unsolicited presents of expensive jewelry to American officials illustrate the point all too well. Now while Palestinians, armed with a few rifles and stones, are bravely defying Israel's military, the leadership is still acting like a supplicant in trying to reopen negotiations with Israel and the United States. The same things can be said about the Arab regimes and even their intellectual sectors, who roundly proclaim their enmity toward Israel and the United States while in fact either collaborating with them politically and economically, or loudly and clamorously denouncing normalization. The sad thing is that this contradiction is generally perceived not as a contradiction but as a necessary part of life today. I would have thought that, instead of denouncing Israel from top to bottom, the smarter thing would have been to cooperate with sectors inside the country who stand for civil and human rights, who oppose the settlement policy, who are ready to take a stand on military occupation, who believe in coexistence and equality, who are disgusted with official repression of the Palestinians. For only in this way is there any hope of changing Israeli policy, given the gigantic disparity in military power between all of the Arabs and Israel. I would also have thought it the better part of honesty to have dissociated oneself from crude anti-Semitic attacks such as those emanating from Damascus recently: what do those do except display to the world a mindset that is both sectarian and viciously stupid?

I know perfectly well that passions regarding Israeli repression of Palestinians today are genuine and that people everywhere are disgusted with the policies of the Sharon government. But is that passion enough of an excuse to abandon rationality altogether, and for intellectuals in particular to flail around incoherently instead of trying in a serious way to come up with a serious political and moral stand based on knowledge rather than uninformed and blind ignorance, which cannot under any circumstances be described as a political position? Or take the recent campaign against the translation of Arabic books into Hebrew (see *Al-Hayat*, May 10, 2001). One would have thought that the more Arabic literature was available in Israel, the better able Israelis would be to understand us as a people and to stop treating us as animals or less-than-human. Instead we have the sorry spectacle of serious Arab writers actually denouncing their colleagues for "allowing" themselves to "normalize" with Israel, which is the idiotic phrase used as an accusation for collaborating with the enemy. Isn't it the case, as Julien Benda was the first to say, that intellectuals are supposed to go against collective passions instead of trading in them demagogically? How on earth is a Hebrew translation an act of collaboration? Getting translated into a foreign language is always a victory for the writer. Always and in each case. Isn't it a far more intelligent and useful thing than the craven "normalization" of the various countries that have trade and diplomatic relationships with the enemy even as Palestinians are being killed like so many flies by the Israeli army and air force? Aren't Hebrew translations of Arabic literature a way of entering Israeli life culturally, making a positive effect in it, changing people's minds from bloody passion to reasonable understanding of Israel's Arab Others, especially when it is Israeli publishers who have gone and published the translations as a sign of cultural protest against Israel's barbarous Arab policy?

All these confusions and contradictions I have described are signs of a deeper Arab malaise. When we mistake puerile acts of defiance for real resistance, and when we assume that know-nothing ignorance is a political act (when in fact it is nothing of the sort), and when we shed all dignity and clamor for American patronage and attention, surely our sense of dignity and self-respect is in tatters. Who hasn't cringed at the memory of Arafat on the White House lawn in 1993 repeating his three thank-yous with fawning abjection, and who hasn't felt that our leaders lack a sense of self-esteem when they are unable to decide whether America is the enemy or our only hope? Instead of adhering to a policy based on principles and norms of decent behavior, we wallow instead in futile acts of defiance based on silly, unreflective dogmas about opposition to Israel, while at the same time we only offer our besieged Palestinian compatriots lip service and patriotic formulas. No model helps us to guide our actions. The Arab world today is the triumph of mediocrity and opportunism, but given the leadership's failures on nearly every front, it becomes the intellectual's role to provide honest analyses and indications of what is reasonable and just, instead of joining the chorus of hand-clapping flatterers who decorate the royal and presidential courts and the corporate boardrooms with their oily, unremittingly approving presences.

I shall conclude with a concrete example of what I mean. Amid all the din about normalization, I have noticed one startling absence, namely, the current status of the Palestinian refugees living in every major Arab country, whose condition everywhere—there are no exceptions—is unacceptably miserable. Wherever there are Palestinians in the Arab world, there are rules and regulations forbidding them full status as residents, forbidding them work and travel, requiring them to register with the police on a monthly basis, and so on. It's not only Israel that treats Palestinians badly, it is the Arab countries who do so also. Now see if there is a sustained campaign by Arab intellectuals against this invidious *local* treatment of the Palestinian refugees: you won't see or hear one. What excuse is there for the horrible refugee camps in which so many of them live, even in places like Gaza and the West Bank; what right do local *mokhabarat* forces have to harass them and generally make their lives miserable? And why is there no protracted press campaign to end this appalling state of affairs? Why, because it is much easier (and less risky) to rail against normalization and Hebrew translations than it is to dramatize the unacceptable condition of Palestinian refugees in the Arab world, who are always being told that they cannot be "normalized" because it would implement Israel's design. What rubbish!

We must return to basic values and honesty of discussion. There can be no military solution to what ails us, Arabs and Jews alike. This truth leaves only the power of mind and education to do the job that armies have been unable to accomplish for over half a century. Whether Israeli intellectuals have failed or not in their mission is not for us to decide. What concerns us is the shabby state of discourse and analysis in the Arab world. For that, as citizens, we must take responsibility and try first of all to release ourselves from the jejune clichés and unthinking formulas that clutter our writing and speaking.

Al-Ahram, May 17–23, 2001
Al-Hayat, May 23, 2001

CHAPTER TWELVE

Enemies of the State

Because of Israel's abominable behavior toward Palestinians, most Arabs—myself included—have tended to direct our criticism less on the general situation in the Arab world than we might ordinarily do. I do not think it is an exaggeration to say, however, that once we start to look at what obtains in the Arab world, most of us are fairly appalled by the overall condition of mediocrity and galloping degeneration that seem to have become our lot. In all significant fields (except perhaps for cooking) we have declined to the bottom of the heap when it comes to quality of life. We have become an embarrassment, as much for our powerlessness and hypocrisy (for instance, vis-à-vis the intifada, for which the Arab states do next to nothing) as for the abysmally poor social, economic, and political conditions that have overtaken every Arab country almost without exception. Illiteracy, poverty, unemployment, and unproductivity have increased alarmingly. And whereas the rest of the world seems to be moving in a democratic direction, the Arab world is going the other way, toward even greater degrees of tyranny, autocracy, and mafia-style rule. As a result more and more of us feel that we should no longer keep silent about this. Yet one scarcely knows where to begin in trying to ameliorate the situation, although honesty about what we have allowed to happen to ourselves is a good way to start.

A small number of instances illustrate what I mean more eloquently than lists of facts and figures, all of which, incidentally, would support what I mean here. A short time ago the Egyptian American intellectual Saadedin Ibrahim, professor of sociology at the American University of Cairo and director of the Ibn Khaldun Center there, was sentenced to seven years prison with hard labor by a state security court. And this after two months of solitary confinement consequent on summary arrest, followed by several months of trial for financial misdemeanor, tarnishing Egypt's image, tampering with the election process, stirring up confessional or sectarian sentiment, as well as being an enemy informer. These are major charges, of course, but what seems amazing is that the court rendered its judgment in a matter of hours after hearing evidence for months.

A huge amount of attention has been lavished on the case for obvious reasons. A prominent intellectual had been brought low in a country whose political centrality and size almost guaranteed much commentary and, especially in the liberal West, a great deal of negative judgment against the system that had seemed to be persecuting a man for his independent, if not always widely popular, opinions. The few Arabs who defended him almost uniformly began by saying that they found his views and his methods distasteful: he was known to favor normalization with Israel, he seemed to prosper financially because of what seemed to be his entrepreneurship, and his ideas in general circulated with more success outside than inside the Arab world. Still, it was meant to be clear to everyone that an example was being made of him; he therefore suffered unjustly, despite his on the whole rather special way of life and success.

I must be one of the few people who has followed the case from a distance, but who knew Ibrahim about thirty years ago and has not seen or heard from him since. I have visited Egypt and the American University several times in the last two decades, but his path and mine never crossed. I don't recall reading anything by him, but I did know of his interest in civil society, his cordial relationship with the power elite in Egypt, Jordan, and elsewhere, as well as his interest in elections and minorities. All of this I gleaned at second or third hand, so I am not in a position to say anything about his ideas. Nor do I think they are really relevant, one way or the other. I assume that he has ideas, and I also assume that, like all intellectuals, he has generated as much hostility as support. That proves nothing and strikes me as entirely normal.

What seems to be incontrovertibly *abnormal,* however, is that he has been systematically punished by the state because of his fame and his criticism of several of the state's policies. The lesson seems to be that if you have the temerity to speak out too much and if you displease the powers that be, you will be severely cut down. Many countries in the world are ruled by emergency decree. Without exception such rule must be opposed and condemned. There can be no reason short of absolute natural catastrophe to suspend unilaterally the rule of law and the protection of impartial justice. Even the worst criminals in a society of laws are entitled to justice and proportional sentence. In the United States, for example, many commentators on the Ibrahim case fail to point out that America (which is not ruled by emergency decree) is one of the worst offenders when it comes to unfair sentencing (usually affecting nonwhites), capital punishment, and a horrible prison system that per capita is the largest and most punitive in the world. In other words, what Egypt does must be looked at from a perspective that includes so-called civilized countries, many of whose journalists have condemned Ibrahim's treatment without also admitting that his case is not unique, neither in the Middle East nor in the West. Thousands of Islamic militants are treated far worse, without much protest from liberal journalists who are passionate defenders of Ibrahim (such as Thomas Friedman) and who have nothing to say either about their own countries' human rights abuses, despite the law, or about the fate of less visible Arab victims of state injustice than Saadedin Ibrahim.

The point, of course, is that justice is justice, and injustice injustice, no matter who is indicted and mistreated. The travesty of due process in the Ibrahim case is an offense not because he is rich and famous but because the offense is a serious one no matter who is its victim. And what is so significant about the case is that it speaks volumes about our current malaise and our sense of distorted priorities when it is assumed that any citizen at all, not just a famous academic, can be subject to the distortions of power in the Arab world. The case tells us that our rulers hold that no one is immune from their wrath and that citizens should maintain a permanent sense of fear and capitulation when it comes to authority, whether secular or religious. When the state is transformed from its role as the people's property and becomes instead the possession of a regime or a ruler, to be used as he/they see fit, we have to admit that as a sovereign people we have been defeated and have entered a phase of advanced degeneration that may be too late to repair or reverse.

Neither a constitution nor an election process has any real meaning if such suspensions of law and justice can take place with the relative acquiescence of an entire people, especially the intellectuals. What I mean is not just that we don't have democracy, but that at bottom we seem to have refused the very concept itself. I became dramatically aware of this eight years ago when, after a lecture I gave in London in which I criticized the Arab governments for their abuse of human freedoms, I was summoned by an Arab ambassador to apologize for my remarks. When I refused even to speak to the man, a friend interceded and arranged for me to have tea with the offended ambassador at my friend's house. What transpired was profoundly revealing. When I repeated my comments, the ambassador lost his temper (he happened also to be a member of the ruling party) and told me in no uncertain terms that, as far as he and his regime were concerned, democracy was little more than AIDS, pornography, and chaos. "We don't want that," he kept repeating with almost insensate rage.

Then I understood that so deep has the authoritarianism in us become that any challenge to it is seen as little short of devilish and therefore unacceptable. Not for nothing have so many people turned to an extremist form of religion as a result of desperation and the absence of hope. When democratic rights were first abrogated in Arab countries in the early years of independence because there seemed to be genuine security concerns, no one realized that the "emergency" would continue for half a century while showing no sign at all of abating in the interests of personal freedom. On the contrary, as the security state has become more insecure—after all, what state in our area can actually provide its citizens with the kind of security and freedom from fear and want that they are entitled to?—the level of repression increases. No one is safe, no one is free of anxiety, no value is preserved by law.

So low has the individual's status sunk that even one's basic right of citizenship, one's right to exist free of personal threat from the state, has all but vanished. As a second instance of what I am describing as a worsening situation, there is the case of the Lebanese journalist Raghida Dergham, a capable woman who has represented *Al-Hayat* in New York for several years. A fine reporter and commentator with an excellent reputation in America, she has brought credit to her profession and her country for several years. She has now been indicted for high treason in her country because she attended a public Washington meeting and debated Uri Lubrani, an Israeli Mossad operative who was one of (and perhaps the chief of) the supervisors of the occupation regime in South Lebanon.

(Before that he had been Israel's connection with the Shah of Iran.) Dergham's passport has been withdrawn, and if she returns to her country, she will immediately be arrested. (Another Lebanese journalist, Samir Kassir, has had his citizenship revoked because something he wrote seems to have angered the authorities.)

The Dergham case is an amazing act of perversity that suggests how far conceptions of the "crime" of "normalization"—a stupid concept when overused either to divert attention from Arab indifference to the Palestinians or to attack other Arabs or to promote ignorance, as I argued in my last article—can be taken. In the first place, Dergham's debate with Lubrani was held in public, in the United States. There was nothing secret about it, and it was nothing more than a debate, certainly not a negotiation. To expect a normal-functioning citizen to obey laws that forbid even mentioning Israel's name is mindless, to say the least. Besides, every Arab government that I know of has had dealings with Israel, secret or open. The whole world, and especially Israel's Palestinian victims, knows that Israel, its army, agents, police, and society exist: what earthly use is there in pretending that it doesn't? But to call what Dergham did high treason is not so much to reveal that the notion of treason has been extended beyond reason and normal practice as to show with what radical hostility the state views its own citizens, particularly those who carry out their professional obligations with skill and conscience. Besides, in most countries except ours, open debate is one of the ways by which the Arab viewpoint is made known. How can that be opposed?

But to Arab governments, sad as it may seem, an enlightened view is something they feel that they must oppose, especially if it displeases the ruler. One can understand and even accept that there can be an adversarial relationship between the state and its citizens, but there is now a situation of such profound antagonism, whereby the individual citizen can be threatened with near extinction by government and ruler, that the entire balance between various interests in the state has lost all meaning. Crime is no longer an objective act, governed by recognized, publicly codified procedures of evidence, trial, punishment, and appeal; it has become the prerogative of the state entirely to define and punish it at will.

At issue is the right to free thought and expression and, underlying that, the right to be free of ludicrously enacted restrictions against individual freedom. Both the cases I have cited were brought against well-known personalities who have the resources and connections to draw attention to what was so unjustly done to them. Yet a whole, mostly hidden population of possible victims exists in Arab societies today, against whom similar measures can and have been taken, either individually or collectively. For them such rubrics as homosexuality, atheism, extremism, terrorism, and fundamentalism have been overused much of the time without sufficient care or nuance, just so that critics of the ruling groups could be silenced or imprisoned. Torture has been as common in Arab prisons, alas, as it has been in Israeli ones.

Most of us live in fear of such a fate, and this is why many intellectuals keep silent or thank their lucky stars that what has happened to Saadedin Ibrahim and Raghida Dergham hasn't happened to them. And certainly these two individuals have been singled out so that an example could be made of their humiliation and punishment. Foolishly, however, other intellectuals also hope that if they behave, join the chorus of condemnation, and be careful to say only the "right" things, they will not suffer a similar fate. At this point, I do not know which is worse, direct censorship practiced by the government, or the self-censorship of caution exercised by each and every one of us so that we can lead our lives inoffensively without going to jail or disappearing in the night. The other day I met a young Iraqi Kurd who had just escaped from his country. There, he told me, if someone wanted to do you harm, they could report you to the police as an enemy of the state: the likelihood is that you and your family would thereafter just disappear. Of how many countries in the world today is this true, and how many of them are Arab? I am too embarrassed to ask.

As the Arab world spins into further incoherence and shame, it is up to every one of us to speak up against these terrible abuses of power. No one is safe unless every citizen protests what in effect is a reversion to medieval practices of autocracy. If we accuse Israel of what it has done to the Palestinians, we must be willing to apply exactly the same standards of behavior to our own countries. This norm is as true for the American as for the Arab and the Israeli intellectual, who must criticize human rights abuses from a universal point of view, not simply when they occur within the domain of an officially designated enemy. Our own cause is strengthened when we take positions that can be applied to all situations, without conditions such as saying "I disagree with his views, but" as a way of lessening the difficulty and the onus of speaking out. The truth is that, as Arabs, all we have left now is the power of speaking out, and unless we exercise that right, the slide into terminal degeneration cannot ever be stopped. The hour is very late . . .

Al-Ahram, June 21–27, 2001
Al-Hayat, June 28, 2001

CHAPTER THIRTEEN

Sharpening the Axe

An ominous air is overtaking the Middle East, now that Ariel Sharon has come to and gone from the United States. A striking resemblance to the period before Israel's 1982 invasion of Lebanon has undoubtedly occurred to anyone with a memory long enough to recall what happened then. The same war criminal, Sharon (who should soon be sharing Slobodan Milosevic's fate in The Hague), came to see then Secretary of State Alexander Haig and then went back with what he informed everyone was an American green light. Thereafter his armies invaded Lebanon. And sure enough, he did the same thing this time with the inexperienced Colin Powell and the intellectually disadvantaged George W. Bush. Both those men have, in the space of less than a month, totally adopted the Israeli lie that the main problem is "the violence," by which it is automatically assumed that violence is what Palestinians practice while restraint is Israel's contribution. So all Sharon now has to do is to invade areas under the control of the Palestinian Authority and then claim that it is being done with restraint and U.S. approval in order to safeguard Israeli security. Perhaps Colin Powell's visit to Palestine and his suggestion that international monitors might supervise the truce will complicate matters slightly, but Sharon's mindset doesn't allow for more than invasion and destruction to Palestinians.

By now it has become clear that no Israeli public official can say anything that isn't an out-and-out lie. Last week a major television debate in the United States between Minister Nabil Shaath and Knesset Speaker Avraham Burg confirmed this sad fact and confirmed yet again that for whatever reason the Authority and its spokesmen seem unable to understand what is happening. Burg sat there and brazenly manufactured one falsehood after another—that as a democrat and a peace lover, he was concerned there was no real Palestinian peace camp; that Israel is trying ever so hard to remain calm while Palestinian terrorists (encouraged by the Authority) threaten his daughter, no less, with brutal killing; that Israel has always wanted peace; that Arafat controls everything; that

Shaath and he (Burg) are exactly the same except that he, Burg, is able to influence Sharon in restraint but Shaath cannot influence Arafat; and on and on. All of it making the point in the style of classical propaganda (to repeat a lie often enough is to believe it) that Israel is victimized by Palestinians, that it wants peace, and that it is waiting for Palestinians to catch up with its magnanimity and restraint.

To this farrago of confections Shaath seemed to have no answer, except to say plaintively that Palestinians also want peace, that they want the Mitchell plan (as if that rubbishy piece of AIPAC-constructed nonsense had already become scripture: have Palestinian leaders like Yasir Abed Rabbo, Shaath, Saeb Erekat, and the others forgotten that as senators, George Mitchell and Warren Rudman, who were almost half the committee that produced that report, were among the highest-paid members of the Israeli lobby?) Rarely have I seen such a concentration of Israeli mendacity received with such cringing servility by Palestinians, and all this while millions of Palestinians are suffering the worst possible collective punishment.

When people like Shaath get a precious opportunity to deal with a criminal like Burg, they should not once let him forget that Israel is indulging in horrendous war crimes, that people by the million are unable to travel, eat, or get health care, that 500 people have been killed, that 2,000 houses have been demolished, that 50,000 trees have been uprooted, that thousands of acres of land have been confiscated, that settlements continue, that all this has occurred during a "peace process." Even a normally excellent and reliable spokesman like Ghassan Khatib has been infected with the virus of talking about violence and the Mitchell report and failing totally to mention the occupation, the occupation, the occupation, the occupation. Can't these redoubtable spokesmen of ours concentrate on the daily reality of our people and their suffering, and can't they once speak as human beings instead of as third-rate imitations of Henry Kissinger and Yitzhak Rabin, who seem to have become their role models? What is wrong with us that we can't ever speak concretely about the central fact of our existence, which is that on every level, for over fifty-three years, we have been oppressed by Israel and continue to be oppressed with blockades, sieges, aerial bombardment, missile and helicopter attacks, and that our refugees have not received one penny of compensation or even the hope of repatriation from the state that dispossessed them and has punished them ever since?

What puzzles me is that even after eight years of deception and betrayal, the official Palestinian mind finds itself incapable of saying what a disaster Oslo was and instead wants it brought back. That's like asking the executioner if he wouldn't mind sharpening his axe a little before having another go. Of course, one needs to stay in whatever political game is going on, and of course, one must be able to respond directly to questions about agreements, truces, and so forth. But above all, what I find so dismaying is that our spokespersons show signs of being so totally remote from the daily horrors of life for average Palestinians that they never even mention it.

To them I want to say that no matter the occasion, no matter the question, no matter the newspaper or TV or radio journalist, every question must first be answered with a few basic points about the military occupation that has been in place for thirty-four years since 1967. This is the source of violence, this is the source of the main problems, and it is the reason Israel can never have real peace. Our entire political position must be based on ending the occupation, and this must take precedence over any and every other consideration. When Erekat or Shaath or Hanan Ashrawi or Khatib is asked something, for example, about the Mitchell report or the Powell visit, the answer should always begin, "So long as there is a military occupation of Palestine by Israel, there can never be peace. Occupation with tanks, soldiers, checkpoints, and settlements is violence, and it is much greater than anything Palestinians have done by way of resistance." Something like that.

These estimable people have to remember that 99 percent of the people reading newspapers or watching TV news all over the world (including Arabs) have simply forgotten—if they ever knew—that Israel is an illegal occupying power and has been for thirty-four years. So we must remind the world of that over and over. Repeat and repeat and repeat. This is not a difficult task, although it is, I believe, absolutely crucial. To remind everyone repeatedly about the Israeli occupation is a necessary repetition, much more so than stupidly inconsequential and sentimental Israeli- and American-style remarks about peace and violence. Can we learn, or are we condemned to repeat our mistakes forever?

Al-Ahram, July 19–25, 2001
Al-Hayat, July 6, 2001

CHAPTER FOURTEEN

The Price of Camp David

In July 2000 Bill Clinton convened a meeting of the Israeli and Palestinian leaderships at the presidential retreat in Camp David so as to finalize a peace agreement that he thought they were ready for. I emphasize Clinton's role in all this because it was characteristic of the man whom Palestinians had placed their hopes in, greeted in Ramallah and Gaza like a hero, and deferred to on every occasion, that he rushed together the two opponents, locked together for decades in a convoluted struggle, in order to be able for his own selfish purposes to say he had engineered a historical achievement.

Yasir Arafat didn't want to go. Ehud Barak was there mainly to extract a promise from the Palestinians that would end the conflict and, more important, end all Palestinian claims against Israel (including the right of return for refugees) once the Oslo process had been concluded. Clinton had always been an opportunist first and last, a Zionist second, and a clumsy politician third. The Palestinians were the weakest party; they were badly led and poorly prepared. Clinton surmised that because his (and Barak's) terms in office were ending, he could produce a peace ceremony based on Palestinian capitulation, a ceremony that would forever enshrine his presidency by erasing the memory of Monica Lewinsky and the developing scandal of Marc Rich's pardon.

This great plan, of course, failed completely. Even American sources recently made public support the Palestinian argument that Barak's "generous offer" was neither an offer nor generous. Robert Malley, a member of Clinton's White House–based National Security Council, has published a report on what took place, and although it is critical of Palestinian tactics during the Camp David summit, it makes clear that Israel wasn't even close to offering what the Palestinians' legitimate national aspirations required. But Malley spoke out in July 2001, a full year after the Camp David summit ended and well after Israel's well-oiled propaganda machine launched the by-now-standard chorus that Arafat had mischievously rejected the best imaginable Israeli offer. This chorus was abetted by Clinton's repeated claim that, whereas Barak was courageous, Arafat was only disappointing. And so the thesis has lodged in public discourse ever since, to Palestine's immense detriment. Unnoticed was the observation made by an Israeli information flunky that after Camp David and Taba, no Palestinians played a consistent role disseminating a Palestinian version of the debacle. Thus Israel has had the field to itself, with results in exploitation and backlash that have been virtually incalculable.

I was well aware of the damage being accordingly done to the intifada as a result of Israel's self-portrayal as a rejected peace-lover last autumn and winter. I made phone calls to members of Arafat's entourage urging them to convince their leader of how Israel was making use of Palestinian silence, which it quickly established was the verbal equivalent of Palestinian violence. Word reached me that Arafat was adamant, that he refused to address his people, the Israelis, or the world, no doubt hoping that fate or his own miraculous powers of noncommunication would affect the Israeli disinformation campaign. In any event, my urging did absolutely no good. Arafat and his numerous lackeys remained ineffective, uncomprehending, and of course largely silent.

We must blame ourselves first of all. Neither our leadership nor our intellectuals seem to have grasped that even a brave anticolonial uprising cannot on its own explain itself, and that what we (and the other Arabs) regard as our right of resistance can be made to seem by Israel like the most unprincipled terrorism or violence. In the meantime, Israel has persuaded the world to forget its own violent occupation and its terrorist collective punishment—to say nothing of its unstoppable ethnic cleansing—against the Palestinian people.

Indeed, we have made matters worse for ourselves by allowing the inadequate Arafat to come and go as he pleases on the question of violence. Every human rights document ever formulated entitles a people to resistance against military occupation, the destruction of homes and property, and the expropriation of land for the purpose of settlements. Arafat and his advisers seem not to have understood that when they blindly entered Israel's unilateral dialectic of violence and terror—verbally speaking—they had in essence given up their right of resistance.

Instead of making clear that any relinquishing of resistance had to be accompanied by Israel's withdrawal and/or equal relinquishing of its occupation, the Palestinian people were made vulnerable by their leadership to charges of terror and violence. Everything Israel did became retaliation. Everything Palestinians did was either violence or terror or (usually) both. The resulting spectacle of a war criminal like Sharon denouncing Palestinian "violence" has been little short of disgusting.

Another consequence of Palestinian ineptitude was that it let the so-called Israeli peace activists off the hook, turning that sad collection of camp-followers into silent allies of Israel's lamentable Sharon-led government. A few brave and principled Israelis like some of the New Historians—Jeff Halper, Michel Warschavsky, and their groups—are an exception. How many times have we heard the official "peaceniks" rant on about their "disappointment" at Palestinian "ingratitude" and violence? How rarely does anyone tell them that their role is to pressure their governments to end the occupation and not (as they always have) to lecture a people under occupation about their magnanimity and disappointed hopes? Would only but the most reactionary French person in 1944 be tolerant of German pleas to be "reasonable" about Germany's occupation of France? No, of course not. But we tolerate the hectoring Israeli "peace" proponents to go on and on about how "generous" Barak has been, without reminding them that every one of their leaders has made his name as a killer or oppressor of Arabs, from 1948 to the present. David Ben-Gurion presided over the Nakbah; Levi Eshkol over the conquests of 1967; Menachem Begin over Deir Yassin and Lebanon; Yitzhak Rabin over the bone-breaking of the first intifada and, before that, over the evacuation of sixty thousand unarmed Palestinian civilians from Ramleh and Lydda in 1948; Peres over the destruction of Qana; Barak personally took part in the assassination of Palestinian leaders; Sharon led the massacre of Qibya and was responsible for Sabra and Shatila. The real role of the Israeli peace camp is to do what it has never seriously done, which is to acknowledge all of that and to prevent further outrages by the Israeli army and air force against a dispossessed and stateless people, not to be free and easy with advice to Palestinians or to express hopes and disappointment to the people whom Israel has oppressed for over half a century.

But once the Palestinian leadership forsook its principles and pretended that it was a great power capable of playing the game of nations, it brought on itself the fate of a weak nation, with neither the sovereignty nor the power to reinforce its gestures or its tactics. So hypnotized is Mr. Arafat with his supposed standing as a president, jumping from Paris to London to Beijing to Cairo on one pointless state visit after another, that he has forgotten that the weapons that the weak and the stateless cannot ever give up are their principles and their people. To occupy and unendingly defend the moral high ground; to keep telling the truth and reminding the world of the full historical picture; to hold on to the lawful right of resistance and restitution; to mobilize people everywhere rather than to appear with the likes of Jacques Chirac and Tony Blair; and to depend neither on the media nor on the Israelis but on oneself to tell the truth. These are what Palestinian leaders forgot first at Oslo and then again at Camp David. When will we as a people assume responsibility for what after all is ours and stop relying on leaders who no longer have any idea what they are doing?

Al-Ahram, July 19–25, 2001
Al-Hayat, July 23, 2001

CHAPTER FIFTEEN

Occupation Is the Atrocity

In the United States, where Israel has its main political base and from which it has received over $92 billion in aid since 1967, the terrible human cost of Thursday's Jerusalem restaurant bombing and Monday's Haifa disaster settles quickly into a familiar explanatory framework. Arafat hasn't done enough to control his terrorists; suicidal Islamic extremists are to be found everywhere, bringing harm on "us" and our strongest allies, driven by sheer human hatred; Israel must defend its security. A thoughtful individual might add: these people have been fighting tirelessly for thousands of years anyway; the violence must be stopped; there's been too much suffering on both sides, although the way Palestinians send their children into battle is another sign of how much Israel has to put up with. And so, exasperated but still restrained, Israel invades unfortified and undefended Jenin with bulldozers and tanks, destroys the Palestine Authority's police buildings plus several others, and then sends out its propagandists to say that it has sent a message to Yasir Arafat to curb his terrorists. In the meantime, he and his coterie are begging for American protection, doubtless forgetting that Israel is the one with U.S. protection and that all he will get, for the six thousandth time, is an injunction to stop the violence.

The fact is that in America, Israel has pretty much won the propaganda war, and America is about to put several million more dollars into a public relations campaign (using stars like Zubin Mehta, Itzhak Perlman, and Amos Oz) to further improve its image. But consider what Israel's unrelenting war against the undefended, basically unarmed, stateless, and poorly led Palestinian people has already achieved. The disparity in power is so vast that it makes you cry. Equipped with the latest in American-built (and freely given) air power, helicopter gunships, uncountable tanks and missiles, and a superb navy as well as a state-of-the-art intelligence service, Israel is a nuclear power abusing a people without any armor or artillery, without an air force (its one pathetic airfield in Gaza is controlled by Israel) or navy or army, with none of the institutions of a modern state. The appallingly unbroken history of Israel's thirty-four-year-old military occupation (the second longest in modern history) of illegally conquered Palestinian land has been obliterated from public memory nearly everywhere, as has been the destruction of Palestinian society in 1948 and the expulsion of 68 percent of its native people, of whom 4.5 million remain refugees today. Behind the reams of newspeak, the stark outlines of Israel's decades-long daily pressure on a people whose main sin is that they happened to be there, in Israel's way, is staggeringly perceptible in its inhuman sadism. The fantastically cruel confinement of 1.3 million people jammed like so many human sardines into the Gaza Strip, plus the nearly 2 million Palestinian residents of the West Bank, has no parallel in the annals of apartheid or colonialism. F-16 jets were never used to bomb South African homelands. They are against Palestinian towns and villages. All entrances and exits to the territories are controlled by Israel (Gaza is completely surrounded by a barbed-wire fence), which also controls the entire water supply. Divided into about sixty-three noncontiguous cantons, completely encircled and besieged by Israeli troops, punctuated by 140 settlements (many of them built under Ehud Barak's premiership) with their own road network banned to "non-Jews," as Arabs are referred to, along with such unflattering epithets as thieves, snakes, cockroaches, and grasshoppers, Palestinians under occupation have now been reduced to 60 percent unemployment and a poverty rate of 50 percent (half the people of Gaza and the West Bank live on less than two dollars a day); they cannot travel from one place to the next; they must endure long lines at Israeli checkpoints, which detain and humiliate the elderly, the sick, the student, and the cleric for hours on end; 150,000 of their olive and citrus trees have been punitively uprooted, 2,000 of their houses demolished, and acres of their land either destroyed or expropriated for military settlement purposes.

Since the Al-Aqsa Intifada began late last September, 609 Palestinians have been killed (four times more than Israeli fatalities) and 15,000 wounded, a dozen times more than on the other side. Regular Israeli army assassinations have picked off alleged terrorists at will, most of the time killing innocents like so many flies. Last week fourteen Palestinians were murdered openly by Israeli forces using helicopter gunships and missiles; they were thus "prevented" from killing Israelis, although at least two children and five innocents were also murdered, to say nothing of many wounded civilians and several destroyed buildings that were part of the somehow acceptable collateral damage. Nameless and faceless, Israel's daily Palestinian victims barely rate a mention on America's news programs, even though—for reasons that I simply cannot understand— Arafat is still hoping that the Americans will rescue him and his crumbling regime.

Nor is this all. Israel's plan is not just to hold land and fill it with dreadful, murderous armed settlers who, defended by the army, wreak havoc on Palestinian orchards, schoolchildren, and homes; it is, as the American researcher Sara Roy has named it, to de-develop Palestinian society, to make life impossible so that they will leave, or give up somehow, or do something crazy like blow themselves up. Since 1967 leaders have been jailed and deported by the Israeli occupation regime, small businesses and farms made unviable by confiscation and sheer destruction, students prevented from studying, universities closed. (In the mid-1980s Palestinian universities on the West Bank were closed for four years.) No Palestinian farmer or business can export to any Arab country directly; their products must pass through Israel. Taxes are paid to Israel. Even after the Oslo peace process began in 1993, the occupation was simply repackaged, only 18 percent of the land given to the corrupt Vichy-like Authority of Yasir Arafat, whose mandate seems to have been only to police and tax his people for Israel's sake. After eight fruitless immiserating years of the Oslo negotiations, masterminded by an American team of former Israeli lobby staffers like Martin Indyk and Dennis Ross, Israel was still in control, the occupation packaged more efficiently, and the phrase "peace process" given a consecrated halo that allowed more abuses, more settlements, more imprisonments, more Palestinian suffering to go on than before. Including a "judaized" East Jerusalem, with Orient House occupied and its contents looted or carted off (there are invaluable records, land deeds, maps that, in a repetition of what it did when it stole PLO archives from Beirut in 1982, Israel has simply stolen), Israel has implanted no less than 400,000 settlers on Palestinian land. To call them vigilantes and hoodlums is not an exaggeration.

It is worth recalling that a couple of weeks after Ariel Sharon's gratuitously arrogant visit to Jerusalem's Haram al-Sharif on September 28,
2000, with a thousand soldiers and guards supplied by Prime Minister
Barak, Israel was condemned for this action by a unanimous Security
Council resolution. Then, as even the merest child could have predicted,
the anticolonial rebellion broke out, with eight killed Palestinians its first
victims. Sharon was swept to power essentially to "subdue" the Palestinians, teach them a lesson, get rid of them. His record as an Arab-killer
goes back thirty years before the Sabra and Shatila massacres that his
forces supervised in 1982, and for which he has now been indicted in a
Belgian court. Still, Arafat wants to negotiate with him and come perhaps
to a cozy arrangement with him so as to safeguard the very Authority that
Sharon is systematically dismantling, destroying, razing to the ground.

But Sharon isn't a fool, either. With every Palestinian act of resistance,
his forces ratchet up the pressure a notch higher, tightening the siege more,
taking more land, making more and deeper incursions into Palestinian
towns like Jenin and Ramallah, cutting off more supplies, openly assassinating Palestinian leaders, making life more intolerable, and redefining
the terms of his government's actions: that it once made "generous concessions" while "defending" itself, that it "prevents" terrorism, that it
"secures" areas, that it "reestablishes" control, and so on. Meanwhile he
and his minions attack and dehumanize Arafat, even saying that he is the
"arch-terrorist" (although he literally can't move without Israeli permission), and that "we" have no war with the Palestinian people. What a
boon for that people! With such "restraint," why should a massive invasion, carefully bruited about to terrorize the Palestinians even more sadistically, be necessary? Israel knows that it can retake their buildings at will
(witness the wholesale theft of Jerusalem's Orient House, plus nine other
buildings, offices, libraries, and archives there and in Abu Dis), just as it
has all but eliminated the Palestinians as a people.

This is the real story of Israel's pretended "victimization," constructed
with such premeditated care and evil intent for months now. Language
has been sundered from reality. Pity not the inept, clumsy, pathetic Arab
governments that can and will do nothing to stop Israel: pity the people
who bear the wounds in their flesh and in the emaciated bodies of their
children, some of whom believe that martyrdom is the only way out for

them. And Israel, stuck in a futureless campaign, flailing about mercilessly? As James Cousins, the Irish poet and critic, said in 1925, the colonizer is in the grip of "false and selfish pre-occupations that stand in the way of its attention to the natural evolution of its own national genius and pull[ed] from the path of open rectitude into the twisted byways of dishonest thought, speech, and action, in the artificial defense of a false position." All colonizers have gone that way, learning or stopping at nothing, until at last, as Israel turned tail from its twenty-two-year occupation of Lebanon, they exit the territory, leaving behind an exhausted and crippled people. If this was supposed to fulfill Jewish aspirations, why did it require so many new victims from another people who had nothing to do with Jewish exile and persecution in the first place?

With Arafat and Company in command, there is no hope. What is the man doing, grotesquely fetching up in the Vatican and Lagos and other miscellaneous places, pleading without dignity or even intelligence for imaginary observers, Arab aid, and international support, instead of staying with his people and trying to aid them with medical supplies, morale-boosting measures, and real leadership? He must go. What we need is a unified leadership of people who are on the ground, who are actually doing the resisting, and who are really with and of their people—not the fat, cigar-chomping bureaucrats who want their business deals preserved and their VIP passes renewed and have lost all trace of decency or credibility. A united leadership that takes positions and plans mass actions designed not to return to Oslo (can you believe the folly of that idea?) but to press on with resistance and liberation, instead of confusing people with talk of negotiations and the stupid Mitchell plan.

Arafat is finished: why don't we admit that he can neither lead, nor plan, nor do anything that makes any difference except to him and his Oslo cronies who have benefited materially from their people's misery? He is the main obstacle to our people's future. All the polls show that his presence blocks whatever forward movement might be possible. We need a united leadership to make decisions, not simply to grovel before the pope and the moronic George W. Bush, even as the Israelis are killing his heroic people with impunity. A leader must lead the resistance, reflect the realities on the ground, respond to his people's needs, plan, think, and expose himself to the same dangers and difficulties that everyone experiences. The struggle for liberation from Israeli occupation is where every Palestinian worth anything now stands: Oslo cannot be restored or repackaged as Arafat and Company might desire. It's over for them, and the sooner they pack and get out, the better for everyone.

Al-Ahram, August 16–22, 2001
Al-Hayat, August 20, 2001

CHAPTER SIXTEEN

Propaganda and War

Never has the media been so influential in determining the course of war as during the Al-Aqsa Intifada, which, as far as the Western media are concerned, has essentially become a battle over images and ideas. Israel has already poured hundreds of millions of dollars into what in Hebrew is called *hasbara,* or information for the outside world (hence, propaganda). This has included an entire range of efforts: lunches and free trips for influential journalists; seminars for Jewish university students who, over a week in a secluded country estate, can be primed to "defend" Israel on the campus; bombarding congressmen and women with invitations and visits; pamphlets and, most important, money for election campaigns; directing (or, as the case requires, harassing) photographers and writers of the current intifada into producing certain images and not others; lecture and concert tours by prominent Israelis; training commentators to make frequent references to the Holocaust and Israel's predicament today; many advertisements in the newspapers attacking Arabs and praising Israel; and on and on. Because so many powerful people in the media and publishing business are strong supporters of Israel, the task is made vastly easier.

Although these are only a few of the devices used to pursue the aims of every modern government, whether democratic or not, since the 1930s and 1940s—to produce consent and approval on the part of the consumer of news—no country and no lobby more than Israel's has used them in the United States so effectively and for so long.

Orwell called this kind of misinformation *newspeak* or *doublethink,* the intention to cover criminal actions, especially killing people unjustly, with a veneer of justification and reason. In the case of Israel, which has always had the intention to silence or make Palestinians invisible as it robs them of their land, this has been in effect a suppression of the truth, or a large part of it, as well as a massive falsification of history. What for the past few months Israel has successfully wanted to prove to the world is that it is an innocent victim of Palestinian violence and terror, and that Arabs and Muslims have no other reason to be in conflict with Israel except for an irreducibly irrational hatred of Jews. Nothing more or less. And what has made this campaign so effective is a long-standing sense of Western guilt for anti-Semitism. What could be more efficient than to displace that guilt onto another people, the Arabs, and thereby feel not only justified but positively assuaged that something good has been done for a much-maligned and harmed people? To defend Israel at all costs—even though it is in military occupation of Palestinian land, has a powerful military, and has been killing and wounding Palestinians in a ratio of four or five to one—is the goal of propaganda. That plus going on with what it does, but seeming to be a victim just the same.

Without any doubt, however, the extraordinary success of this unparalleled and immoral effort has been in large part due not only to the campaign's carefully planned and executed detail but also to the fact that the Arab side has been practically nonexistent. When our historians look back to the first fifty years of Israel's existence, an enormous historical responsibility shall rest damningly on the shoulders of the Arab leaders who have criminally—yes, criminally—allowed this to go on without even the most meager and half-hearted response. Instead, each of them has fought all of the others, or has relied on the hopelessly self-serving theory that by trying to ingratiate themselves with the American government (even becoming clients of the United States), they would assure themselves of longevity in power, regardless of whether Arab interests were being served or not. So deeply ingrained has this notion become that even the Palestinian leadership has subscribed to it, with the result that as the intifada rolls on, the average American hasn't the slightest inkling that there is a narrative of Palestinian suffering and dispossession at least as old as Israel itself. Meanwhile Arab leaders come running to Washington begging for American protection without even understanding that three generations of Americans have been brought up on Israeli propaganda to believe that Arabs are lying terrorists with whom it is wrong to do business, much less to protect.

Since 1948 Arab leaders have never bothered to confront Israeli propaganda in the United States. All the immense amounts of Arab money invested in military spending (first on Soviet, then on Western arms) have come to naught because Arab efforts have neither been protected by information nor explained by patient, systematic organizing. The result is that literally hundreds of thousands of lost Arab lives have gone for nothing, nothing at all. The world's only superpower's citizens have been led to believe that everything Arabs do and are is wasteful, violent, fanatical, and anti-Semitic. Israel is "our" only ally. And so $92 billion in aid since 1967 has gone unquestioningly from the U.S. taxpayer to the Jewish state. As I said earlier, a total absence of planning and thought vis-à-vis the U.S. political and cultural arena is hugely (but not exclusively) to blame for the astounding amount of Arab land and lives lost to Israel (subsidized by the United States) since 1948, a major political crime that I hope the Arab leaders one day answer for.

I recall that during the siege of Beirut in 1982, a large nongovernmental group of very successful Palestinian businessmen and prominent intellectuals gathered in London to establish an endowment to help Palestinians on all levels. With the PLO trapped in Beirut and incapable of doing much, it was felt that a mobilization of this sort might help us to help ourselves. I also recall that as the funds were quickly gathered, a decision was made after much discussion that fully half the money would go for information in the West; it was felt that since—as usual—Palestinians were being oppressed by Israel with scarcely a voice lifted in the West to support the victims, it was imperative that money should be spent for advertisements, media time, tours, and the like in order to make it more difficult to kill and further oppress Palestinians without complaint or awareness. This was especially important, we felt, in America, where taxpayers' money was being spent in subsidizing Israel's illegal wars, settlements, and conquests. For about two years, this policy was followed; then, for reasons I have never fully understood, efforts to help the Palestinians in the United States were abruptly terminated. When I asked why, I was told by a Palestinian gentleman who had made a fortune in the Gulf that "throwing money away" in America was a waste. The philanthropy now continues exclusively for the Occupied Territories and Lebanon, where this association does much good but very little in comparison with projects funded by the European Union and numerous American foundations.

Some weeks ago the American-Arab Anti-Discrimination Committee (ADC), by far the largest and most effective Arab American organization in the United States, commissioned a public opinion poll on current American perspectives on the Palestinian-Israeli conflict. A very wide and deep sample of the population was polled, with quite startling, not to say disheartening, results. Israelis are still believed to be a pioneering democratic people, even though no Israeli leader did very well in the poll. Seventy-three percent of the American people approve of the idea of a Palestinian state, a very surprising result. The interpretation of that statistic is that when you ask an educated American who watches television and reads elite newspapers whether he/she identifies with the Palestinian struggle for independence and freedom, the answer is mostly yes. But if the same person is asked what his idea is about Palestinians, the answer is almost always negative—violence and terrorism. Images of the Palestinians seem to be that they are uncompromising, aggressive, and "alien," that is, not like "us." Even when asked about the stone-throwing young people, whom we believe are Davids fighting against Goliath, most Americans see aggression rather than heroism. Americans still blame the Palestinians for obstructing the peace process, Camp David most particularly. Suicide bombing is viewed as "inhuman" and is condemned universally.

What Americans think of Israelis is not a great deal better, but there is a much greater identification with them as people. The most disturbing thing is that hardly any of the questioned Americans knew anything at all about the Palestinian story, nothing about 1948, nothing at all about Israel's illegal thirty-four-year-old military occupation. The main narrative model that dominates American thinking still seems to be Leon Uris's 1950 novel *Exodus*. Just as alarming is the fact that the most negative things in the poll were what Americans thought and said about Yasir Arafat, his uniform (seen as needlessly "militant"), his speech, his presence.

Overall, then, the conclusion is that Palestinians are viewed neither in terms of a story that is theirs, nor in terms of a human image with which people can easily identify. So successful has Israeli propaganda been that it would seem that Palestinians really have few, if any, positive connotations. They are almost completely dehumanized.

Fifty years of unopposed Israeli propaganda in America has brought us to the point where, because we do not resist or contest these terrible mis-representations in any significant way with images and messages of our own, we are losing thousands of lives and acres of land without troubling anyone's conscience. The correspondent of the *Independent*, Phil Reeves, writes passionately today (August 27, 2001) that Palestinians are dying or being crushed by Israel and the world looks on silently.

It is therefore up to Arabs and Palestinians everywhere to break the silence, in a rational, organized, and effective way, not by shooting off guns or by wailing or complaining. God knows we have reason to do all of the above, but cold logic is necessary now. In the American mind, analogies with South Africa's liberation struggle or with the horrible fate of the Native Americans most emphatically do not occur. We must make those analogies above all by humanizing ourselves and thus reversing the cynical, ugly process whereby American columnists like Charles Krauthammer and George Will audaciously call for more killing and bombing of Palestinians, a suggestion they would not dare do for any other people. Why should we passively accept the fate of flies or mosquitoes, to be killed wantonly with American backing anytime war criminal Sharon decides to wipe out a few more of us?

To that end, I was pleased to learn from ADC president Ziad Asali that his organization is about to embark on an unprecedented public information campaign in the mass media to redress the balance and present the Palestinians as human beings—can you believe the irony of such a necessity?—as women who are teachers and doctors as well as mothers, as men who work in the field and are nuclear engineers, as people who have had years and years of military occupation and are still fighting back. (Incidentally, one astounding result of the poll is that less than 3 or 4 percent of the sample had any idea that there *was* an Israeli occupation in the first place. So even the main fact of Palestinian existence has been obscured by Israeli propaganda.) This effort has never before been made in the United States: there have been fifty years of silence, which is about to be broken.

Even though it is modest, the announced ADC campaign is also a major step forward. Consider that the Arab world seems to be in a state of moral and political paralysis, its leaders encumbered by their ties both to Israel and, more important, to the United States, their people kept in a state of anxiety and repression. As they and their brave Lebanese comrades did in 1982 when 19,000 were killed by Israeli military power, Palestinians in Gaza and the West Bank are dying not only because Israel has the power to use force with impunity but because, for the first time in modern history, the active alliance between propaganda in the West and military force worked out by Israel and its supporters has enabled the sustained collective punishment of Palestinians with American tax dollars, $5 billion of which go to Israel annually. With neither history nor humanity, media representations of Palestinians show them only as aggressive rock-throwing people of violence and have made it possible for the dimwitted but politically astute George W. Bush to blame the Palestinians for violence. This new ADC campaign sets out to restore history and humanity to the Palestinians, to show them (as they have always been) as people "like us," fighting for the right to live in freedom, to raise their children, to die in peace. Once even the glimmerings of this story penetrate the American consciousness, the truth will, I hope, begin to dissipate the vast cloud of evil propaganda with which Israel has covered reality. Since it is clear that the media campaign can go only so far, the hope is that Arab Americans will feel empowered enough to enter the political battle in the United States to try to break, modify, or fray the link that binds U.S. policy so tightly to Israel. And then we can hope again.

Al-Ahram, August 30–September 5, 2001
Al-Hayat, September 9, 2001

PART TWO

September 11,
the War on Terror, the West Bank
and Gaza Reinvaded

CHAPTER SEVENTEEN

Collective Passion

S pectacular horror of the sort that struck New York (and to a lesser degree Washington) has ushered in a new world of unseen, unknown assailants, terror missions without political message, senseless destruction. For the residents of this wounded city, the consternation, fear, and sustained sense of outrage and shock will certainly continue for a long time, as will the genuine sorrow and affliction that such carnage has cruelly imposed on so many. New Yorkers have been fortunate that Mayor Rudy Giuliani, a normally rebarbative and unpleasantly combative, even retrograde figure, known for his virulently Zionist views, has rapidly attained Churchillian status. Calmly, unsentimentally, and with extraordinary compassion, he has marshaled the city's heroic police, fire, and emergency services to admirable effect and, alas, with huge loss of life. Giuliani's was the first voice to caution against panic and jingoistic attacks on the city's large Arab and Muslim communities, the first to express the common sense of anguish, the first to press everyone to try to resume life after the shattering blows.

Would that that were all. The national television reporting has of course brought the horror of those dreadful winged juggernauts into every household, unremittingly, insistently, not always edifyingly. Most commentary has stressed, indeed magnified the expected and the predictable in what most Americans feel: terrible loss, anger, outrage, a sense of violated vulnerability, a desire for vengeance and unrestrained retribution. There has been nothing to speak of on all the major television channels but repeated reminders of what happened, of who the terrorists were (as yet nothing proven, which hasn't prevented the accusations from being reiterated hour after hour), of how America has been attacked, and so on. Beyond formulaic expressions of grief and patriotism, every politician and accredited pundit or expert has dutifully repeated how we shall not be defeated, not be deterred, not stop until terrorism is exterminated.

This is a war against terrorism, everyone says, but where, on what fronts, for what concrete ends? No answers are provided, except the vague suggestion that the Middle East and Islam are what "we" are up against, and that terrorism must be destroyed.

What is most depressing, however, is how little time is spent trying to understand America's role in the world and its direct involvement in the complex reality beyond the two coasts that have for so long kept the rest of the world extremely distant and virtually out of the average American's mind. You'd think that "America" was a sleeping giant rather than a superpower almost constantly at war, or in some sort of conflict, all over the Islamic domains. Usama bin Laden's name and face have become so numbingly familiar to Americans as in effect to obliterate any history that he and his shadowy followers might have had (e.g., as useful conscripts in the jihad raised twenty years ago by the United States against the Soviet Union in Afghanistan) before they became stock symbols of everything loathsome and hateful to the collective imagination. Inevitably then, collective passions are being funneled into a drive for war that uncannily resembles Captain Ahab in pursuit of Moby Dick, rather than what is in fact going on, an imperial power injured at home for the first time, pursuing its interests systematically in what has become a suddenly reconfigured geography of conflict, without clear borders or visible actors. Manichean symbols and apocalyptic scenarios are bandied about, with future consequences and rhetorical restraint thrown to the winds.

Rational understanding of the situation is what is needed now, not more drum-beating. George W. Bush and his team clearly want the latter, not the former. Yet to most people in the Islamic and Arab worlds, the official United States is synonymous with arrogant power, known mainly for its sanctimoniously munificent support not only of Israel but of numerous repressive Arab regimes, and its inattentiveness even to the possibility of dialogue with secular movements and people who have real grievances. Anti-Americanism in this context is not based on a hatred of modernity or on technology envy, as accredited pundits like Thomas Friedman keep repeating; it is based on a narrative of concrete interventions, specific depredations and—in the cases of the Iraqi people's suffering under U.S.-imposed sanctions and U.S. support for the thirty-four-year-old Israeli occupation of Palestinian territories—cruel and inhumane policies administered with a stony coldness.

Israel is now cynically exploiting the American catastrophe by intensifying its military occupation and oppression of the Palestinians. Since September 11, Israeli military forces have invaded Jenin and Jericho and have repeatedly bombed Gaza, Ramallah, Beit Sahour, and Beit Jala, exacting great civilian casualties and enormous material damage. All of this, of course, is done brazenly with U.S. weaponry and the usual lying cant about fighting terrorism. Israel's supporters in the United States have resorted to hysterical cries like "we are all Israelis now," making the connection between the World Trade Center and Pentagon bombings and Palestinian attacks on Israel an absolute conjunction of "world terrorism," in which Bin Laden and Arafat are interchangeable entities. What might have been a moment for Americans to reflect on the probable causes of what took place, which many Palestinians, Muslims, and Arabs have condemned, has been turned into a huge propaganda triumph for Sharon; Palestinians are simply not equipped to defend themselves against both Israeli occupation in its ugliest and most violent forms *and* the vicious defamation of their national struggle for liberation.

Political rhetoric in the United States has overridden these things by flinging about words like *terrorism* and *freedom,* whereas, of course, such large abstractions have mostly hidden sordid material interests, the efficacy of the oil, defense, and Zionist lobbies now consolidating their hold on the entire Middle East, and an age-old religious hostility to (and ignorance of) "Islam" that takes new forms every day. The commonest thing is to get TV commentary, run stories, hold forums, or announce studies on Islam and violence or on Arab terrorism or any such thing, using the predictable experts (the likes of Judith Miller, Fouad Ajami, and Steven Emerson) to pontificate and throw around generalities without context or real history. Why no one thinks of holding seminars on Christianity (or Judaism for that matter) and violence is probably too obvious to ask.

It is important to remember (although this is not at all mentioned) that China will soon catch up with the United States in oil consumption, and it has become even more urgent for the United States to control both Persian Gulf and Caspian Sea oil supplies more tightly: an attack on Afghanistan, including the use of former Soviet Central Asian republics as staging grounds, therefore consolidates a strategic arc for the United States from the Gulf to the northern oil fields that will be very difficult for anyone in the future to pry loose. As pressure on Pakistan mounts daily, we can be certain that a great deal of local instability and unrest will follow in the wake of the events of September 11.

Intellectual responsibility, however, requires a still more critical sense of the actuality. There *has* been terror, of course, and nearly every struggling modern movement at some stage has relied on terror. This was as true of Mandela's ANC as it was of all the others, Zionism included. And yet bombing defenseless civilians with F-16s and helicopter gunships has the same structure and effect as more conventional nationalist terror. All terror is especially bad when it is attached to religious and political abstractions and reductive myths that keep veering away from history and sense. This is where the secular consciousness has to step forward and try to make itself felt, whether in the United States or in the Middle East. No cause, no god, no abstract idea can justify the mass slaughter of innocents, most particularly when only a small group of people are in charge of such actions and feel themselves to represent the cause without having been elected or having a real mandate to do so.

Besides, as much as Islam has been quarreled over by Muslims, there isn't a single Islam: there are *Islams,* just as there are Americas. This diversity is true of all traditions, religions, and nations, even though some of their adherents have futilely tried to draw boundaries around themselves and pin down their creeds neatly. Yet history is far more complex and contradictory than is represented by demagogues who are much less representative than either their followers or opponents claim. The trouble with religious or moral fundamentalists is that today their primitive ideas of revolution and resistance, including a willingness to kill and be killed, seem all too easily attached to technological sophistication and what appear to be gratifying acts of horrifying symbolic savagery. (With astonishing prescience in 1907, Joseph Conrad drew the portrait of the archetypal terrorist, whom he called laconically "the Professor" in his novel *The Secret Agent;* this is a man whose sole concern is to perfect a detonator that will work under any circumstances and whose handiwork results in a bomb exploded by a poor boy sent, unknowingly, to destroy the Greenwich Observatory as a strike against "pure science.") The New York and Washington suicide bombers seem to have been middle-class, educated men, not poor refugees. Instead of getting a wise leadership that stresses education, mass mobilization, and patient organization in the service of a cause, the poor and the desperate are often conned into the magical thinking and quick bloody solutions that such appalling models provide, wrapped in lying religious claptrap. This remains true in the Middle East generally, in Palestine in particular, but also in the United States, surely the most religious of all countries. It is also a major failure of the class of secular intellectuals not to have redoubled their efforts to provide analysis and models to offset the undoubted sufferings of the large mass of their people, immiserated and impoverished by globalism and an unyielding militarism with scarcely anything to turn to except blind violence and vague promises of future salvation.

On the other hand, immense military and economic power such as the United States possesses is no guarantee of wisdom or moral vision, particularly when obduracy is thought of as a virtue and exceptionalism is believed to be the national destiny. Skeptical and humane voices have been largely unheard in the present crisis, as "America" girds itself for a long war to be fought somewhere out there, along with allies who have been pressed into service on very uncertain grounds and for imprecise ends. We need to step back from the imaginary thresholds that supposedly separate people from each other into supposedly clashing civilizations and reexamine the labels, reconsider the limited resources available, and decide somehow to share our fates with one another as in fact cultures mostly have done, despite the bellicose cries and creeds.

"Islam" and "the West" are simply inadequate as banners to follow blindly. Some will run behind them, of course, but for future generations to condemn themselves to prolonged war and suffering without so much as a critical pause, without looking at interdependent histories of injustice and oppression, and without trying for common emancipation and mutual enlightenment seems far more willful than necessary. Demonization of the Other is not a sufficient basis for any kind of decent politics, certainly not now, when the roots of terror in injustice and misery can be addressed and the terrorists themselves easily isolated, deterred, or otherwise put out of business. It takes patience and education, but it is more worth the investment than still greater levels of large-scale violence and suffering. The immediate prospects are for destruction and suffering on a very large scale, with U.S. policy-makers milking the apprehensions and anxieties of their constituencies with cynical assurance that few will attempt a countercampaign against the inflamed patriotism and belligerent warmongering that has for a time postponed reflection, understanding, even common sense. Nevertheless, those of us with a possibility for reaching people who are willing to listen—and there are many such people, in the United States, Europe, and the Middle East, at least—must try to do so as rationally and as patiently as possible.

Al-Ahram, September 20–26, 2001
Al-Hayat, September 23, 2001
Le Monde Supplement, September 27, 2001
The Observer, September 16, 2001

CHAPTER EIGHTEEN

Backlash, Backtrack

For the 7 million Americans who are Muslims (only 2 million of them Arab) and have lived through the catastrophe and backlash of September 11, it's been a harrowing, especially unpleasant time. Not only were there several Arab and Muslim innocent casualties of the atrocities, but also an almost palpable air of hatred directed at the group as a whole that has taken many forms. George W. Bush immediately seemed to align America and God with each other, declaring war on the "folks"—who are now, as he says, wanted dead or alive—who perpetrated the horrible deeds. And this means, as no one needs any further reminding, that Usama bin Laden, the elusive Muslim fanatic who represents Islam to the vast majority of Americans, has taken center stage. TV and radio have run file pictures and potted accounts of the shadowy (former playboy, they say) extremist almost incessantly, as they have of the Palestinian women and children caught "celebrating" America's tragedy.

Pundits and hosts refer nonstop to "our" war with Islam, and words like "jihad" and "terror" have aggravated the understandable fear and anger that seem widespread all over the country. Two people (one a Sikh) have already been killed by enraged citizens who seem to have been encouraged by remarks like those of Deputy Secretary of Defense Paul Wolfowitz to literally think in terms of "ending countries" and nuking our enemies. Hundreds of Muslim and Arab shopkeepers, students, *hijab*-ed women, and ordinary citizens have had insults hurled at them, while posters and graffiti announcing their imminent death spring up all over the place. The director of the leading Arab American organization told me this morning that he averages ten messages an hour of insult, threat, and bloodcurdling verbal attack. A Gallup poll released yesterday states that 49 percent of the American people said yes (49 percent no) to the idea that Arabs, including those who are American citizens, should carry special identification; 58 percent demand (41 percent don't) that Arabs, including those who are Americans, should undergo special, more inten-sive security checks in general.

Then the official bellicosity slowly diminishes as George W. discovers that his allies are not quite as unrestrained as he is, as (undoubtedly) some of his advisers, chief among them the altogether more sensible-seeming Colin Powell, suggest that invading Afghanistan is not quite as simple as sending in the Texas militias might have been, even as the enormously con-fused reality forced on him and his staff dissipates the simple Manichean imagery of good versus evil that he has been maintaining on behalf of his people. A noticeable de-escalation sets in, even though reports of police and FBI harassment of Arabs and Muslims continue to flood in. Bush visits a Washington mosque; he calls on community leaders and the Con-gress to damp down hate speech; he starts trying to make at least rhe-torical distinctions between "our" Arab and Muslim friends (the usual ones—Jordan, Egypt, Saudi Arabia) and the still undisclosed terrorists. In his speech to the joint session of Congress, Bush did say that the United States is not at war with Islam, but he said regrettably nothing about the rising wave both of incidents and rhetoric that has assailed Muslims, Arabs, and people resembling Middle Easterners all across the country. Powell here and there expresses displeasure with Israel and Sharon for exploiting the crisis by oppressing Palestinians still more, but the general impression is that U.S. policy is still on the same course it has always been on—only now a huge war seems to be in the making.

But there is little positive knowledge of Arabs and Islam in the public sphere to fall back on and balance the extremely negative images that float around: the stereotypes of lustful, vengeful, violent, irrational, fanati-cal people persist anyway. Palestine as a cause has not yet gripped the imagination here, especially not after the Durban conference. Even my own university, justly famous for its intellectual diversity and the hetero-geneity of its students and staff, rarely offers a course on the Koran. Philip Hitti's *History of the Arabs,* by far the best modern one-volume book in English on the subject, is out of print. Most of what is available is polemical and adversarial: the Arabs and Islam are occasions for con-troversy, not cultural and religious subjects like others. Film and TV are packed with horrendously unattractive, bloody-minded Arab terrorists; they were there, alas, before the terrorists of the World Trade Center and

Pentagon hijacked the planes and turned them into instruments of mass slaughter that reeks of criminal pathology much more than of any religion.

There seems to be a minor campaign in the print media to hammer home the thesis that "we are all Israelis now," and that what has occasionally occurred in the way of Palestinian suicide bombs is more or less exactly the same as the World Trade Center and Pentagon attacks. In the process, of course, Palestinian dispossession and oppression are simply erased from memory; also erased are the many Palestinian condemnations of suicide bombing, including my own. The overall result is that any attempt to place the horrors of what occurred on September 11 in a context that includes U.S. actions and rhetoric is either attacked or dismissed as somehow condoning the terrorist bombardment.

Intellectually, morally, politically, such an attitude is disastrous since the equation between understanding and condoning is profoundly wrong and very far from being true. What most Americans find difficult to believe is that, in the Middle East and Arab world, U.S. actions as a state—unconditional support for Israel; the sanctions against Iraq that have spared Saddam Hussein and condemned hundreds of thousands of innocent Iraqis to death, disease, and malnutrition; the bombing of the Sudan; the U.S. "green light" for Israel's 1982 invasion of Lebanon (during which almost 20,000 civilians lost their lives, in addition to the massacres of Sabra and Shatila); the use of Saudi Arabia and the Gulf generally as a private U.S. fiefdom; the support of repressive Arab and Islamic regimes—are deeply resented and not incorrectly are seen as being done in the name of the American people. There is an enormous gap between what the average American citizen is aware of and the often unjust and heartless policies that, whether he/she is conscious of them, are undertaken abroad. Every U.S. veto of a UN Security Council resolution condemning Israel for settlements, the bombing of civilians, and so forth, may be brushed aside by, say, the residents of Iowa or Nebraska as unimportant events and probably correct, whereas to an Egyptian, Palestinian, or Lebanese citizen these things are wounding in the extreme and remembered very precisely.

In other words, there is a dialectic between specific U.S. actions on the one hand and consequent attitudes toward America on the other that has literally very little to do with jealousy or hatred of America's prosperity, freedom, and all-around success in the world. On the contrary, every Arab or Muslim to whom I have ever spoken expressed mystification as to why so extraordinarily rich and admirable a place as America (and so likable a group of individuals as Americans) has behaved internationally with such callous obliviousness of lesser peoples. Surely also many Arabs and Muslims are aware of the hold on U.S. policy of the pro-Israeli lobby and the dreadful racism and fulminations of pro-Israeli publications like *The New Republic* and *Commentary*, to say nothing of bloodthirsty columnists like Charles Krauthammer, William Safire, George Will, Norman Podhoretz, and A. M. Rosenthal, whose columns regularly express hatred and hostility toward Arabs and Muslims. These are usually to be found in the mainstream media (e.g., the editorial pages of the *Washington Post*), where everyone can read them as such, rather than being buried in the back pages of marginal publications.

So we are living through a period of turbulent, volatile emotion and deep apprehension, with the promise of more violence and terrorism dominating consciousness, especially in New York and Washington, where the terrible atrocities of September 11 are still very much alive in the public awareness. I certainly feel it, as does everyone around me.

But what is nevertheless encouraging, despite the appalling general media performance, is the slow emergence of dissent, petitions for peaceful resolution and action, and a gradually spreading, if still very spotty and relatively small, demand for alternatives to more bombing and destruction. This kind of thoughtfulness has been very remarkable in my opinion. First of all, there have been very widely expressed concerns about what may be the erosion of civil liberties and individual privacy as the government demands and seems to be getting the powers to wiretap telephones, to arrest and detain Middle Eastern people on suspicion of terrorism, and generally to induce a state of alarm, suspicion, and mobilization that could amount to paranoia resembling McCarthyism. Depending on how one reads it, the American habit of flying the flag everywhere can seem patriotic, of course, but patriotism can also lead to intolerance, hate crimes, and all sorts of unpleasant collective passions. Numerous commentators have warned about this, and as I said earlier, even the president in his speech said that "we" are not at war with Islam or Muslim people.

But the danger is there and has been duly noted by other commentators, I am happy to say.

Second, there have been many calls and meetings to address the whole matter of military action, which, according to a recent poll, 92 percent of the American people seem to want. Because, however, the administration hasn't exactly specified what the aims of this war are ("eradicating terrorism" is more metaphysical than it is actual), nor the means, nor the plan, there is considerable uncertainty as to where we may be going militarily. But generally speaking, the rhetoric has become less apocalyptic and religious—the idea of a crusade has disappeared almost completely—and more focused on what might be necessary beyond general words like "sacrifice" and "a long war, unlike any others." In universities, colleges, churches, and meeting houses there are a great many debates on what the country should be doing in response; I have even heard that families of the innocent victims have said in public that they do not believe that military revenge is an appropriate response. The point is that there is considerable reflection at large as to what the United States should be doing, but I am sorry to report that the time for a critical examination of U.S. policies in the Middle East and Islamic worlds has not yet arrived. I hope that it will.

If only more Americans and others can grasp that the main long-range hope for the world is this community of conscience and understanding, that whether in protecting constitutional rights, or in reaching out to the innocent victims of American power (as in Iraq), or in relying on understanding and rational analysis, "we" can do a great deal better than we have so far. Of course, this won't lead directly to changed policies on Palestine, or to a less skewed defense budget, or to more enlightened environmental and energy attitudes: but where else but in this sort of decent backtracking is there room for hope? Perhaps this constituency may grow in the United States, but speaking as a Palestinian, I must also hope that a similar constituency should be emerging in the Arab and Muslim world. We must start thinking about ourselves as responsible for the poverty, ignorance, illiteracy, and repression that have come to dominate *our* societies, evils that we have allowed to grow despite our complaints about Zionism and imperialism. How many of us, for example, have openly and honestly stood up for *secular* politics and have condemned the use of religion in the Islamic world as roundly and as earnestly as we have denounced the manipulation of Judaism and Christianity in Israel and the West? How many of us have denounced all suicidal missions as immoral and wrong, even though we have suffered the ravages of colonial settlers and inhuman collective punishment? We can no longer hide behind the injustices done to us, any more than we can passively bewail the American support for our unpopular leaders. A new *secular* Arab politics must now make itself known, without for a moment condoning or supporting the militancy (it is madness) of people willing to kill indiscriminately. There can be no more ambiguity on that score.

I have been arguing for years that our main weapons as Arabs today are not military but moral, and that one reason why, unlike the struggle against apartheid in South Africa, the Palestinian struggle for self-determination against Israeli oppression has not caught the world's imagination is that we cannot seem to be clear about our goals and our methods, and we have not stated unambiguously enough that our purpose is coexistence and inclusion, not exclusivism and a return to some idyllic and mythical past. The time has come for us to be forthright and to start immediately to examine, reexamine, and reflect on our own policies as so many Americans and Europeans are now doing. We should expect no less of ourselves than we should of others. Would that all people took the time to try to see where our leaders seem to be taking us, and for what reason. Skepticism and reevaluation are necessities, not luxuries.

Al-Ahram, September 27–October 6, 2001
Al-Hayat, October 10, 2001
London Review of Books, October 4, 2001

CHAPTER NINETEEN

Adrift in Similarity

Samuel Huntington's article "The Clash of Civilizations?" appeared in the Spring 1993 issue of *Foreign Affairs*, where it immediately attracted a surprising amount of attention and reaction. Because the article was intended to supply Americans with an original thesis about "the new phase" in world politics after the end of the cold war, Huntington's terms of argument seemed compellingly large, bold, even visionary. He very clearly had his eye on rivals in the policy-making ranks, theorists such as Francis Fukuyama and his "end of history" ideas, as well as the legions who had celebrated the onset of globalism, tribalism, and the dissipation of the state. But they, he allowed, had understood only *some* aspects of this new period. He was about to announce *the* "crucial, indeed a central aspect" of what "global politics is likely to be in the coming years." Unhesitatingly he pressed on:

"It is my hypothesis that the fundamental source of conflict in this new world will not be primarily ideological or primarily economic. The great divisions among humankind and the dominating source of conflict will be cultural. Nation states will remain the most powerful actors in world affairs, but the principal conflicts of global politics will occur between nations and groups of different civilizations. The clash of civilizations will dominate world politics. The fault lines between civilizations will be the battle lines of the future."(22)

Most of the argument in the pages that followed relied on a vague notion of something Huntington called "civilization identity," and "the interactions among seven or eight [*sic*] major civilizations," of which the conflict between two of them, Islam and the West, gets the lion's share of his attention. In this belligerent kind of thought, he relies heavily on a 1990 article by the veteran Orientalist Bernard Lewis, whose ideological colors are manifest in the title "The Roots of Muslim Rage." In both articles, the personification of enormous entities called "the West" and

"Islam" is recklessly affirmed, as if hugely complicated matters like identity and culture existed in a cartoonlike world where Popeye and Bluto bash each other mercilessly, with one always more virtuous pugilist getting the upper hand over his adversary. Certainly neither Huntington nor Lewis has much time to spare for the internal dynamics and plurality of every civilization, or for the fact that the major contest in most modern cultures concerns the definition or interpretation of each culture, or for the unattractive possibility that a great deal of demagogy and downright ignorance is involved in presuming to speak for a whole religion or civilization. No, the West is the West, and Islam Islam. The challenge for Western policy-makers, says Huntington, is to make sure that the West gets stronger and fends off all the others, Islam in particular.

More troubling is Huntington's assumption that his perspective, which is to survey the entire world from a perch outside all ordinary attachments and hidden loyalties, is the correct one, as if everyone else were scurrying around looking for the answers that he has already found. In fact, Huntington is an ideologist, someone who wants to make "civilizations" and "identities" into what they are not, shut-down, sealed-off entities that have been purged of the myriad currents and countercurrents that animate human history and that over centuries have made it possible for that history to contain not only wars of religion and imperial conquest but also exchange, cross-fertilization, and sharing. This far less visible history is ignored in the rush to highlight the ludicrously compressed and constricted warfare that "The Clash of Civilizations?" argues is the reality. When he published his book by the same title in 1996, he tried to give his argument a little more subtlety and many, many more footnotes; all he did, however, was to confuse himself and demonstrate what a clumsy writer and inelegant thinker he is. The basic paradigm of the West vs. the rest (the cold war opposition reformulated) remained untouched, and this is what has persisted, often insidiously and implicitly, in discussions since the terrible events of September 11.

The carefully planned mass slaughter and horrendous, pathologically motivated suicide bombing by a small group of deranged militants has been turned into proof of Huntington's thesis. Instead of seeing it for what it is, the capture of big ideas (I use the word loosely) by a tiny band of crazed fanatics for criminal purposes, international luminaries from former Pakistani prime minister Benazir Bhutto to Italian prime minister

Silvio Berlusconi have pontificated about Islam's troubles, and the latter has used Huntington to rant on about the West's superiority, how "we" have Mozart and Michelangelo and they don't. (He has since made a half-hearted apology for his insult to "Islam.")

But why not instead see parallels, admittedly less spectacular in their destructiveness, for Usama bin Laden and his followers in cults like the Branch Davidians or the disciples of Reverend Jim Jones at Guyana or the Japanese Aum Shinrikyo? Even the normally sober British weekly *The Economist,* in its issue of September 22–28, can't resist reaching for the vast generalization and praises Huntington extravagantly for his "cruel and sweeping, but nonetheless acute" observations about Islam. "Today," the journal says with unseemly solemnity, Huntington writes that "the world's billion or so Muslims are 'convinced of the superiority of their culture, and obsessed with the inferiority of their power.' " Did he canvas 100 Indonesians, 200 Moroccans, 500 Egyptians, 50 Bosnians? Even if he did, what sort of sample is that?

Uncountable are the editorials in every American and European newspaper and magazine of note adding to this vocabulary of gigantism and apocalypse, each use of which is plainly designed not to edify but to inflame the reader's indignant passion as a member of the "West" and to instruct what we need to do. Churchillian rhetoric is used inappropriately by self-appointed combatants in the West's, and especially America's, war against its haters, despoilers, and destroyers, with scant attention to complex histories that defy such reductiveness and that have seeped from one territory into another, in the process overriding the boundaries that are supposed to separate us all into divided armed camps.

This is the problem with unedifying labels like *Islam* and *the West*: they mislead and confuse the mind, which is trying to make sense of a disorderly reality that won't be pigeonholed or strapped down as easily as all that. I remember a man who rose from the audience after a lecture I had given at a West Bank university in 1992 and started to attack my ideas as "Western," as opposed to the strict Islamic ones he espoused. I interrupted him: "Why are you wearing a suit and tie?" was the first simpleminded retort that came to mind. "They're Western, too." He sat down with an embarrassed smile on his face, but I recalled the incident when information on the September 11 terrorists started to come in, how they had mastered all the technical details required to do their homicidal evil on the World Trade Center, the Pentagon, and the aircraft they had commandeered. Where does one draw the line between "Western" technology and, as Berlusconi declared, "Islam's" inability to be a part of "modernity"?

One cannot easily do so, of course, but how finally inadequate are the labels, generalizations, cultural assertions. At some level, for instance, primitive passions and sophisticated knowhow converge in ways that give the lie to a fortified boundary not only between "West" and "Islam" but also between past and present, us and them, to say nothing of the very concepts of identity and nationality about which there is literally unending disagreement and debate. A unilateral decision to draw lines in the sand, to undertake crusades, to oppose their evil with our good, to extirpate terrorism, and in Paul Wolfowitz's nihilist vocabulary, to end nations entirely doesn't make the supposed entities any easier to see; rather, it speaks to how much simpler it is to make bellicose statements for the purpose of mobilizing collective passions than to reflect, examine, sort out what it is we are dealing with in reality, the interconnectedness of innumerable lives, "ours" as well as "theirs."

In a remarkable series of three articles published between January and March 1999 in *Dawn*, Pakistan's most respected weekly, the late Eqbal Ahmad, writing for a Muslim audience, analyzed what he called the roots of the religious right, coming down very harshly on the mutilations of Islam by absolutists and fanatical tyrants whose obsession with regulating personal behavior promotes "an Islamic order reduced to a penal code, stripped of its humanism, aesthetics, intellectual quests, and spiritual devotion." And this "entails an absolute assertion of one, generally de-contextualized, aspect of religion and a total disregard of another. The phenomenon distorts religion, debases tradition, and twists the political process wherever it unfolds." As a timely instance of this debasement, Ahmad proceeds first to present the rich, complex, pluralist meaning of the word *jihad,* then goes on to show that, in the word's current confinement to indiscriminate war against presumed enemies, it is impossible "to recognize . . . Islamic religion, society, culture, history or politics as lived and experienced by Muslims through the ages." The modern Islamists, Ahmad concludes, are "concerned with power not with the soul, with the mobilization of people for political purposes rather than with sharing and alleviating their sufferings and aspirations. Theirs is a very limited and time bound agenda." What has made matters worse is that similar distortions and zealotry occur in the "Jewish" and "Christian" universes of discourse.

It was Joseph Conrad, more powerfully than any of his readers at the end of the nineteenth century could have imagined, who understood that the distinctions between civilized London and "the heart of darkness" quickly collapsed in extreme situations, and that the heights of European civilization could instantaneously reverse into the most barbarous practices without preparation or transition. And it was Conrad also in *The Secret Agent* (1907) who described terrorism's affinity for abstractions like "pure science" (and by extension for "Islam" or "the West"), as well as the terrorist's ultimate moral degradation.

For there are closer ties between apparently warring civilizations than most of us would like to believe, and as both Freud and Nietzsche showed, the traffic across carefully maintained, even policed boundaries moves with often-terrifying ease. But then such fluid ideas, full of ambiguity and skepticism about notions that we hold on to, scarcely furnish us with suitable, practical guidelines for situations such as the one we face now; hence the altogether more reassuring battle orders (a crusade, good versus evil, freedom against fear, etc.) drawn out of Huntington's opposition between Islam and the West, from which in the first days official discourse drew its vocabulary. There's since been a noticeable de-escalation in that discourse, but to judge from the steady amount of hate speech and actions, plus reports of law enforcement efforts, directed against Arabs, Muslims, and Indians all over the country, the paradigm stays on.

One further reason for its persistence is the increased presence of Muslims all over Europe and the United States. Think of the populations today of France, Italy, Germany, Spain, Britain, America, and even Sweden, and you must concede that Islam is no longer on the fringes of the West but at its center. But what is so threatening about that presence? Buried in the collective culture are memories of the first great Arab-Islamic conquests that began in the seventh century and that, as the celebrated Belgian historian Henri Pirenne wrote in his landmark book *Mohammed and Charlemagne* (1939), shattered once and for all the ancient unity of the Mediterranean, destroyed the Christian-Roman synthesis, and gave rise to a new civilization dominated by northern powers

(Germany and Carolingian France), whose mission, he seemed to be saying, was to resume defense of the "West" against its historical-cultural enemies. What Pirenne left out, alas, was that in the creation of this new line of defense the West drew on the humanism, science, philosophy, sociology, and historiography of Islam, which had already interposed itself between Charlemagne's world and classical antiquity. Islam was inside from the start, as even Dante, great enemy of Muhammad, had to concede when he placed the Prophet at the very heart of his Inferno.

Then there is the persisting legacy of monotheism itself, the Abrahamanic religions, as Louis Massignon aptly called them. Beginning with Judaism and Christianity, each is a successor haunted by what came before: for Muslims, Islam fulfills and ends the line of prophecy. There is still no decent history or demystification of the many-sided contest among these three followers—not one of them by any means a monolithic, unified camp—of the most jealous of all Gods, even though the bloody modern convergence on Palestine furnishes a rich secular instance of what has been so tragically irreconcilable about them. Not surprisingly, then, Muslims and Christians speak readily of crusades and jihads, both of them eliding the Judaic presence with often sublime insouciance. Such an agenda, says Eqbal Ahmad, "is very reassuring to the men and women who are stranded in the middle . . . between the deep waters of tradition and modernity."

But we are all swimming in those waters, Westerners and Muslims and others alike. And since the waters are part of the ocean of history, trying to plow or divide them with barriers is futile. These are tense times, but it is better to think in terms of powerful and powerless communities, the secular politics of reason and ignorance, and universal principles of justice and injustice, than to wander off in search of vast abstractions that may give momentary satisfaction but little self-knowledge or informed analysis. The "clash of civilizations" thesis is a gimmick like *The War of the Worlds,* better for reinforcing defensive self-pride than for critical understanding of the bewildering interdependence of our time.

Al-Ahram, October 11–17, 2001
Al-Hayat, October 12, 2001
The Nation, October 22, 2001

CHAPTER TWENTY

A Vision to Lift the Spirit

With the bombs and missiles falling on Afghanistan in the high-altitude U.S. destruction wrought by Operation Enduring Freedom, the Palestine question may seem tangential to the altogether more urgent events in Central Asia. But it would be a mistake to think so, and not just because Usama bin Laden and his followers (no one knows how many there are in theory or in practice) have tried to capture Palestine as a rhetorical part of their unconscionable campaign of terror. But so too has Israel, for its own purposes. With the killing of cabinet minister Rehavam Ze'evi on October 17 as retaliation by the Popular Front for the Liberation of Palestine for the assassination of its leader by Israel last August, General Sharon's sustained campaign against the Palestinian Authority as Israel's Bin Laden has risen to a new, semihysterical pitch. Israel has been assassinating Palestinian leaders and militants (more than sixty of them to date) for the past several months and couldn't have been surprised that its illegal methods would sooner or later prompt Palestinian retaliation in kind. But why one set of killings should be acceptable and others not is a question Israel and its supporters are unable to answer. And so the violence goes on, with Israel's occupation the more deadly and the vastly more destructive, causing huge civilian suffering: in the period between October 18 and 21, six Palestinian towns were reoccupied by Israeli forces; five more Palestinian activists were assassinated, plus twenty-one civilians killed and 160 injured; curfews were imposed everywhere, and all this Israel has the gall to compare with the U.S. war against Afghanistan and terrorism.

Thus the frustration and subsequent impasse in pressing the claims of a people dispossessed for fifty-three years and militarily occupied for thirty-four years have definitively gone beyond the main arena of struggle and are willy-nilly tied in all sorts of ways to the global war against terrorism. Israel and its supporters worry that the United States will sell them out, all the while protesting contradictorily that Israel isn't the issue in the new war. Palestinians, Arabs, and Muslims generally have either felt uneasiness or a creeping guilt by association that attaches to them in the public realm, despite efforts by political leaders to keep dissociating Bin Laden from Islam and the Arabs: but they, too, keep referring to Palestine as the great symbolic nexus of their disaffection,

In official Washington, George W. Bush and Colin Powell have more than once revealed unambiguously that Palestinian self-determination is an important, perhaps even a central, issue. The turbulence of war and its unknown dimensions and complications (its consequences in places like Saudi Arabia and Egypt are likely to be dramatic, if as yet unknown) have stirred up the whole Middle East in striking ways, so that the need for some genuinely positive change in the status of the 7 million stateless Palestinians is sure to grow in importance, even though a number of quite dispiriting things about the present impasse are evident enough now. The main problem is whether or not the United States and the parties are going to resort only to the stopgap measures that brought us the disastrous Oslo agreement.

The immediate experience of the Al-Aqsa Intifada has universalized Arab and Muslim powerlessness and exasperation to a degree never before as magnified as it is now. The Western media hasn't at all conveyed the crushing pain and humiliation imposed on Palestinians by Israel's collective punishment, its house demolitions, its invasions of Palestinian areas, its air bombings and killings, as have the nightly broadcasts by Al-Jazeera satellite television, or admirable daily reporting in *Ha'aretz* by the Israeli journalist Amira Hass and commentators like her. At the same time, I think, there is widespread understanding among Arabs that the Palestinians (and, by extension, the other Arabs) have been traduced and hopelessly misled by their leaders. An abyss visibly separates nattily suited negotiators who make declarations in luxurious surroundings and the dusty hell of the streets of Nablus, Jenin, Hebron, and elsewhere. Schooling is inadequate; unemployment and poverty rates have climbed to alarming heights; anxiety and insecurity fill the atmosphere, with governments either incapable of stopping or unwilling to stop the rise of Islamic extremism or an astonishingly flagrant corruption at the very top. Above all, the brave secularists who protest at human rights abuses, fight clerical tyranny, and try to speak and act on behalf of a new modern democratic Arab order are pretty much left alone in their fight, unassisted by the official culture, their books and careers sometimes thrown as a sop to mounting Islamic fury. A huge dank cloud of mediocrity and incompetence hangs over everyone, and this in turn has given rise to magical thinking and/or a cult of death that is more prevalent than ever.

I know it is often argued that suicide bombings are the result either of frustration and desperation or of the criminal pathology of deranged religious fanatics. But these are inadequate explanations. The New York and Washington suicide terrorists were middle-class, far-from-illiterate men, perfectly capable of modern planning of audacious as well as terrifyingly deliberate destruction. The young men sent out by Hamas and Islamic Jihad do what they are told with a conviction that suggests clarity of purpose, if not of much else. The real culprit is a system of primary education that is woefully piecemeal, cobbled together from the Koran, rote exercises based on outdated fifty-year-old textbooks, hopelessly large classes, woefully ill-equipped teachers, and a nearly total inability to think critically. Along with the oversized Arab armies—all of them burdened with unusable military hardware and no record of any positive achievement—this antiquated educational apparatus has produced the bizarre failures in logic and moral reasoning, as well as the insufficient appreciation of human life, that lead either to leaps of religious enthusiasm of the worst kind or to a servile worship of power.

Similar failures in vision and logic operate on the Israeli side. How it has come to seem morally possible, or even justifiable, for Israel to maintain and defend its thirty-four-year-old occupation fairly boggles the mind, but even Israeli "peace" intellectuals remain fixated on the supposed absence of a Palestinian peace camp, forgetting that a people under occupation doesn't have the same luxury as the occupier to decide whether or not an interlocutor exists. In the process, military occupation is taken as an acceptable given and is scarcely mentioned; Palestinian terrorism becomes the cause, not the effect, of violence, even though one side possesses a modern military arsenal (unconditionally supplied by the United States), the other is stateless, virtually defenseless, savagely persecuted at will, and herded inside 160 little cantons, schools closed, life made impossible. Worst of all, the daily killing and wounding of Palestinians is accompanied by the growth of Israeli settlements and by the 400,000 settlers who dot the Palestinian landscape without respite.

A recent report issued by Peace Now in Israel states the following:

1. At the end of June 2001 there were 6593 housing units in different stages of active construction in settlements.
2. During the Barak administration 6045 housing units were begun in settlements. In fact settlement building in the year 2000 reached the highest since 1992, with 4499 starts.
3. When the Oslo agreements were signed there were 32,750 housing units in the settlements. Since the signing of the Oslo agreements 20,371 housing units have been constructed, representing an increase of 62% in settlement units.

The essence of the Israeli position is its total irreconcilability with what the Jewish state wants—peace and security, even though everything it does assures neither one nor the other.

The United States has underwritten Israel's intransigence and brutality: there are no two ways about it—$92 billion and unending political support, all for the world to see. Ironically, this was far truer during, rather than either before or after, the Oslo process. The plain truth of the matter is that anti-Americanism in the Arab and Muslim worlds is tied directly to the United States' behavior, lecturing the world on democracy and justice while openly supporting their exact opposites. There also is an undoubted ignorance about the United States in the Arab and Islamic worlds, and there has been far too great a tendency to use rhetorical tirades and sweeping general condemnation instead of rational analysis and critical understanding of America. The same is true of Arab attitudes toward Israel.

Both the Arab governments and the intellectuals have failed in important ways on this matter. Governments have failed to devote any time or resources to an aggressive cultural policy that puts across an adequate representation of Arab and Muslim culture, tradition, and contemporary society, with the result that these things are unknown in the West, leaving unchallenged pictures of Arabs and Muslims as violent, oversexed fanatics. The intellectual failure is no less great. It is simply inadequate to keep repeating clichés about struggle and resistance that imply a military program of action when none is either possible or really desirable. Our defense against unjust policies is a moral one, and we must first occupy the moral high ground and then promote understanding of that position in Israel and the United States, something we have never done. We have refused interaction and debate, disparagingly calling them only normalization and collaboration. Refusing to compromise in putting forth our just position (which is what I am calling for) cannot possibly be construed as a concession, especially when it is made directly and forcefully to the occupier or the author of unjust policies of occupation and reprisal. Why do we fear confronting our oppressors directly, humanely, persuasively, and why do we keep believing in precisely the vague ideological promises of redemptive violence that are little different from the poison spewed by Bin Laden and the Islamists? The answer to our needs lies in principled resistance, well-organized civil disobedience against military occupation and illegal settlement, and an educational program that promotes coexistence, citizenship, and the worth of human life.

But we are now in an intolerable impasse, requiring more than ever a genuine return to the all-but-abandoned bases of peace that were proclaimed at Madrid in 1991, UN Security Council Resolutions 242 and 338, land for peace. There can be no peace without pressure on Israel to withdraw from the Occupied Territories, including Jerusalem, and—as the Mitchell report affirmed—to dismantle its settlements. This can obviously be done in a phased way, with some sort of immediate emergency protection for undefended Palestinians, but the great failing of Oslo must be remedied now at the start: a clearly articulated end to occupation, the establishment of a viable, genuinely independent Palestinian state, and the existence of peace through mutual recognition. These goals have to be stated as the *objective* of negotiations, a beacon shining at the end of the tunnel. Palestinian negotiators have to be firm about this and not use the reopening of talks—if any should now begin, in this atmosphere of harsh Israeli war on the Palestinian people—as an excuse simply to return to Oslo. In the end, though, only the United States can restore negotiations, with European, Islamic, Arab, and African support, but it must be done through the United Nations, which must be the essential sponsor of the effort.

And since the Palestinian-Israeli struggle has been so humanly impoverishing, I would suggest that important symbolic gestures of recognition and responsibility, undertaken perhaps under the auspices of a Mandela or a panel of impeccably credentialed peacemakers, should try to establish justice and compassion as crucial elements in the proceedings. Unfortunately, it is perhaps true that neither Arafat nor Sharon is suited to so high an enterprise. The Palestinian political scene must absolutely be overhauled to represent seamlessly what every Palestinian longs for—peace with dignity and justice and, most important, decent, equal coexistence with Israeli Jews. We need to move beyond the undignified shenanigans, the disgraceful backing and filling of a leader who hasn't in a long time come anywhere near experiencing the sacrifices of his long-suffering people. The same is true of Israelis who are led abysmally by the likes of General Sharon. What we need is a vision that can lift the much-abused spirit beyond the sordid present, something that will not fail when presented unwaveringly as what people need to aspire to.

Al-Ahram, October 25–31, 2001
Al-Hayat, November 10, 2001

CHAPTER TWENTY-ONE

Suicidal Ignorance

The extraordinary turbulence of the present moment during the U.S. military campaign against Afghanistan, now in the middle of its second month, has crystallized a number of themes and counterthemes that deserve some clarification here. I shall list them without too much discussion and qualification as a way of broaching the current stage of development in the long and terribly unsatisfactory history of relationships between the United States and Palestine.

We should start by perhaps restating the obvious, that every American I know (including myself, I must admit) firmly believes that the terrible events of September 11 inaugurated a rather new stage in world history. Even though numerous Americans know rationally that other atrocities and disasters have occurred in history, there is still something unique and unprecedented in the World Trade Center and Pentagon bombings. A new reality, therefore, seems to proceed from that day, most of it focused on the United States itself, its sorrow, its anger, its psychic stresses, its ideas about itself. I would go so far as saying that today almost the least likely argument to be listened to in the United States in the public domain is one that suggests that there are historical reasons why America, as a major world actor, has drawn such animosity to itself by virtue of what it has done; this is considered simply to be an attempt to justify the existence and actions of Bin Laden, who has become a vast, overdetermined symbol of everything America hates and fears: in any case, such talk is and will not be tolerated in mainstream discourse for the time being, especially not in the mainstream media or in what the government says. The assumption seems to be that American virtue or honor in some profoundly inviolate way has been wounded by an absolutely evil terrorism, and that any minimizing or explanation of that is an intolerable idea even to contemplate, much less to investigate rationally. That such a state of affairs is exactly what the pathologically crazed world-vision of Bin

Laden himself seems to have desired all along—a division of the universe into his forces and those of the Christians and Jews—seems not to matter.

As a result of that, therefore, the political image that the government and the media—which have mostly acted without independence from the government, although certain questions are being asked and criticism articulated about the conduct of the war itself, not its wisdom or efficacy—wish to project is American "unity." There really is a feeling being manufactured by the media and the government that a collective "we" exists and that "we" all act and feel together, as witnessed by such perhaps unimportant surface phenomena as flag-flying and the use of the collective "we" by journalists in describing events all over the world in which the United States is involved. We bombed, we said, we decided, we acted, we feel, we believe, etc., etc. Of course this has only marginally to do with the reality, which is far more complicated and far less reassuring. There is plenty of unrecorded or unregistered skepticism, even outspoken dissent, but it seems hidden by overt patriotism. So American unity is being projected with such force as to allow very little questioning of U.S. policy, which in many ways is heading toward a series of unexpected events in Afghanistan and elsewhere, the meaning of which many people will not realize until too late. In the meantime, American unity needs to state to the world that what America does and *has done* cannot brook serious disagreement or discussion. Just like Bin Laden, Bush tells the world, you are either with us, or you are with terrorism and hence against us. So on the one hand America is not at war with Islam but only with terrorism, and on the other hand in complete contradiction with that, since only America decides who or what Islam and terrorism are, "we" are against Muslim terrorism and Islamic rage as "we" define them. That there has been so far an effective Lebanese and Palestinian demurral at the American condemnation of Hizbollah and Hamas as terrorist organizations is no assurance that the campaign to brand Israel's enemies as "our" enemies will stop.

In the meantime, both George W. Bush and Tony Blair have realized that indeed something needs to be done about Palestine, even though I believe there is no serious intention of changing U.S. foreign policy to accommodate what is going to be done. In order for that to happen, the United States must look at its own history, just as its media flacks such as the egregious Thomas Friedman and Fouad Ajami keep preaching at Arab and Muslim societies that that is what *they* must do, but of course never consider that that is something that everyone, *including Americans,* needs also do. No, we are told over and over, American history is about freedom and democracy, and only those: no mistakes can be admitted, or radical reconsiderations announced. *Everyone else* must change their ways; however, America remains as it is. Then Bush declares that the United States favors a Palestinian state with recognized boundaries next to Israel and adds that this has to be done according to UN resolutions, without specifying which ones and refusing to meet Yasir Arafat personally.

This may seem like a contradictory step also but in fact it isn't. For the past six weeks there has been an astonishingly unrelenting and minutely organized media campaign in the United States more or less pressing the Israeli vision of the world on the American reading and watching public, with practically nothing to counter it. Its main themes are that Islam and the Arabs are the true causes of terrorism, Israel has been facing such terrorism all its life, Arafat and Bin Laden are basically the same thing, and most of the United States' Arab allies (especially Egypt and Saudi Arabia) have played a clear negative role in sponsoring anti-Americanism, supporting terrorism, and maintaining corrupt, undemocratic societies. Underlying the campaign has been the (at best) dubious thesis that anti-Semitism is on the rise. All of this adds up to a near promise that anything to do with Palestinian (or Lebanese) resistance to Israeli practices—never more brutal, never more dehumanizing and illegal than today—has to be destroyed after (or perhaps while) the Taliban and Bin Laden have been destroyed. That this also happens to mean, as the Pentagon hawks and their right-wing media machine keep reminding Americans relentlessly, that Iraq must be attacked next, and indeed all the enemies of Israel in the region along with Iraq must totally be brought low, is lost on no one. So brazenly has the Zionist propaganda apparatus performed in the weeks since September 11 that very little opposition to these views is encountered. Lost in this extraordinary farrago of lies, bloodthirsty hatred, and arrogant triumphalism is the simple reality that America is not Israel, and Bin Laden not the Arabs or Islam.

This concentrated pro-Israeli campaign, over which Bush and his people have little real political control, has kept the U.S. administration from anything like a real reassessment of U.S. policies toward Israel and the Palestinians. Even during the opening rounds of the American counter-propaganda campaign directed to the Muslim and Arab world, there has been a remarkable unwillingness to treat the Arabs as seriously as all other peoples have been treated. Take as an example an Al-Jazeera discussion program a week ago in which Bin Laden's latest video was played in its entirety. A hodgepodge of accusations and declarations, it accused the United States of using Israel to bludgeon the Palestinians without respite; Bin Laden of course crazily ascribed this to a Christian and Jewish crusade against Islam, but most people in the Arab world are convinced—because it is patently true—that America has simply allowed Israel to kill Palestinians at will with U.S. weapons and unconditional political support in the UN and elsewhere. The Doha-based moderator of the program then called on a U.S. official, Christopher Ross, who was in Washington, to respond, and then Ross, a decent but by no means remarkable or even fluent Arabic speaker, read a long statement whose message was that the United States, far from being against Islam and the Arabs, was really their champion (e.g., in Bosnia and Kosovo), plus the fact that the United States supplied more food to Afghanistan than anyone else, upheld freedom and democracy, and so on.

All in all, it was standard U.S. government issue. Then the moderator asked Ross to explain why, given everything that he said about U.S. support for justice and democracy, the United States backed Israeli brutality in its military occupation of Palestine. Instead of taking an honest position that respected his listeners and affirmed that Israel is a U.S. ally and "we" choose to support it for internal political reasons, Ross chose instead to insult their basic intelligence and defended the United States as the only power that has brought the two sides to the negotiating table. When the moderator persisted in his questioning about U.S. hostility to Arab aspirations, Ross persisted in his line, too, more or less claiming that only the United States had the Arabs' interests at heart. As an exercise in propaganda, Ross's performance was poor, of course; but as an indication of the possibility of any serious change in U.S. policy, Ross (inadvertently) at least did Arabs the service of indicating that they would have to be fools to believe in any such change.

Whatever else it says, Bush's America remains a unilateralist power, in the world, in Afghanistan, in the Middle East, everywhere. It shows no sign of having understood what Palestinian resistance is all about, or why Arabs resent its horrendously unjust policies in turning a blind eye to Israel's maleficent sadism against the Palestinian people as a whole. It still refuses to sign the Kyoto convention, or the War Crimes Court agreement, or the anti–land mine conventions, or pay its UN dues. Bush can still stand up and lecture the world as if he were a schoolmaster telling a bunch of unruly little vagrants why they must behave according to American ideas.

In short, there is absolutely no reason at all why Yasir Arafat and his ever-present coterie should grovel at American feet. Our only hope as a people is for Palestinians to show the world that we have our principles, we occupy the moral high ground, and we must continue an intelligent and well-organized resistance to a criminal Israeli occupation, which no one seems to mention anymore. My suggestion is that Arafat should stop his world tours and come back to his people (who keep reminding him that they no longer really support what he does: only 17 percent say they back what he is doing) and respond to their needs as a real leader must. Israel has been destroying the Palestinian infrastructure, destroying towns and schools, killing innocents, invading at will, without Arafat paying enough serious attention. He must lead the nonviolent protest marches on a daily, if not hourly, basis and not let a group of foreign volunteers do our work for us.

It is a self-sacrificing spirit of human and moral solidarity with his people that Arafat's leadership so fatally lacks. I am afraid that this terrible absence has now almost completely marginalized him and his ill-fated and ineffective Authority. Certainly Sharon's brutality has played a major role in destroying it, too, but we must remember that before the intifada began, most Palestinians had already lost their faith, and for good reason. What Arafat never seems to have understood is that we are and have always been a movement standing for, symbolizing, getting support for, and embodying principles of justice and liberation. This alone will enable us to free ourselves from Israeli occupation, not the covert maneuvering in the halls of Western power, where until today Arafat and his people are treated with contempt. Whenever, as in Jordan, Lebanon, and during the Oslo process, he has behaved as if he and his movement were just like another Arab state, he has always been defeated; only when he finally understands that the Palestinian people demand liberation and justice, not a police force and a corrupt bureaucracy, will he begin to lead them. Otherwise he will flounder disgracefully and will bring disaster and misfortune on us.

On the other hand, and I shall conclude with this now, leaving the subject for my next article to develop in detail, we must not as Palestinians or Arabs fall into an easy rhetorical anti-Americanism. It is not acceptable to sit in Beirut or Cairo meeting halls and denounce American imperialism (or Zionist colonialism, for that matter) without a whit of understanding that these are complex societies not always truly represented by their governments' stupid or cruel policies. We have never addressed the currents in Israel and America that it is possible, and indeed vital, for us to address and in the end to come to an agreement with. In this respect, we need to make our resistance respected and understood, not hated and feared as it is now by virtue of suicidal ignorance and indiscriminate belligerence.

One more thing. It is also far too easy for a small group of unexceptional expatriate Arab academics in America to keep appearing on the media here in order to denounce Islam and the Arabs, without having the courage or the decency to say these things in Arabic to the Arab societies and peoples they so easily rail against in Washington and New York. Neither is it acceptable for Arab and Muslim governments to pretend to be defending their people's interests at the United Nations and in the West generally, while doing very little for their people at home. Most Arab countries now wallow in corruption, the terror of undemocratic rule, and a fatally flawed educational system that still has not faced up to the realities of a secular world.

But I shall leave that all until my next article.

Al-Ahram, November 15–21, 2001
Al-Hayat, November 22, 2001

CHAPTER TWENTY-TWO

Israel's Dead End

The world is closing on us, pushing us through the last passage, and we tear off our limbs to pass through." Thus Mahmoud Darwish, writing in the aftermath of the PLO's exit from Beirut in September 1982. "Where shall we go after the last frontiers, where should the birds fly after the last sky?" Nineteen years later what was happening then to the Palestinians in Lebanon is happening to them in Palestine. Since the Al-Aqsa Intifada began last September, Palestinians have been sequestered by the Israeli army in no fewer than 220 discontinuous little ghettos and subjected to intermittent curfews often lasting for weeks at a stretch. No one, young or old, sick or well, dying or pregnant, student or doctor, can move without spending hours at barricades, manned by rude and deliberately humiliating Israeli soldiers. As I write, two hundred Palestinians are unable to receive kidney dialysis, because for "security reasons" the Israeli military won't allow them to travel to medical centers. Have any of the innumerable members of the foreign media covering the conflict done a story about these brutalized young Israeli conscripts, trained to punish Palestinian civilians as the main part of their military duty? I think not.

Yasir Arafat was not allowed to leave his office in Ramallah to attend the emergency meeting of the Islamic Conference foreign ministers on December 10 in Qatar; his speech was read by an aide. The airport fifteen miles away in Gaza and Arafat's two aging helicopters had been destroyed the previous week by Israeli planes and bulldozers, with no one and no force to check, much less prevent, the daily incursions of which this particular feat of military daring was a part. Gaza airport was the only direct port of entry into Palestinian territory, the only civilian airport in the world wantonly destroyed since World War II. Since last May, Israeli F-16s (generously supplied by the United States) have regularly bombed and strafed Palestinian towns and villages, Guernica-style, destroying property and killing civilians and security officials (there is no

Palestinian army, navy, or air force to protect the people); Apache attack helicopters (again supplied by the United States) have used their missiles to murder seventy-seven Palestinian leaders, for alleged terrorist offenses, past or future. A group of unknown Israeli intelligence operatives have the authority to decide on these assassinations, presumably with the approval on each occasion of the Israeli cabinet and, more generally, that of the United States. The helicopters have also done an efficient job of bombing Palestinian Authority installations, police as well as civilian. During the night of December 5, the Israeli army entered the five-story offices of the Palestinian Central Bureau of Statistics in Ramallah and carried off the computers, as well as most of the files and reports, thereby effacing virtually the entire record of collective Palestinian life. In 1982 the same army under the same commander entered West Beirut and carted off documents and files from the Palestinian Research Center, before flattening its structure. A few days later came the massacres of Sabra and Shatila.

The suicide bombers of Hamas and Islamic Jihad have of course been at work, as Sharon knew perfectly well they would be when, after a ten-day lull in the fighting in late November, he suddenly ordered the murder of the Hamas leader Mahmoud Abu Hanoud: an act designed to provoke Hamas into retaliation and thus allow the Israeli army to resume the slaughter of Palestinians. After eight years of barren peace discussions, 50 percent of Palestinians are unemployed and 70 percent live in poverty on less than two dollars a day. Every day brings with it unopposable land grabs and house demolitions. The Israelis even make a point of destroying trees and orchards on Palestinian land. Although five or six Palestinians have been killed in the last few months for every one Israeli, the old warmonger has the gall to keep repeating that Israel has been the victim of the same terrorism as that meted out by Bin Laden.

The crucial point in all this is that Israel has been in illegal military occupation since 1967; it is the longest such occupation in history and the only one anywhere in the world today: this is the original and continuing violence against which all the Palestinian acts of violence have been directed. On December 10, for instance, two children aged three and thirteen were killed by Israeli bombs in Hebron, yet at the same time an EU delegation was demanding that Palestinians curtail their violence and acts of terrorism. Five more Palestinians were killed on December 11, all of them civilian, victims of helicopter bombings of Gaza's refugee camps. To make matters worse, as a result of the September 11 attacks, the word *terrorism* is being used to blot out legitimate acts of resistance against military occupation, and any causal or even narrative connection between the dreadful killing of civilians (which I have always opposed) and the thirty-plus years of collective punishment is proscribed.

Every Western pundit or official who pontificates about Palestinian terrorism needs to ask how forgetting the fact of the occupation is supposed to stop terrorism. Arafat's great mistake, a consequence of frustration and poor advice, was to try to make a deal with the occupation when he authorized "peace" discussions between scions of two prominent Palestinian families and the Mossad in 1992 at the American Academy of Arts and Sciences in Cambridge. These discussions only discussed Israeli security; nothing at all was said about Palestinian security, nothing at all, and the struggle of his people to achieve an independent state was left to one side. Indeed, Israeli security to the exclusion of anything else has become the recognized international priority that allows General Anthony Zinni and Javier Solana to preach to the PLO while remaining totally silent on the occupation. Yet Israel has scarcely gained more from these discussions than the Palestinians have. The Israeli mistake has been to imagine that by conning Arafat and his coterie into interminable discussions and tiny concessions, Israel would get a general Palestinian quiescence. Every official Israeli policy thus far has made things worse rather than better for Israel. Ask yourself: is Israel more secure and more accepted now than it was ten years ago?

The terrible and, in my opinion, stupid suicide raids against civilians in Haifa and Jerusalem over the weekend of December 1 should of course be condemned, but in order for these condemnations to make any sense, the raids must be considered in the context of Abu Hanoud's assassination earlier in the week, along with the killing of five children by an Israeli booby-trap in Gaza—to say nothing of the houses destroyed, the Palestinians killed throughout Gaza and the West Bank, the constant tank incursions, the endless grinding away of Palestinian aspirations, minute by minute, for the past thirty-five years. In the end, desperation only produces poor results, none worse than the green light that George W. and Colin Powell seem to have given Sharon when he was in Washington on

December 2 (all too reminiscent of the green light Al Haig gave Sharon in May 1982). With their support went the usual ringing declarations turning the people under occupation and their hapless, inept leader into worldwide aggressors who had to "bring to justice" their own criminals even as Israeli soldiers were systematically destroying the entire Palestinian police structure that was supposed to do the arresting!

Arafat is hemmed in on all sides, an irony of his bottomless wish to be all things Palestinian to everyone, enemies and friends alike. He is at once a tragically heroic figure and a bumbling one. No Palestinian today is going to disavow his leadership, for the simple reason that despite all his wafflings and mistakes, he is being punished and humiliated because he is a *Palestinian* leader, and in that capacity his mere existence offends purists (if that's the right word) like Sharon and his American backers. Except for the health and education ministries, both of which have done a decent job, Arafat's Palestinian Authority has not been a brilliant success. Its corruption and brutality stem from Arafat's apparently whimsical, but actually very meticulous, way of keeping everyone dependent on his largesse; he alone controls the budget, and he alone decides what goes on the front pages of the five daily newspapers. Above all, he manipulates and sets up *against* one another the twelve or fourteen—some say nineteen or twenty—independent security services, each of which is structurally loyal to its own leaders and to Arafat at the same time without being able to do much more for its people than arrest them when enjoined to do so by Arafat, Israel, and the United States. The 1996 elections were designed for a term of three years, but Arafat has shilly-shallied with the idea of calling new ones, which would almost certainly challenge his authority and popularity in a serious way.

He and Hamas have had a well-publicized entente of sorts since the latter's June bombings: Hamas wouldn't go after Israeli civilians if Arafat left the Islamic parties alone. Sharon killed off the entente with Abu Hanoud's assassination: Hamas retaliated, and there was nothing to stop Sharon squeezing the life out of Arafat, with American support. Having destroyed Arafat's security network, his jails and offices, and having physically imprisoned him, Sharon has made demands that he knows can't be met (even though Arafat, with a few cards up his sleeve, has managed, astonishingly, to half-comply). Sharon stupidly believes that, having dispensed with Arafat, he can make a series of independent agreements with local warlords and divide 40 percent of the West Bank and most of Gaza into several noncontiguous cantons whose borders would be controlled by the Israeli army. How this is supposed to make Israel more secure eludes most people, but not, alas, the ones with the relevant power.

That still leaves out three players, or groups of players, two of whom in his racist way Sharon gives no weight to. First, the Palestinians themselves, many of whom are far too intransigent and politicized to accept anything less than unconditional Israeli withdrawal. Israel's policies, like all such aggressions, produce the opposite effect to the one intended: to suppress is to provoke resistance. Were Arafat to disappear, Palestinian law provides for sixty days of rule by the speaker of the Assembly (an unimpressive and unpopular Arafat hanger-on called Abu 'Ala, much admired by Israelis for his "flexibility"). After that, a succession struggle would ensue between other Arafat cronies such as Abu Mazen and two or three of the leading (and capable) security chiefs—notably, Jibril Rajoub of the West Bank and Mohammed Dahlan in Gaza. None of these people have Arafat's stature or anything resembling his (perhaps now lost) popularity. Temporary chaos is the likely result: we must face it, Arafat's presence has been an organizing focus for Palestinian politics, in which millions of other Arabs and Muslims have a very large stake.

Arafat has always tolerated, indeed supported, a plurality of organizations that he manipulates in various ways, balancing them against one another so that no one predominates except his Fateh. New groups are emerging, however, secular, hardworking, committed, dedicated to a democratic polity in an independent Palestine. Over these groups the Palestinian Authority has no control at all. But it should also be said that no one in Palestine is willing to accede to the Israeli-U.S. demand for an end to "terrorism," although it will be difficult to draw a line in the public mind between suicidal adventurism and actual resistance to the occupation, as long as Israel continues its bombings and oppression of all Palestinians, young and old.

The second group are the leaders in the rest of the Arab world who have a vested interest in Arafat, despite their evident exasperation with him. He is cleverer and more persistent than they are, and he knows the

hold he has on the popular mind in their countries, where he has cultivated two separate Arab constituencies, the Islamists and the secular
nationalists. Both feel under attack, even though the latter has hardly
been noticed by the vast number of Western experts and Orientalists who
take Bin Laden—rather than the much larger number of Muslim and
non-Muslim secular Arabs who detest what Bin Laden stands for and
what he has done to be the paradigmatic Muslim. In Palestine, for
example, recent polls have found that Arafat and Hamas are now about
equal in popularity (both hover between 20 and 25 percent), with the
majority of citizens favoring neither. (But even as he has been cornered,
Arafat's popularity has shot up.) The same division, with the same significant plague-on-both-your-houses majority, exists in the Arab countries,
where most people are put off either by the corruption and brutality of
the regimes or by the reductiveness and extremism of the religious
groups—most of which are more interested in the regulation of personal
behavior than in matters like globalization or producing electricity and
jobs.

Arabs and Muslims might well turn against their own rulers were
Arafat seen as being choked to death by Israeli violence and Arab indifference. So he is necessary to the present landscape. His departure would
seem natural only when a new collective leadership emerged among a
younger generation of Palestinians. When and how that will happen is
impossible to tell, but I'm quite certain that it will happen.

The third group of players includes the Europeans, the Americans, and
the rest, and frankly, I don't think they know what they're doing. Most of
them would gladly be rid of Palestine as a problem and, in the spirit of
Bush and Powell, would not be unhappy if the vision of a Palestinian state
were somehow realized, as long as someone else did it. Besides, they
would find functioning in the Middle East difficult if they didn't have
Arafat to blame, snub, insult, prod, pressure, or give money to. The mission of the European Union and General Zinni seems senseless and will
have no effect on Sharon and his people. The Israeli politicians have concluded correctly that the Western governments are, in general, on their
side, and they can continue what they do best, regardless of Arafat and
his people's fruitless begging to negotiate. A slowly emerging group of
Palestinians, both in Palestine and in the diaspora, is beginning to learn

and use tactics that solidly place a moral onus on the West and Israel to address the issue of Palestinian rights, not just of the Palestinian presence. In Israel, for example, an audacious Knesset member, the Palestinian Azmi Bishara, has been stripped of his parliamentary immunity and will soon be on trial for incitement to violence. Why? Because he has long stood for the Palestinian right of resistance to occupation, arguing that, like every other state in the world, Israel should be the state of all its citizens, not just of the Jewish people. For the first time, a major Palestinian challenge on Palestinian rights is being mounted *inside* Israel (not on the West Bank), with all eyes on the proceedings. At the same time, the Belgian Attorney General's Office has confirmed that a war crimes case against Sharon can go forward in that country's courts. A painstaking mobilization of secular Palestinian opinion is under way and will slowly overtake the Palestinian Authority. The moral high ground will soon be reclaimed from Israel, as the occupation becomes the focus of attention and as more and more Israelis realize that there is no way to continue indefinitely a thirty-five-year-old occupation. Besides, as the U.S. war against terrorism spreads, more unrest is almost certain; far from closing things down, U.S. power is likely to stir them up in ways that may not be containable. It's no mean irony that the renewed attention on Palestine came about because the Americans and Europeans need to maintain the anti-Taliban coalition.

Al-Ahram, December 20–26, 2001
Al-Hayat, December 20, 2001
London Review of Books, January 3, 2002

CHAPTER TWENTY-THREE

Emerging Alternatives in Palestine

Since it began fifteen months ago, the Palestinian intifada has little to show for itself politically, despite the remarkable fortitude of a militarily occupied, unarmed, poorly led, and still dispossessed people that has defied the pitiless ravages of Israel's war machine. In the United States the government and, with a handful of exceptions, the "independent" media have echoed each other in harping on Palestinian violence and terror, with no attention at all paid to the thirty-five-year-old Israeli military occupation, the longest in modern history: as a result, American official condemnations of Yasir Arafat's Palestinian Authority after September 11 as harboring and even sponsoring terrorism have coldly reinforced the Sharon government's preposterous claim that Israel is the victim, the Palestinians the aggressors in the four-decade war that the Israeli army has waged against civilians, property, and institutions without mercy or discrimination. The result today is that the Palestinians are locked up in 220 ghettos controlled by the army; American-supplied Apache helicopters, Merkava tanks, and F-16s mow down people, houses, olive groves, and fields on a daily basis; schools and universities as well as businesses and civil institutions are totally disrupted; hundreds of innocent civilians have been killed and tens of thousands injured; Israel's assassinations of Palestinian leaders continue; unemployment and poverty stand at about 50 percent—and all this while General Anthony Zinni drones on about Palestinian "violence" to the wretched Arafat who can't even leave his office in Ramallah because he is imprisoned there by Israeli tanks, while his several tattered security forces scamper about trying to survive the destruction of their offices and barracks.

To make matters worse, the Palestinian Islamists have played into Israel's relentless propaganda mills and its ever-ready military by occasional bursts of wantonly barbaric suicide bombings that finally forced Arafat in mid-December to turn his crippled security forces against

Hamas and Islamic Jihad, arresting militants, closing offices, occasionally firing at and killing demonstrators. Every demand that Sharon makes, Arafat hastens to fulfill, even as Sharon makes still another one, provokes an incident, or simply says—with U.S. backing—that he is unsatisfied and that Arafat remains an "irrelevant" terrorist (whom he sadistically forbade from attending Christmas services in Bethlehem) whose main purpose in life is to kill Jews. To this logic-defying congeries of brutal assaults on the Palestinians, on the man who for better or worse is their leader, and on their already humiliated national existence, Arafat's baffling response has been to keep asking for a return to negotiations, as if Sharon's transparent campaign against even the possibility of negotiations weren't actually happening, and as if the whole idea of the Oslo peace process hadn't already evaporated. What surprises me is that, except for a small number of Israelis (most recently David Grossman), no one comes out and says openly that Palestinians are being persecuted by Israel as *its* natives.

A closer look at the Palestinian reality tells a somewhat more encouraging story. Recent polls have shown that between them, Arafat and his Islamist opponents (who refer to themselves unjustly as "the resistance") get somewhere between 40 and 45 percent popular approval. This means that a silent majority of Palestinians is neither for the Authority's misplaced trust in Oslo (or for its lawless regime of corruption and repression) nor for Hamas's violence. Ever the resourceful tactician, Arafat has countered by delegating Dr. Sari Nusseibeh, a Jerusalem notable, president of Al-Quds University, and Fateh stalwart, to make trial-balloon speeches suggesting that if Israel were to be just a little nicer, the Palestinians might give up their right of return. In addition, a slew of Palestinian personalities close to the Authority (or, more accurately, whose activities have never been independent of the Authority) have signed statements and gone on tour with Israeli peace activists who are either out of power or otherwise seem ineffective as well as discredited. These dispiriting exercises are supposed to show the world that Palestinians are willing to make peace at any price, even to accommodate the military occupation. Arafat is still undefeated so far as his relentless eagerness to stay in power is concerned.

Yet at some distance from all this, a new secular nationalist current is slowly emerging. It's too soon to call this a party or a bloc, but it is now a visible group with true independence and popular status. It counts Dr. Haidar Abdel Shafi and Dr. Mustafa Barghuti (not to be confused with his distant relative, Tanzim activist Marwan Barghuti) among them, along with Ibrahim Dakkak, Professors Ziad Abu Amr, Ahmad Harb, Ali Jarbawi, Fouad Moughrabi, Legislative Council members Rawia al-Shawa and Kamal Shirafi, writers Hassan Khadr and Mahmoud Darwish, Raja Shehadeh, Rima Tarazi, Ghassan Khatib, Naseer Aruri, Elia Zureik, and myself. In December 2001, a collective statement was issued that was well covered in the Arab and European media (it went unmentioned in the United States) calling for Palestinian unity and resistance and the unconditional end of Israeli military occupation, while keeping deliberately silent about returning to Oslo. We believe that negotiating an improvement in the occupation is tantamount to prolonging it. Peace can come only after the occupation ends. The declaration's boldest sections focus on the need to improve the internal Palestinian situation, above all to strengthen democracy; "rectify" the decision-making process (which is totally controlled by Arafat and his men); restore the law's sovereignty and an independent judiciary; prevent the further misuse of public funds; and consolidate the functions of public institutions so as to give every citizen confidence in those that are expressly designed for public service. The final and most decisive demand calls for new parliamentary elections.

However else this declaration may have been read, the fact that so many prominent independents with, for the most part, functioning health, educational, professional, and labor organizations as their base have said these things was lost neither on other Palestinians (who saw it as the most trenchant critique yet of the Arafat regime) nor on the Israeli military. In addition, just as the Authority jumped to obey Sharon and Bush by rounding up the usual Islamist suspects, a nonviolent International Solidarity Movement was launched by Dr. Barghuti that comprised about 550 European observers (several of them European Parliament members), who flew in at their own expense. With them was a well-disciplined band of young Palestinians who, while disrupting Israeli troop and settler movement along with the Europeans, prevented rock-throwing or firing from the Palestinian side. This effectively froze out the Authority and the Islamists and set the agenda for making Israel's occupation itself the focus of attention. All this occurred while the United States was vetoing a Security Council resolution mandating an international group of unarmed observers to interpose themselves between the Israeli army and defenseless Palestinian civilians.

The first result was that on January 3, after Barghuti held a press conference with about twenty Europeans in East Jerusalem, the Israelis arrested, detained, and interrogated him twice, breaking his knee with rifle butts and injuring his head, on the pretext that he was disturbing the peace and had illegally entered Jerusalem (even though he was born in it and has a medical permit to enter it). None of this of course has deterred him or his supporters from continuing the nonviolent struggle, which, I think, is certain to take control of the already-too-militarized intifada, center it nationally on ending occupation and settlements, and steer Palestinians toward statehood and peace. Israel has more to fear from someone like Barghuti, who is a self-possessed, rational, and respected Palestinian, than from the bearded Islamic radicals whom Sharon loves to misrepresent as Israel's quintessential terrorist threat. All they do is to arrest him, which is typical of Sharon's bankrupt policy.

So where is the Israeli and American left that is quick to condemn "violence" while saying not a word about the disgraceful and criminal occupation itself? I would seriously suggest that they should join brave activists like Jeff Halper and Luisa Morgantini at the barricades (literal and figurative), stand side by side with this major new secular Palestinian initiative, and start protesting the Israeli military methods that are directly subsidized by taxpayers and their dearly bought silence. Having for a year wrung their collective hands and complained about the absence of a Palestinian peace movement (since when does a militarily occupied people have responsibility for a peace movement?), the alleged peaceniks who can actually influence Israel's military have a clear political duty to organize against the occupation right now, unconditionally and without making unseemly demands on the already laden Palestinians.

Some of them have. Several hundred Israeli reservists have refused military duty in the Occupied Territories, and a whole spectrum of journalists, activists, academics, and writers (including Amira Hass, Gideon Levy, David Grossman, Ilan Pappe, Danny Rabinowitz, and Uri Avnery) have kept up a steady attack on the criminal futility of Sharon's campaign against the Palestinian people. Ideally, there should be a similar chorus in the United States where, except for a tiny number of Jewish voices making public their outrage at Israel's military occupation, there is far too much complicity and drum-beating. The Israeli lobby has been temporarily successful in identifying the war against Bin Laden with Sharon's single-minded, collective assault on Arafat and his people. Unfortunately, the Arab American community is both too small and too beleaguered as it tries to fend off the ever expanding Ashcroft dragnet, racial profiling, and curtailment of civil liberties here.

Most urgently needed, therefore, is coordination between the various secular groups who support Palestinians, a people whose major obstacle is geographical dispersion (even more than Israeli depredations). To end the occupation and all that has gone with it is a clear enough imperative. Now let us do it. And Arab intellectuals needn't feel shy about actually joining in.

Al-Ahram, January 10–16, 2002
Al-Hayat, January 18, 2002

CHAPTER TWENTY-FOUR

The Screw Turns, Again

History has no mercy. There are no laws in it against suffering and cruelty, no internal balance that restores a people much sinned against to their rightful place in the world. Cyclical views of history have always seemed to me flawed for that reason, as if the turning of the screw means that present evil can later be transformed into good. Nonsense. Turning the screw of suffering means more suffering, not a path to salvation. The most frustrating thing about history, however, is that so much in it escapes language, escapes attention and memory altogether. Historians have therefore resorted to metaphors and poetic figures to fill in the spaces, and this is why the first great historian, Herodotus, was also known as the Father of Lies: so much in what he wrote embellished and, to a great extent also, concealed the truth that it is the powers of his imagination that make him so great a writer, not the vast number of facts he deployed.

Living in the United States at this moment is a terrible experience. While the main media and the government echo each other about the Middle East, there are alternative views available through the Internet, the telephone, satellite channels, and the local Arabic and Jewish press. Nevertheless, so far as what is readily available to the average American—drowned in a storm of media pictures and stories almost completely cleansed of anything in foreign affairs but the patriotic line issued by the government—the picture is a startling one. America is fighting the evils of terrorism. America is good, and anyone who objects is evil and anti-American. Resistance against America, its policies, its arms and ideas is little short of terrorist. What I find just as startling is that influential and, in their own way, sophisticated American foreign policy analysts keep saying that they cannot understand why the whole world (and the Arabs and Muslims in particular) will not accept the American message, and why the rest of the world—including Europe, Asia, Africa, and Latin

America—persists in its criticism of American policy for the war in Afghanistan, for its unilateral renunciation of six international treaties, for its total, unconditional support of Israel, for its astonishingly obdurate policy on prisoners of war. The difference between realities as perceived by Americans on the one hand and by the rest of the world on the other is so vast and irreconcilable as to defy description.

Words alone are inadequate to explain how an American secretary of state, who presumably has all the facts at his command, can without a trace of irony accuse Palestinian leader Yasir Arafat of not doing enough against terror and of buying fifty tons of arms to defend his people, while Israel is supplied with everything that is most lethally sophisticated in the American arsenal at no expense to Israel. (At the same time, it needs to be said that PLO handling of the *Karine A* incident has been incompetent and bungling beyond even its own poor standards.) Meanwhile, Israel has Arafat locked up in his Ramallah headquarters, his people totally imprisoned, leaders assassinated, innocents starved, the sick dying, life completely paralyzed, and yet the Palestinians are accused of terrorism. The idea, much less the reality, of a thirty-five-year-old military occupation has simply slid away from the media and the U.S. government alike. Do not be surprised tomorrow if Arafat and his people are accused of besieging Israel while blockading its citizens and towns. No, those are not Israeli planes bombing Tul Karm and Jenin, those are Palestinian terrorists wearing wings, and those are Israeli towns being bombed.

As for Israel on the U.S. media, its spokesmen have become so practiced at lying, creating falsehoods the way a sausage-maker makes sausages, that nothing is beyond them. Yesterday I heard an Israel Defense (even the name sticks in one's throat) Ministry official answering an American reporter's questions about house destruction in Rafah: those were empty houses, he said without hesitation, they were terrorist nests used for killing Israeli citizens; we have to defend Israeli citizens against Palestinian terror. The occupation wasn't even referred to by the journalist, and neither was the fact that the "citizens" referred to were settlers. As for the several hundred poor homeless Palestinians whose pictures appeared fleetingly in the U.S. media after the (American-made) bulldozers had done their demolition, they were gone from memory and awareness completely.

As for the Arab nonresponse, that has exceeded in disgrace and shamefulness the already abysmally low standards set by our governments for the past fifty years. Such a callous silence, such a stance of servility and incompetence in facing the United States and Israel, is as astonishing and unacceptable in its own way as what Sharon and Bush are about. Are the Arab leaders so fearful of offending the United States that they are willing to accept not only Palestinian humiliation but their own as well? And for what? Simply to be allowed to go on with corruption, mediocrity, and oppression. What a cheap bargain they have made between the furtherance of their narrow interests and American forbearance! No wonder there is scarcely an Arab alive today for whom the word *regime* connotes little more than amused contempt, unadulterated bitterness, and (except for the circle of advisers and sycophants) angry alienation. At least with the recent press conferences by high Saudi officials criticizing U.S. policy toward Israel, there is a welcome break in the silence, although the disarray and dysfunction concerning the upcoming Arab summit continues to add to our already well-stocked cupboard of poorly managed incidents that demonstrate a needless disunity and posturing.

I do think that the adjective *wicked* (*shar*) is the correct one here for what is being done to the truth of the Palestinian experience of suffering imposed by Sharon collectively on the whole of the West Bank and Gaza. That it cannot adequately be described or narrated, that the Arabs say or do nothing in support of the struggle, that the United States is so terrifyingly hostile, that the Europeans are (except for their recent declaration, which has no measures of implementation in it) so useless, all this has driven many of us to despair, I know, and to a kind of hopeless frustration that is one of the results aimed for by Israeli officials and their U.S. counterparts. To reduce people to the heedlessness of not caring anymore, and to make life so miserable that it seems necessary to give up life itself, comprise a state of desperation that Sharon so clearly wants. This is what he was elected to do and what, if his policies fail, will cause him to lose his office, whereupon Benjamin Netanyahu will be brought in to try to finish the same dreadful and inhuman (but ultimately suicidal) task.

In the face of such a situation, passivity and helpless anger—even a kind of bitter fatalism—are, I truly believe, inappropriate intellectual and political responses. Examples to the contrary still abound. Palestinians have neither been intimidated nor persuaded to give up, and that is a sign of great will and purpose. Looked at from that point of view, all of Israel's collective measures and constant humiliations have proved ineffective; as one of their generals put it, stopping the resistance by besieging Palestinians is like trying to drink the sea with a spoon. It just doesn't work. But having taken note of that, I also firmly believe that we have to go beyond stubborn resistance toward a creative one, toward getting beyond the tired old methods for defying the Israelis but not sufficiently advancing Palestinian interests in the process. Take decision-making as a simple case in point. It's all very well for Arafat to sit out his own imprisonment in Ramallah and to repeat endlessly that he wants to negotiate, but it just is not a political program, nor is its personal style sufficient to mobilize his own people as well as his allies. Certainly it is good to take note of the European declaration in support of the Authority, but surely it is more important to say something about the Israeli reservists who refused service on the West Bank and Gaza. Without identifying and trying to work in concert with Israeli resistance to Israeli oppression, we are still standing at square one.

The point, of course, is that every turning of the screw of cruel collective punishment dialectically creates a new space for new kinds of resistance, of which suicide bombing is simply not a part, any more than Arafat's personal style of defiance (all too reminiscent of what he said twenty and thirty years ago in Amman and Beirut and Tunis) is new. These forms of resistance and defiance aren't new and aren't up to what is now being done by opponents of Israel's military occupation in both Palestine and Israel. Why not make a specific point of singling out Israeli groups who have opposed house demolitions, or apartheid, or assassinations, or any of the lawless displays of Israeli macho bullying? There is no way that the occupation is going to be defeated unless Palestinian and Israeli efforts combine to work together to end the occupation, in specific and concrete ways. And that, therefore, means that Palestinian groups (with or without the Authority's guidance) have to take initiatives that they have been shy of taking (because of understandable fears of normalization), initiatives that actively solicit and involve Israeli resistance as well as European, Arab, and American resistance. In other words, with the disappearance of Oslo, Palestinian civil society has been released from that fraudulent peace process's strictures, and this new empowerment means going beyond such traditional interlocutors as the now completely discredited Labor Party and its hangers-on, in the direction of more courageous, innovative antioccupation drives. If the Authority wants to keep calling on Israel to return to the negotiating table, that's fine, of course, if any Israelis can be found to sit there with it. But that doesn't mean that Palestinian NGOs have to repeat the same chorus, or that they have to keep worrying about normalization, which was all about normalization with the Israeli state, not progressive currents and groups in its civil society that actively support real Palestinian self-determination and the end of occupation, of settlements, of collective punishment.

Yes, the screw turns, but it not only brings more Israeli repression, it also dialectically reveals new opportunities for Palestinian ingenuity and creativity. There are already considerable signs of progress (noted in my last column) in Palestinian civil society: an intensified focus on them is required, especially as fissures in Israeli society disclose a frightened, closed-off, and horrifyingly insecure populace badly in need of awakening. It always falls to the victim, not the oppressor, to show new paths for resistance, and in this the signs are that Palestinian civil society is beginning to take the initiative. This is an excellent omen in a time of despondency and instinctual retrogression.

Al-Ahram, January 31–February 6, 2002
Al-Hayat, March 7, 2002

CHAPTER TWENTY-FIVE

Thoughts About America

I don't know a single Arab or Muslim American who does not now feel that he or she belongs to the enemy camp, and that being in the United States at this moment provides us with an especially unpleasant experience of alienation and widespread, quite specifically targeted hostility. For despite the occasional official statements saying that Islam and Muslims and Arabs are not enemies of the United States, everything else about the current situation argues the exact opposite. Hundreds of young Arab and Muslim men have been picked up for questioning and, in far too many cases, detained by the police or the FBI. Anyone with an Arabic or Muslim name is usually made to stand aside for special attention during airport security checks. There have been many reported instances of discriminatory behavior against Arabs, so that speaking Arabic or even reading an Arabic document in public is likely to draw unwelcome attention. And of course, the media have run far too many "experts" and "commentators" on terrorism, Islam, and the Arabs whose endlessly repetitious and reductive line is so hostile and so misrepresents our history, society, and culture that the media itself has become little more than an arm of the war on terrorism in Afghanistan and elsewhere, as now seems to be the case with the projected attack to "end" Iraq. There are U.S. forces already in several countries with important Muslim populations like the Philippines and Somalia, the buildup against Iraq continues, and Israel prolongs its sadistic collective punishment of the Palestinian people, all with what seems like great public approval in the United States.

While true in some respects, this picture is quite misleading. America is more than what Bush and Rumsfeld and the others say it is. I have come to deeply resent the notion that I must accept the picture of America as being involved in a "just war" against something unilaterally labeled as terrorism by Bush and his advisers, a war that has assigned us the role either of silent witnesses or as defensive immigrants who should be grateful to be allowed residence in the United States. The historical realities are different: America is an immigrant republic and has always been one. It is a nation of laws passed not by God but by its citizens. Except for the mostly exterminated Native Americans, the original Indians, everyone who now lives here as an American citizen originally came to these shores as an immigrant from somewhere else, even Bush and Rumsfeld. The Constitution does not provide for different levels of Americanness, nor for approved or disapproved forms of "American" behavior, including things that have come to be called "un-" or "anti-American" statements or attitudes. That is the invention of American Talibans who want to regulate speech and behavior in ways that remind one eerily of the unregretted former rulers of Afghanistan. And even if Mr. Bush insists on the importance of religion in America, he is not authorized to force such views on the citizenry or to speak for everyone when he makes proclamations in China and elsewhere about God and America and himself. The Constitution expressly separates church and state.

There is worse. By passing the Patriot Act last November, Bush and his compliant Congress have suppressed or abrogated or abridged whole sections of the First, Fourth, Fifth, and Eighth Amendments, instituted legal procedures against individuals that give them no recourse either to a proper defense or to a fair trial, allowed secret searches, eavesdropping, and detention without limit, and given the treatment of the prisoners at Guantánamo Bay, allowed the U.S. executive branch to abduct prisoners, detain them indefinitely, and decide unilaterally whether they are prisoners of war and whether the Geneva conventions apply to them, which is not a decision to be taken by individual countries. Moreover, as Congressman Dennis Kucinich (Democrat of Ohio) said in a magnificent speech given on February 17, the president and his men were not authorized to declare war (Operation Enduring Freedom) against the world without limit or reason, were not authorized to increase military spending to over $400 billion per year, were not authorized to repeal the Bill of Rights, and, he added for the first time by a prominent, publicly elected official, "we did not ask that the blood of innocent people, who perished on September 11, be avenged with the blood of innocent villagers in Afghanistan." I strongly recommend that Congressman Kucinich's speech, which was made with the best of American principles and values in mind, be published in full in Arabic so that people in our part of the world can understand that America is not a monolith for the use of George Bush and Dick Cheney but in fact contains many voices and currents of opinion that this government is trying to silence or make irrelevant.

The problem for the world today is how to deal with the unparalleled and unprecedented power of the United States, which in effect has made no secret of the fact that it does not need coordination with or approval of others in the pursuit of what a small circle of men and women around Bush believe are its interests. So far as the Middle East is concerned, it does seem that since September 11 there has been almost an Israelization of U.S. policy: and in effect Ariel Sharon and his associates have cynically exploited the single-minded attention to "terrorism" by George Bush and used it as a cover for their continued failed policy against the Palestinians. The point here is that Israel is not the United States, and mercifully, neither is the United States Israel: thus even though Israel commands Bush's support for the moment, it is a small country whose continued survival as an ethnocentric state in the midst of an Arab-Islamic sea depends not just on an expedient if not infinite dependence on the United States but rather on accommodation with its environment. That is why I think Sharon's policy has finally been revealed to a significant number of Israelis as suicidal, and why more and more Israelis are taking the reserve officers' position against serving the military occupation as a model for their approach and resistance. This is the best thing to have emerged from the intifada. It proves that Palestinian courage and defiance in resisting occupation have finally borne fruit.

What hasn't changed, however, is the U.S. position, which has been escalating toward a more and more metaphysical sphere, in which Bush and his people identify themselves (as in the very name of the military campaign Operation Enduring Freedom) with righteousness, purity, the good, and manifest destiny, and the country's external enemies with an equally absolute evil. Anyone reading the world press in the past few weeks can ascertain that people outside of the United States are both mystified by and aghast at the vagueness of U.S. policy, which claims for itself the right to imagine and create enemies on a world scale, then prosecute wars on them without much regard for accuracy of definition, specificity of aim, concreteness of goal, or, worst of all, the legality of such actions.

What does it mean to defeat "evil terrorism" in a world like ours? It cannot mean eradicating everyone who opposes the United States, an infinite and strangely pointless task, nor can it mean changing the world map to suit the United States, substituting people we think are "good guys" for evil creatures like Saddam Hussein. The radical simplicity of all this is attractive to Washington bureaucrats; their domain is purely theoretical because they sit behind desks in the Pentagon, and they tend to see the world as a distant target for the United States' very real and virtually unopposed power. For if you live ten thousand miles away from any known evil state and you have at your disposal acres of warplanes, nineteen aircraft carriers, and dozens of submarines, plus a million and a half people under arms, all of them willing to serve their country idealistically in the pursuit of what Bush and Condoleezza Rice keep referring to as evil, the chances are that you will be willing to use all that power sometime, somewhere, especially if the administration keeps asking for (and getting) billions of dollars to be added to the already swollen defense budget.

From my point of view, the most shocking thing of all is that with few exceptions most prominent intellectuals and commentators in this country have tolerated the Bush program, tolerated and in some flagrant cases tried to go beyond it toward more self-righteous sophistry, more uncritical self-flattery, more specious argument. What they will not accept is that the world we live in, the historical world of nations and peoples, is moved and can be understood by politics, not by huge general absolutes like good and evil, with America always on the side of good, its enemies on the side of evil. When Thomas Friedman tiresomely sermonizes to Arabs that they have to be more self-critical, missing in anything he says is the slightest tone of *self*-criticism. Somehow, he thinks, the atrocities of September 11 entitle him to preach at others, as if only the United States had suffered such terrible losses and as if lives lost elsewhere in the world were not worth lamenting quite as much or drawing as large moral conclusions from.

One notices the same discrepancies and blindness when Israeli intellectuals concentrate on their own tragedies and leave out of the equation the much greater suffering of a dispossessed people without a state, or an army, or an air force, or a proper leadership—that is, Palestinians, whose suffering at the hands of Israel continues minute by minute, hour by hour. This sort of moral blindness, this inability to evaluate and weigh the comparative evidence of sinner and sinned-against (to use a moralistic language that I normally avoid and detest), is very much the order of the day, and it must be the critical intellectual's job not to fall into—and actively to campaign against falling into—the trap. It is not enough to say blandly that all human suffering is equal, then to go on basically bewailing one's own miseries: it is far more important to see what the strongest party does, and to question rather than justify that. The intellectual's is a voice in opposition to and critical of great power, which is consistently in need of a restraining and clarifying conscience and a comparative perspective, so that the victim will not, as is often the case, be blamed and so that real power will not be encouraged to do its will.

A week ago I was stunned when a European friend asked me what I thought of a declaration by sixty American intellectuals that was published in all the major French, German, Italian, and other continental papers but that did not appear in the United States at all, except on the Internet, where few people took notice of it. This declaration took the form of a pompous sermon about the American war against evil and terrorism being "just" and in keeping with American values, as defined by these self-appointed interpreters of our country. Paid for and sponsored by something called the Institute for American Values, whose main (and financially well-endowed) aim is to propagate ideas in favor of families, "fathering" and "mothering," and God, the declaration was signed by Samuel Huntington, Francis Fukuyama, and Daniel Patrick Moynihan, among many others, but was basically written by a conservative feminist academic, Jean Bethke Elshtain, and its main arguments about a "just" war were inspired by Michael Walzer, a supposed socialist who is allied with the pro-Israel lobby in this country and whose role is to justify everything Israel does by recourse to vaguely leftist principles. In signing this declaration, Walzer has given up all pretension to leftism and, like Sharon, allies himself with an interpretation (and a questionable one at that) of America as a righteous warrior against terror and evil, the more to make it appear that Israel and the United States are similar countries with similar aims.

Nothing could be further from the truth, since Israel is not the state of its citizens but of all the Jewish people, while the United States is most assuredly *only* the state of its citizens. Moreover, Walzer never has the courage to state boldly that in supporting Israel, he is supporting a state structured by ethnoreligious principles, which (with typical hypocrisy) he would oppose in the United States if this country were declared to be white and Christian.

Walzer's inconsistencies and hypocrisies aside, the document is really addressed to "our Muslim brethren" who are supposed to understand that America's war is not against Islam but against those who oppose all sorts of principles that it would be hard to disagree with. Who could oppose the principle that all human beings are equal, that killing in the name of God is a bad thing, that freedom of conscience is excellent, and that "the basic subject of society is the human person, and the legitimate role of government is to protect and help to foster the conditions for human flourishing"? In what follows, however, America turns out to be the aggrieved party, and even though some of its mistakes in policy are acknowledged very briefly (and without mentioning anything specific in detail), it is depicted as hewing to principles unique to the United States, such as that all people possess inherent moral dignity and status, that universal moral truths exist and are available to everyone, that civility is important where there is disagreement, and that freedom of conscience and religion are a reflection of basic human dignity and are universally recognized. Fine. For although the authors of this sermon say it is often the case that such great principles are contravened, no sustained attempt is made to say where and when those contraventions actually occur (as they do all the time), or whether they have been more contravened than followed, or anything as concrete as that. Yet in a long footnote, Walzer and his colleagues set forth a list of how many American "murders" have occurred at Muslim and Arab hands, including those of the Marines in Beirut in 1983, as well as other military combatants. Somehow a list of that kind is worth making for these militant defenders of America, whereas the murder of Arabs and Muslims—including the hundreds of thousands killed with American weapons by Israel with U.S. support, or the hundreds of thousands killed by U.S.-maintained sanctions against the innocent civilian population of Iraq—need neither be mentioned nor tabulated. What sort of dignity is there in the humiliation of Palestinians by Israel, with American complicity and even cooperation, and where is the nobility and moral conscience of saying nothing as Palestinian children are killed, millions besieged, and millions more kept as stateless refugees? Or for that matter, the millions killed in Vietnam, Colombia, Turkey, and Indonesia with American support and acquiescence?

All in all this declaration of principles and complaint addressed by American intellectuals to their Muslim brethren seems like neither a statement of real conscience nor of true intellectual criticism against the arrogant use of power, but rather the opening salvo in a new cold war declared by the United States in full ironic cooperation, it would seem, with those Islamists who have argued that "our" war is with the West and with America. Speaking as someone with a claim on America and the Arabs, I find this sort of hijacking rhetoric profoundly objectionable. While it pretends to the elucidation of principles and the declaration of values, it is in fact exactly the opposite, an exercise in *not knowing*, in blinding readers with a patriotic rhetoric that encourages ignorance as it overrides real politics, real history, and real moral issues. Despite its vulgar trafficking in great "principles and values," it merely waves them around in a bullying way designed to cow foreign readers into submission. I have a feeling that this document wasn't published here because it would be so severely criticized by American readers that it would be laughed out of court.

Whatever the case, the publication of "What Are American Values?" augurs a new and degraded era in the production of intellectual discourse. For when the intellectuals of the most powerful country in the history of the world align themselves so flagrantly with that power, pressing that power's case instead of urging restraint, reflection, genuine communication, and understanding, we are back to the bad old days of the intellectual war against communism, which we now know brought far too many compromises, collaborations, and fabrications on the part of intellectuals and artists who should have played an altogether different role. Subsidized and underwritten by the government (the CIA especially, which went so far as to provide for the subvention of magazines like *Encounter*, underwrote scholarly research, travel, and concerts as well as artistic exhibitions), those militantly unreflective and uncritical intellectuals and artists in the 1950s and 1960s brought the whole notion of intellectual honesty and complicity a new and disastrous dimension. For along with that effort went also the domestic campaign to stifle debate, intimidate critics, and restrict thought. For many Americans, like myself, this is a shameful episode in our history, and we must be on our guard against and resist its return.

Al-Ahram, February 28–March 6, 2002
Al-Hayat, March 7, 2002

CHAPTER TWENTY-SIX

What Price Oslo?

The television images on Al-Jazeera have been burningly clear. There is a kind of Palestinian heroism in evidence there that is *the* story of our time. An entire army, navy, and air force supplied munificently and unconditionally by the United States has been wreaking destruction on the 18 percent of the West Bank and 60 percent of Gaza afforded Palestinians after ten years of negotiations with Israel and the United States. Palestinian hospitals, schools, refugee camps, civilian residences have been at the receiving end of a merciless, criminal assault by Israeli troops huddled inside their helicopter gunships, F-16s, and Merkavas, and still the poorly armed resistance fighters take on this preposterously more powerful force undaunted and unyielding. In the United States, CNN and newspapers like the *New York Times,* to their discredit, fail ever to mention that "the violence" is uneven and that there aren't two sides involved here but only one state, turning all its great power against a stateless, repeatedly refugeed, and dispossessed people, bereft of arms and real leadership, with the aim of destroying this people, "dealing them a terrible blow," as the war criminal who leads Israel has put it shamelessly. As an index of how deranged Sharon has become, I might quote here what he said to *Ha'aretz* on March 5, 2002: "The PA is behind the terror, it's all terror. Arafat is behind the terror. Our pressure is aimed at ending the terror. Don't expect Arafat to act against the terror. We have to cause them heavy casualties and then they'll know they can't keep using terror and win political achievements."

Besides symptomatically revealing the workings of an obsessed mind bent on destruction and sheer, unadulterated hatred, Sharon's words indicate the failures of reason and criticism loosed on the world since last September. Yes, there was a terrorist outrage, but there's more to the world than terror. There is politics, and struggle, and history, and injustice, and resistance, and yes, state terror as well. With scarcely a peep from the American professoriat or intelligentsia, we have all succumbed entirely to the promiscuous misuse of language and sense, by which everything we don't like has become terror and what we do is pure and simple good, to fight terror, no matter how much wealth and lives and destruction are involved. Swept away are all the Enlightenment precepts by which we attempt to educate our students and our fellow citizens, replaced by a disproportionate orgy of vindictiveness and self-righteous wrath of the kind that only the wealthy and the powerful, it would seem, have the right to use and act upon. No wonder then that such a fourth-rate thug as Sharon feels entitled (by emulation and derivation) to do what he does, when in the greatest democracy on earth, laws, constitutional rights, writs of habeas corpus, and reason itself are consigned to the rubbish bin in the pursuit of terror and terrorism. As educators and as citizens, we have failed in our mission by allowing ourselves to be bamboozled in this way, without so much as an organized public discussion about a defense budget that has shot up to $400 billion and 40 million people remain without health insurance.

Israelis, Arabs, and Americans are told that love of country requires such expenditures and such destruction because a good cause is at stake. Nonsense. What is at stake are material interests that keep rulers in power, corporations making profits, and people in a state of manufactured consent, just so long as they don't get up one morning and start to think about where, in this mad technologized rush to bomb and kill, we are going.

Israel is now waging a war against civilians, pure and simple, although you will never hear it put that way in the United States. This is a racist war and, in its strategy and tactics, a colonial one as well. People are being killed and made to suffer disproportionately because they are not Jews. What an irony! Yet CNN never refers to "occupied" territories (always rather to "violence in Israel," as if the main battlefields were the concert halls and cafés of Tel Aviv and not in fact the ghettos and besieged refugee camps of Palestine that have already been surrounded by no less than 150 illegal Israeli settlements). For the past ten years, the great fraud of Oslo was foisted on the world by the United States, with hardly an awareness that only 18 percent of the West Bank was given up, and 60 percent of Gaza. No one knows geography, and it's better not to know, since the reality on the ground is so astonishing, considering the verbal hoopla and self-congratulation.

And that pseudo-pundit—the insufferably conceited Thomas Friedman—still has the gall to say that "Arab TV" shows one-sided pictures, as if "Arab TV" should be showing things from Israel's point of view the way CNN does, with "Mideast violence" the catchall word for the ethnic cleansing that Israel is wreaking on the Palestinians in their ghettos and camps. Has Friedman (or CNN, for that matter) ever tried to point out the difference between an attacking army fighting a colonial war on the territory of the people it has occupied for thirty-five years, and the people defending against that butchery? Of course not, for indeed why should Friedman ever bother to say honestly that there is no Palestinian occupation, there are no Palestinian F-16s, no Apache helicopters, no gunboats, no Merkava tanks, in short, no Palestinian occupation of Israel. So much for Friedman's credentials as an honest commentator and reporter, who has utterly failed in unadorned terms both to explain the U.S. view and to understand the Arab and Palestinian cause. Can he not see that he and his writings are part of the problem, that in their maundering self-justifications and their dishonesty, showing no sign of the self-criticism he keeps hectoringly expecting of others, he actually aggravates the ignorance and the misperceptions rather than reducing them? Poor journalist and educator, he.

The picture you get here is that Israelis are battling for their lives instead of for their settlements and military bases on the occupied lands of Palestine. No maps have been run for months in the American media. On March 8, hitherto the bloodiest day for Palestinians of the sixteen-month intifada, CNN's main evening news specified the death of forty "people" and failed even to mention the death of several Red Crescent workers killed while their ambulances were prevented callously by Israeli tanks from getting to the wounded. Just "people," and no pictures of the hell they've been living in in this the thirty-fifth year of military occupation. Tul Karm, undergoing a siege of sieges with twenty-four-hour curfews, electricity and water cut off, systematic round-ups and the removal of eight hundred young men, the wanton smashing of refugee houses, immense destruction of property (and I'm not speaking of nightclubs or sports facilities but of shacks and lean-tos that have furnished twice-displaced refugees with hovels for bare subsistence), and limitless cases of unexampled sadistic cruelty to unarmed and undefended civilians who are pushed and beaten and left to bleed to death, women allowed to give birth to stillborn babies while they wait needlessly at Israeli roadblocks, old men made to strip and take off their shoes and walk barefoot for a gum-chewing eighteen-year-old waving around an M-16 that my taxes have paid for. Bethlehem, its town center and university destroyed, flattened from five thousand feet by valiant Israeli bombers swooshing in with their marvelous F-16s, which I've paid for, too. Balata camp, Aida and Deheisheh and Azza camps, the tiny villages of Khadr and Husam, all battered into rubble without even a mention by the U.S. press, whose New York editors so obviously have no problems with it, with a few exceptions here and there. The uncounted dead and wounded, the unburied and unassisted, to say nothing of the hundreds of thousands of lives maimed, distorted, and catastrophically marked by wantonly caused suffering, all of it ordered at a safe distance from the action in leafy, calm West Jerusalem by men for whom the West Bank and Gaza are distant rat holes filled with insects and rodents that must be "subdued" and driven out, taught a lesson in the accepted jargon of Israel's superb military. Today, in the biggest attack of all, Ramallah has been invaded and is being ravaged by 140 Israeli tanks, thus completing Israel's reconquest of the already-occupied Palestinian territories.

The Palestinian people are paying the heavy, heavy, unconscionable price of Oslo, which after ten years of negotiating left them with bits of land lacking coherence and continuity, security institutions designed to assure their subservience to Israel, and a life that impoverished them so that the Jewish state could thrive and prosper. In vain during those ten years did some of us warn that the distance between the U.S.-Israeli language of peace and the appalling realities on the ground was never bridged, never even intended to be bridged. Words and phrases like *peace process* and *terrorism* took hold without any real referent. Land confiscations were either overlooked or referred to as "bilateral negotiations" that were taking place between a state consolidating its hold on territory that it wanted at all costs, and a mediocre set of uninformed negotiators whom it took four years to acquire, much less use, a reliable map of the land they were negotiating over. The worst misrepresentation of all is that in the fifty-four years since 1948, never has a narrative of Palestinian heroism and suffering ever been allowed to emerge. We are all depicted as basically violent fanatic extremists who are little more than the terrorists whom George W. Bush and his cabal have imposed on the consciousness of a stunned and systematically misinformed population, aided and un-critically abetted by an entire army of commentators and media stars—the Blitzers, Zahns, Lehrers, Rathers, Brokaws, Russerts, and their ilk. The Israeli lobby is scarcely needed with such faithful disciples trailing happily in its ranks.

But now that the Saudi peace proposal has become the point of discussion and of hope, it is necessary, I think, to put it in its real, as opposed to its supposed, context. First of all, this is the recycled Reagan plan of 1982, the Fahd plan of 1983, the Madrid plan of 1991, and so on: in other words, it follows a series of plans many times put forward that in the end both Israel and the United States have not only refused to implement but have actively torpedoed. The way I see it, the only negotiations worth having should be on the phases of a total Israeli withdrawal and not, as was the case with Oslo, bargaining over what pieces of land Israel was willing very grudgingly to give up. There's been too much Palestinian blood spilled, too much Israeli contempt and racist violence dispensed, for any serious return to Oslo-style negotiations brokered by that most biased of honest brokers, the United States. Everyone is aware, however, that the old Palestinian negotiators haven't given up on their dreams and illusions, and that meetings have been occurring throughout the raids and bombings. But I would argue that due weight should be given to decades of Palestinian suffering and the real human costs of Israel's destructive policies before any negotiations accord undue status to Israeli governments that have trampled on Palestinian rights the way they have demolished our houses and killed our people. Any Arab-Israeli negotiations that do not factor in history—and for this task a team of historians, economists, and geographers with a conscience is needed—are not worth having, just as Palestinians must now elect a new set of negotiators and representatives in the hope of salvaging something from the present calamity.

In short, in whatever meetings that now occur between Israeli and Palestinian representatives, the gravity of Israeli depredations against our people has to be given attention and not simply brushed aside as so much past history. Oslo, in effect, pardoned the occupation, excusing it for all the buildings and lives destroyed over the first twenty-five years of occupation. After so much further suffering, Israel cannot be excused and allowed to walk away from the table without even a rhetorical demand that it needs to atone for what it did.

I will be told that politics is about what is possible, not about what is desired, and that we should be grateful to get even a small Israeli pullback. I disagree strongly. Negotiations can only be about *when* the total withdrawal will take place, not about how many percentages Israel is willing to concede. A conqueror and a vandal cannot concede anything: he must simply return what he's taken and pay for the abuses that are his responsibility, just as Saddam Hussein should and did pay for his occupation of Kuwait. We are still a considerable distance from that goal, although in the meantime the extraordinary unbowed bravery of all Palestinians in Gaza and the West Bank has in effect politically and morally defeated Sharon, who will lose his seat in the not too distant future. But that in two decades his armies can invade Arab cities at will, killing and sowing destruction without so much as a collective Arab peep, speaks reams for the Arab world's great leaders!

Lastly, what the various Arab rulers who are so delicately silent now while Palestine is being raped on TV think they are doing, I don't know, but I can imagine that deep in their souls they must feel no small amount of shame and disgrace. Powerless militarily, politically, economically, and above all morally, they have little credibility and no real standing, except as obedient pawns on the American-Israeli chessboard. Perhaps they feel they are playing a waiting game. Perhaps. But they (like Arafat and his men) haven't even learned the power of systematically disseminating information as a way of protecting their people from the onslaughts of those who consider all Arabs militant, extremist, terrorist fanatics. The good news is that the time for that sort of irresponsible and contemptible behavior is very short. Will the new generation do any better?

It is for a whole new attitude toward secular education to decide the answer, whether collectively we go down again to disorganization, corruption, and mediocrity or whether at last we can become a nation.

Al-Ahram, March 14–20, 2002
Al-Hayat, March 31, 2002

CHAPTER TWENTY-SEVEN

Thinking Ahead

Anyone with any connection at all to Palestine is today in a state of stunned outrage and shock. While almost a repeat of what happened in 1982, the current Israeli all-out colonial assault on the Palestinian people (with George W. Bush's astoundingly ignorant and grotesque support) is indeed worse than Sharon's two previous mass forays in 1971 and 1982 against the Palestinian people. The political and moral climate today is a good deal cruder and more reductive, the media's destructive role (which has played the part almost entirely of singling out Palestinian suicide attacks and isolating them from their context in Israel's thirty-five-year-old illegal occupation of the Palestinian territories) is greater in favoring the Israeli view of things, the United States' power is more unchallenged, the war against terrorism has more completely taken over the global agenda, and so far as the Arab environment is concerned, there is greater incoherence and fragmentation than ever before.

Sharon's homicidal instincts have been enhanced (if that's the right word) by all of the above, and magnified to boot. This in effect means that he can do more damage with more impunity than before, although he is also more deeply undermined than before in all his efforts as well as in his entire career by the failure that comes with single-minded negation and hate, which in the end nourish neither political nor even military success. Conflicts between peoples such as this contain more elements than can be eliminated by tanks and air power, and a war against unarmed civilians— no matter how many times Sharon lumberingly and mindlessly trumpets his stupid mantras about terror—can never bring a really lasting political result of the sort his dreams tell him he can have. Palestinians will not go away. Besides, Sharon will almost certainly end up disgraced and rejected by his people. He has no plan, except to destroy everything about Palestine and the Palestinians. Even in his enraged fixation on Arafat and terror, he is failing to do much more than raise the man's prestige, while essentially drawing attention to the blind monomania of his own position.

In the end he is Israel's problem to deal with. For us, our main consideration now is morally to do everything in our power to make certain that despite the enormous suffering and destruction imposed on us by a criminal war, we must go on. When a renowned and respected retired politician like Zbigniew Brzezinski says explicitly on national television that Israel has been behaving like the white supremacist regime of apartheid South Africa, one can be certain that he is not alone in this view, and that an increasing number of Americans and others are slowly growing not only disenchanted but also disgusted with Israel as a hugely expensive and draining ward of the United States, costing far too much, increasing American isolation, and seriously damaging the country's reputation with its allies and its citizens. The question is what in this most difficult of moments can we rationally learn about the present crisis that we need to include in our plans for the future?

What I have to say now is highly selective, but it is the modest fruit of many years of working on behalf of the Palestinian cause as someone who is from both Arab and Western worlds. I neither know nor can say everything, but here are some of the handful of thoughts I can contribute at this very difficult hour. Each of the four points that follow here is related to the other.

1. For better or for worse, Palestine is not just an Arab and Islamic cause; it is important to many different, contradictory, and yet intersecting worlds. To work for Palestine is necessarily to be aware of these many dimensions and constantly to educate oneself in them. For that we need a highly educated, vigilant, and sophisticated leadership and democratic support. Above all we must, as Nelson Mandela never tired of saying about *his* struggle, be aware that Palestine is one of the great moral causes of our time. Therefore we need to treat it as such. It's not a matter of trade, or bartering negotiations, or making a career. It is a just cause that should allow Palestinians to capture the moral high ground and keep it.

2. There are different kinds of power, military of course being the most obvious. What has enabled Israel to do what it has been doing to the Palestinians for the past fifty-four years is a carefully and scientifically planned campaign to validate Israeli actions and, simultaneously, devalue and efface Palestinian actions. This is a matter not just of maintaining a powerful military but of organizing opinion, especially in the United States and Western Europe, and it is a power derived from slow, methodi-

cal work where Israel's position is seen as one to be easily identified with, whereas the Palestinians are thought of as Israel's enemies, hence repugnant, dangerous, against "us." Since the end of the cold war, Europe has faded into near insignificance so far as the organization of opinion, images, and thought is concerned. America (outside of Palestine itself) is the main arena of battle. We have simply never learned the importance of systematically organizing our political work in this country on a mass level, so that for instance the average American will not immediately think of "terrorism" when the word *Palestinian* is pronounced. That kind of work quite literally protects whatever gains we might make through our on-the-ground resistance to Israel's occupation.

What has enabled Israel to deal with us with impunity therefore has been that we are unprotected by any body of opinion that would deter Sharon from practicing his war crimes and saying that what he has done is to fight terrorism. Given the immense diffusionary, insistent, and repetitive power of the images broadcast by CNN, for example, in which the phrase "suicide bomb" is numbingly repeated a hundred times an hour for the American consumer and taxpayer, it is the grossest negligence not to have had a team of people like Hanan Ashrawi, Leila Shahid, Ghassan Khatib, and Afif Safieh—to mention just a few—sitting in Washington ready to go on CNN or any of the other channels just to tell the Palestinian story, provide context and understanding, and give us a moral and narrative presence that has positive, rather than merely negative, value. We need a future leadership that understands this as one of the basic lessons of modern politics in an age of electronic communication. Not to have understood this is part of the tragedy of today.

3. There is simply no use operating politically and responsibly in a world dominated by one superpower without having a profound familiarity with and knowledge of that superpower, America, its history, its institutions, its currents and countercurrents, its politics and culture. And above all, a perfect working knowledge of its language. To hear our spokesmen, as well as the other Arabs, saying the most ridiculous things about America, throwing themselves on its mercy, cursing it in one breath, asking for its help in another, all in a miserably inadequate fractured English, shows a state of such primitive incompetence as to make one cry. America is not monolithic. We have friends, and we have possible friends.

We can cultivate, mobilize, and use our communities and their affiliated communities here as an integral part of our politics of liberation, just as the South Africans did, or as the Algerians did in France during their struggle for liberation. Planning, discipline, coordination. We have not at all understood the politics of nonviolence. Moreover, neither have we understood the power of trying to address Israelis directly, the way the African National Congress addressed the white South Africans, as part of a politics of inclusion and mutual respect. Coexistence is our answer to Israeli exclusivism and belligerence. This is not conceding: it is creating solidarity and therefore isolating the exclusivists, the racists, the fundamentalists.

4. The most important lesson of all for us to understand about ourselves is manifest in the terrible tragedies of what Israel is now doing in the Occupied Territories. The fact is that we are a people and a society, and despite Israel's ferocious attack against the Palestinian Authority, our society still functions. We are a people because we have a functioning society that goes on—and has gone on for the past fifty-four years—despite every sort of abuse, every cruel turn of history, every misfortune we have suffered, every tragedy we have gone through as a people. Our greatest victory over Israel is that people like Sharon and his kind do not have the capacity to see that, and this is why they are doomed despite their great power and their awful, inhuman cruelty. We have surmounted the tragedies and memories of our past, whereas such Israelis as Sharon have not. He will go to his grave only as an Arab-killer and a failed politician who brought more unrest and insecurity to his people. It must surely be the legacy of a leader that he should leave something behind upon which future generations will build. Sharon, Shaul Mofaz, and all the others associated with them in this bullying, sadistic campaign of death and carnage will leave nothing except gravestones. Negation breeds negation.

As Palestinians, I think we can say that we have left a vision and a society that has survived every attempt to kill it. And that is something. It is for the generation of my children and yours to go on from there, critically, rationally, with hope and forbearance.

Al-Ahram, April 4–10, 2002
Al-Hayat, April 7, 2002
Le Monde, April 11, 2002

CHAPTER TWENTY-EIGHT

What Has Israel Done?

Despite Israel's effort to restrict coverage of its extraordinarily destructive invasion of the West Bank's Palestinian towns and refugee camps, information and images have nevertheless seeped through. The Internet has provided hundreds of verbal as well as pictorial eyewitness reports, as have Arab and European TV coverage, most of it unavailable or blocked or spun out of existence from the mainstream U.S. media. That evidence provides stunning proof of what Israel's campaign has actually (has always) been about, the irreversible conquest of Palestinian land and society. The official line (which the United States has basically supported, along with nearly every American media commentator) is that Israel has been defending itself by retaliating for the suicide bombings that have undermined its security and even threatened its existence. That claim has gained the status of an absolute truth moderated neither by what Israel has done nor by what in fact has been done to it.

"Plucking out the terrorist network," "destroying the terrorist infrastructure," "attacking terrorist nests" (note the total dehumanization involved in every one of these phrases) are repeated so often and so unthinkingly that they have therefore given Israel the right to do what it has wanted to do, which in effect is to destroy Palestinian civil life, with as much damage, as much sheer wanton destruction, killing, humiliation, vandalism, and purposeless but overwhelming technological violence as possible. No other state on earth could have done what Israel has done with as much approbation and support as the United States has given it. None has been more intransigent and destructive, more out of touch with its own realities than Israel.

There are signs, however, that the amazing, not to say grotesque, nature of these claims (Israel's "fight for existence") is slowly being eroded by the harsh and nearly unimaginable devastation wrought by the Jewish state and its homicidal prime minister, Ariel Sharon. Take this front-page report, "Attacks Turn Palestinian Plans into Bent Metal and Piles of Dust," by the *New York Times*'s Serge Schmemann (no Palestinian propagandist) on April 11: "There is no way to assess the full extent of the damage to the cities and towns—Ramallah, Bethlehem, Tul Karm, Qalqilya, Nablus, and Jenin—while they remain under a tight siege, with patrols and snipers firing in the streets. But it is safe to say that the infrastructure of life itself and of any future Palestinian state—roads, schools, electricity pylons, water pipes, telephone lines—has been devastated." By what inhuman calculus did Israel's army, using fifty tanks, 250 missile strikes a day, and dozens of F-16 sorties, besiege Jenin's refugee camp for over a week, a one-square-kilometer patch of shacks housing fifteen thousand refugees and a few dozen men armed with automatic rifles and with no defenses whatever, no leaders, no missiles, no tanks, nothing, and call it a response to terrorist violence and the threat to Israel's survival? There are reported to be hundreds buried in the rubble that Israeli bulldozers are now trying to heap over the camp's ruins. Are Palestinian civilian men, women, children no more than rats or cockroaches that can be killed and attacked in the thousands without so much as a word spoken compassionately or in their defense? And what about the capture of thousands of Palestinian men who have been taken off by Israeli soldiers without a trace, the destitution and homelessness of so many ordinary people trying to survive in the ruins created by Israeli bulldozers all over the West Bank, the siege that has now gone on for months and months, the cutting off of electricity and water in all Palestinian towns, the long days of total curfew, the shortage of food and medicine, the wounded who have bled to death, the systematic attacks on ambulances and aid workers that even the mild-mannered Kofi Annan has decried as outrageous? Those actions will not be pushed so easily into the memory hole. Its friends must ask Israel how its suicidal policies can possibly gain it peace, acceptance, and security.

A monstrous transformation of an entire people, by the most formidable and feared propaganda machine in the world, into little more than "militants" and "terrorists" has allowed not just Israel's military but its fleet of writers and defenders to efface a terrible history of suffering and abuse in order to destroy the civil existence of the Palestinian people with impunity. Gone from public memory are the destruction of Palestinian society in 1948 and the creation of a dispossessed people; the conquest of the West Bank and Gaza and their military occupation since 1967; the invasion of 1982 with its 17,500 Lebanese and Palestinian dead and the Sabra and Shatila massacres; and the continuous assault on Palestinian schools, refugee camps, hospitals, and civil installations of every kind. What antiterrorist purpose is served by destroying the building and then removing the records of the Ministry of Education, the Ramallah Municipality, the Central Bureau of Statistics, various institutes specializing in civil rights, health, and economic development, hospitals, and radio and television stations? Isn't it clear that Sharon is bent not only on "breaking" the Palestinians but on trying to eliminate them as a people with national institutions?

In such a context of disparity and asymmetrical power, it seems deranged to keep asking the Palestinians, who have neither army, nor air force, nor tanks, nor defenses of any kind, nor functioning leadership, to "renounce" violence and to require no comparable limitation on Israel's actions. Even the matter of suicide bombers, which I have always opposed, cannot be examined from a viewpoint that permits a hidden racist standard to value Israeli lives over the many more Palestinian lives that have been lost, maimed, distorted, and foreshortened by long-standing Israeli military occupation, and the systematic barbarity openly used by Sharon against Palestinians since the beginning of his career in the 1950s until now.

There can be no conceivable peace, in my opinion, that doesn't tackle the real issue, which is Israel's utter refusal to accept the sovereign existence of a Palestinian people that is entitled to rights over what Sharon and most of the people supporting him consider exclusively to be the land of Greater Israel, that is, the West Bank and Gaza. A profile of Sharon in the April 6–7, 2002, issue of the *Financial Times* concluded with an extremely telling extract from his autobiography, which the *FT* prefaced with "he has written with pride of his parents' belief that Jews and Arabs could live side by side." Then the relevant quote from Sharon's book: "But they believed without question that only they had rights over the land. And no one was going to force them out, regardless of terror or anything else. When the land belongs to you physically . . . that is when you have power, not just physical power but spiritual power."

In 1988 the PLO made the concession that partition of historical Palestine into two states would be acceptable. This was reaffirmed on numerous occasions and certainly again in the Oslo documents. *But only the Palestinians explicitly recognized the notion of partition. Israel never has.* This is why there are now more than 170 settlements on Palestinian lands, why a three-hundred-mile network of roads connecting them to one another and totally impeding Palestinian movements exists (according to Jeff Halper of the Israeli Committee Against House Demolition, it costs $3 billion and has been funded by the United States), and why no Israeli prime minister from Rabin on has ever conceded any *real Palestinian sovereignty* to the Palestinians, and why of course the settlements have increased on an annual basis. The merest glance at a recent map of the territories reveals what Israel has been doing throughout the peace process, and what the consequent geographical discontinuity and shrinkage in Palestinian life has been. In effect, then, Israel considers itself and the Jewish people to own the land of Israel in its entirety: there are land-ownership laws in Israel itself guaranteeing this, but on the West Bank and Gaza the network of settlements and roads, and the absence of any concessions on sovereign land rights to the Palestinians, serve the same function.

What boggles the mind is that no official—no American, Palestinian, Arab, UN, European, or any other—has challenged Israel on this point, which has been threaded through all of the Oslo documents, procedures, agreements. Which is why of course after nearly ten years of "peace negotiations" Israel still controls the West Bank and Gaza. These lands are more directly controlled (owned?) by more than a thousand Israeli tanks and thousands of soldiers today, but the underlying principle is the same. No Israeli leader (and certainly not Sharon and his Land of Israel supporters, who are the majority in his government) has either officially recognized the Occupied Territories as occupied territories or gone on to recognize that Palestinians could or might theoretically have sovereign rights, that is, without Israeli control over borders, water, air, security on what most of the world considers Palestinian land. So to speak about the "vision" of a Palestinian state, as has become fashionable, is mere vision, alas, unless the questions of land ownership and sovereignty are openly and officially conceded by the Israeli government. None ever has, and if I am right, none will in the near future. It needs to be remembered that Israel is the only state in the world today that has never had internationally declared borders; the only state that is not the state of its citizens but of the whole Jewish people; the only state where over 90 percent of the land is held in trust for the use only of the Jewish people. That it is also the only state in the world never to have recognized any of the main provisions of international law (as argued recently by Richard Falk) suggests the depth and structural knottiness of the absolute rejectionism that Palestinians have had to face.

This is why I have been skeptical about discussions and meetings about peace, which is a lovely word but in the present context simply means that Palestinians will have to stop resisting Israeli control over their land. It is among the many deficiencies of Arafat's terrible leadership (to say nothing of the even more lamentable Arab leaders in general) that he neither made the decade-long Oslo negotiations ever focus on land ownership, thus never putting the onus on Israel to declare itself constitutively willing to give up title to Palestinian land, nor asked that Israel be required to deal with *any* of its responsibility for the sufferings of his people. Now I worry that he may simply be trying to save himself again, whereas what we really need are international monitors to protect us as well as new elections to assure a real political future for the Palestinian people.

The profound question facing Israel and its people is this: is it willing juridically to assume the rights and obligations of being a country like any other, and forswear the kind of impossible land-ownership assertions for which Sharon and his parents and his soldiers have been fighting since day one? In 1948 Palestinians lost 78 percent of Palestine. In 1967 they lost the last 22 percent. Both times to Israel. Now the international community must lay upon Israel the obligation to accept the principle of real, as opposed to fictional, partition, and to accept the principle of limiting Israel's untenable extraterritorial claims, those absurd biblically based pretentions, and laws that have so far allowed it to override another people completely. Why is that kind of fundamentalism tolerated unquestioningly? But so far all we hear is that Palestinians must give up violence and condemn terror. Is nothing substantive ever demanded of Israel, and can it go on doing what it has without a thought for the consequences?

That is the real question of its existence: whether it can exist as a state like all others, or must always be above the constraints and duties of all other states in the world today. The record is not reassuring.

Al-Ahram, April 18–24, 2002
Al-Hayat, April 21, 2002

CHAPTER TWENTY-NINE

Crisis for American Jews

Afew weeks ago a vociferous pro-Israel demonstration was held in Washington, at roughly the same moment that the siege of Jenin was taking place. All of the speakers were prominent public figures, including several senators, leaders of major Jewish organizations, and other celebrities, each of whom expressed unfailing solidarity with everything Israel was doing. The administration was represented by Paul Wolfowitz, the number-two man at the Department of Defense, an extreme right-wing hawk who has been speaking about "ending" countries like Iraq ever since last September. Also known as a rigorous hard-line supporter of Israel, in his speech he did what everyone else did—celebrated Israel and expressed total unconditional support for it—but unexpectedly referred also in passing to "the sufferings of the Palestinians." Because of that phrase, he was booed so loudly and so long that he was unable to continue his speech, leaving the platform in a kind of disgrace.

The moral of this incident is that public American Jewish support for Israel today simply does not tolerate any allowance for the existence of an actual Palestinian people, except in the context of terrorism, violence, evil, and fanaticism. Moreover, this refusal to see, much less hear anything about, the existence of "another side" far exceeds the fanaticism of anti-Arab sentiment among Israelis, who are of course on the front line of the struggle in Palestine. To judge by the recent antiwar demonstration of sixty thousand people in Tel Aviv, the increasing number of military reservists who refuse service in the Occupied Territories, the sustained protest of (admittedly only a few) intellectuals and groups, and some of the polls that show a majority of Israelis willing to withdraw in return for peace with the Palestinians, there is at least a dynamic of political activity among Israeli Jews. But not so in the United States.

Two weeks ago the weekly magazine *New York*, which has a circulation of about a million, ran a dossier entitled "Crisis for American Jews," whose theme was that "in New York, as in Israel, [it is] an issue of survival." I won't try to summarize the main points of this extraordinary claim except to say that it painted such a picture of anguish about "what is most precious in my life, the state of Israel," according to one of the prominent New Yorkers quoted in the magazine, that you would think that the existence of this most prosperous and powerful of all minorities in the United States was actually being threatened. One of the other people quoted even went so far as to suggest that American Jews are on the brink of a second holocaust. Certainly, as the author of one of the articles said, most American Jews support what Israel did on the West Bank, enthusiastically; one American Jew said, for instance, that his son is now in the Israeli army and that he is "armed, dangerous and killing as many Palestinians as possible."

Guilt at being well-off in America plays a role in this kind of delusional thinking, but mostly it is the result of an extraordinary self-isolation in fantasy and myth that comes from education and unreflective nationalism of a kind unique in the world. Ever since the intifada broke out almost two years ago, the American media and the major Jewish organizations have been running all kinds of attacks on Islamic education in the Arab world, in Pakistan, and even in the United States. These attacks have accused Islamic authorities, as well as Yasir Arafat's Palestinian Authority, of teaching youngsters hatred of America and Israel, the virtues of suicide bombing, and unlimited praise for jihad. Little has been said, however, of the results of what American Jews have been taught about the conflict in Palestine: that the land was given to Jews by God, that it was empty, that it was liberated from Britain, that the natives ran away because their leaders told them to, that in effect the Palestinians don't exist except recently as terrorists, that all Arabs are anti-Semitic and want to kill Jews.

Nowhere in all this incitement to hatred does the reality of a Palestinian people exist, and more to the point, there is no connection made between Palestinian animosity and enmity toward Israel and what Israel has been doing to Palestinians since 1948. It's as if an entire history of dispossession, the destruction of a society, the thirty-five-year-old occupation of the West Bank and Gaza, to say nothing of massacres, bombardments, expulsions, land expropriations, killings, sieges, humiliations, years of collective punishment, and assassinations that have gone on for decades were as nothing, since Israel has been victimized by Palestinian rage, hostility, and gratuitous anti-Semitism. It simply does not occur to most American supporters of Israel to see Israel as the actual author of specific actions done in the name of the Jewish people by the Jewish state, and to connect in consequence those actions to Palestinian feelings of anger and revenge.

The problem at bottom is that as human beings the Palestinians do not exist, that is, as human beings with history, traditions, society, sufferings, and ambitions like all other people. Why this should be so for most but by no means all American Jewish supporters of Israel is something worth looking into. It goes back to the knowledge that there was an indigenous people in Palestine—all the Zionist leaders knew it and spoke about it— but the fact, as a fact that might prevent colonization, could never be admitted. Hence the collective Zionist practice of either denying the fact or, more specially in the United States, where the realities are not so available for actual verification, lying about it by producing a counterreality. For decades it has been decreed to schoolchildren that there were no Palestinians when the Zionist pioneers arrived, and so those miscellaneous people who throw stones and fight occupation are simply a collection of terrorists who deserve killing. Palestinians in short do not deserve anything like a narrative or collective actuality, and so they must be transmuted and dissolved into essentially negative images. This is entirely the result of a distorted education, doled out to millions of youngsters who grow up without any awareness at all that the Palestinian people have been totally dehumanized to serve a political-ideological end, namely to keep support high for Israel.

What is so astonishing is that notions of coexistence between peoples play no part in this kind of distortion. Whereas American Jews want to be recognized as Jews and Americans in America, they are unwilling to accord a similar status as Arabs and Palestinians to another people that has been oppressed by Israel since the beginning.

Only if one were to live in the United States for years would one be aware of the depth of the problem, which far transcends ordinary politics. The intellectual suppression of the Palestinians that has occurred because of Zionist education has produced an unreflecting, dangerously skewed sense of reality in which whatever Israel does, it does as a victim: according to the various articles I have quoted above, American Jews in crisis by extension therefore feel the same thing as the most right-wing of Israeli Jews, that they are at risk and their survival is at stake. This has nothing to do with reality, obviously enough, but rather with a kind of hallucinatory state that overrides history and facts with a supremely unthinking narcissism. A recent defense of what Wolfowitz said in his speech didn't even refer to the Palestinians he mentioned but defended President Bush's Middle East policy.

This is dehumanization on a vast scale, and it is made even worse, one has to say, by the suicide bombings that have so disfigured and debased the Palestinian struggle. All liberation movements in history have affirmed that their struggle is about life, not about death. Why should ours be an exception? The sooner we educate our Zionist enemies and show that our resistance offers coexistence and peace, the less able will they be to kill us at will and never refer to us except as terrorists. I am not saying that Sharon and Netanyahu can be changed. I am saying that there is a Palestinian—yes, a Palestinian—constituency, as well as an Israeli and American one, that needs to be reminded by strategy and tactics that force of arms and tanks and human bombs and bulldozers are not a solution but only create more delusion and distortion, on both sides.

Al-Ahram, May 16–22, 2002
Al-Hayat, May 19, 2002

CHAPTER THIRTY

Palestinian Elections Now

Six distinct calls for Palestinian reform and elections are being uttered now: five of them are, for Palestinian purposes, both useless and irrelevant. Sharon wants reform as a way of further disabling Palestinian national life, that is, as an extension of his failed policy of constant intervention and destruction. He wants to be rid of Yasir Arafat, cut up the West Bank into fenced-in cantons, reinstall an occupation authority— preferably with some Palestinians helping out—carry on with settlement activity, and maintain Israeli security the way he's been doing it. He is too blinded by his own ideological hallucinations and obsessions to see that this will bring neither peace nor security and will certainly not bring the "quiet" he keeps prattling on about. Palestinian elections in the Sharonian scheme are quite unimportant.

Second, the United States wants reform principally as a way of combating "terrorism," a catchall of a word that takes no account of history, context, society, or anything else. George W. Bush has a visceral dislike for Arafat and no understanding at all of the Palestinian situation. To say that he and his disheveled administration "want" anything is to dignify a series of spurts, fits, starts, retractions, denunciations, totally contradictory statements, sterile missions by various officials of his administration, and about-faces with the status of an overall desire, which of course doesn't exist. Incoherent, except when it comes to the pressures and agendas of the Israeli lobby and the Christian right whose spiritual head he now is, Bush's policy consists in reality of calls for Arafat to end terrorism, and (when he wants to placate the Arabs) for someone, somewhere, somehow to produce a Palestinian state and a big conference, and finally for Israel to go on getting full and unconditional U.S. support, including most probably ending Arafat's career. Beyond that, U.S. policy waits to be formulated, by someone, somewhere, somehow. One should always keep in mind, though, that the Middle East is a domestic, not a foreign, policy issue in America and subject to dynamics within the society that are difficult to predict.

All this perfectly suits the Israeli demand, which wants nothing more than to make Palestinian life collectively more miserable and more unlivable, whether by military incursions or by impossible political conditions that suit Sharon's frenzied obsession with stamping out Palestinians forever. Of course, there are other Israelis who want coexistence with a Palestinian state, as there are American Jews who want similar things: but neither group has any determining power now at all. Sharon and the Bush administration run the show.

Third is the Arab leaders' demand, which as far as I can tell is a combination of several different elements, none of them directly helpful to the Palestinians themselves. First is fear of their own populations, who have been witnessing Israel's mass and essentially unopposed destruction of the Palestinian territories without any serious Arab interference or attempt at deterrence. The Beirut summit peace plan offers Israel precisely what Sharon has refused, which is land for peace, and it is a proposal without any teeth, much less one with a timetable in it. While it may be a good thing to have it on record as a counterweight to Israel's naked belligerence, we should have no illusions about its real intention, which, like the calls for Palestinian reform, are really tokens offered to seething Arab populations who are quite thoroughly sick with the mediocre inaction of their rulers.

Second is the sheer exasperation of most of the Arab regimes with the whole Palestinian problem. They seem to have no ideological problem with Israel as a Jewish state without any declared boundaries, which has been in illegal military occupation of Jerusalem, Gaza, and the West Bank for thirty-five years, or with Israel's dispossession of the Palestinian people. They are prepared to accommodate nicely those terrible injustices if only Arafat and his people will simply either behave or quietly go away.

Third, of course, is the long-standing desire of the Arab leaders to ingratiate themselves with the United States and, among themselves, to vie for the title of most important U.S. Arab ally. Perhaps they are simply unaware of how contemptuous most Americans are of them, and how little understood or regarded is their cultural and political status in the United States.

Fourth in the chorus of reform are the Europeans. But they only scurry around sending emissaries to see Sharon and Arafat, they make ringing declarations in Brussels, they fund a few projects—and more or less leave it at that, so great is the shadow of the United States over them.

Fifth is Yasir Arafat and his circle of associates, who have suddenly discovered the virtues (theoretically at least) of democracy and reform. I know that I speak at a great distance from the field of struggle, and I also know all the arguments about the besieged Arafat as a potent symbol of Palestinian resistance against Israeli aggression, but I have come to a point where I think none of that has any meaning anymore. Arafat is simply interested in saving himself. He has had almost ten years of freedom to run a petty kingdom and has succeeded essentially in bringing opprobrium and scorn on himself and most of his team; the Authority has become a byword for brutality, autocracy, and unimaginable corruption. Why anyone for a moment believes that at this stage he is capable of anything different, or that his new streamlined cabinet (dominated by the same old faces of defeat and incompetence) is going to produce actual reform, simply defies reason. He is the leader of a long-suffering people, whom in the past year he has exposed to unacceptable pain and hardship, all of it based on a combination of his absence of a strategic plan and his unforgivable reliance on the tender mercies of Israel and the United States via Oslo. Leaders of independence and liberation movements have no business exposing their unarmed people to the savagery of war criminals like Sharon, against whom there was no real defense or advance preparation. Why then provoke a war whose victims will be mostly innocent people when you have neither the military capacity to fight it nor the diplomatic leverage to end it? Having done this now three times (Jordan, Lebanon, West Bank), Arafat should not be given a chance to bring on a fourth disaster.

He has announced that elections will take place in early 2003, but his real concentration is to reorganize the security services. I have long pointed out in these columns that Arafat's security apparatus was always designed principally to serve him and Israel, since the Oslo accords were based on his having made a deal with Israel's military occupation. Israel cared only about its security, for which it held Arafat responsible (a position, by the way, he willingly accepted as early as 1992). In the meantime Arafat played the fifteen or nineteen or whatever the right number of groups was against one another, a tactic he perfected in Fakahani [the

Beirut neighborhood where the PLO had its offices in the 1970s] and that is patently stupid so far as the general good is concerned. He never really reined in Hamas and Islamic Jihad, which suited Israel perfectly so that it would have a ready-made excuse to use the so-called martyrs' (mindless) suicide bombings to further diminish and punish the whole people. If there is one thing that has done us more harm as a cause than Arafat's ruinous regime, it is this calamitous policy of killing Israeli civilians, which further proves to the world that we are indeed terrorists and an immoral movement. For what gain, no one has been able to say.

Having therefore made a deal with the occupation through Oslo, Arafat was never really in a position to lead a movement to end it. And ironically, he is trying to make another deal now, both to save himself and to prove to the United States, Israel, and the other Arabs that he deserves another chance. I myself don't care a whit for what Bush, or the Arab leaders, or Sharon says: I am interested in what we as a people think of our leader, and there I believe we must be absolutely clear in rejecting his entire program of reform, elections, and reorganizing the government and security services. His record of failure is too dismal and his capacities as a leader too enfeebled and incompetent for him to try yet again to save himself for another try.

Sixth, finally, is the Palestinian people, who are now justifiably clamoring both for reform and for elections. As far as I am concerned, this clamor is the only legitimate one of the six I have outlined here. It's important to point out that Arafat's present administration as well as the Legislative Council have overstayed their original term, which should have ended with a new round of elections in 1999. Moreover, the whole basis of the 1996 elections was the Oslo accords, which in effect simply licensed Arafat and his people to run bits of the West Bank and Gaza for the Israelis, without true sovereignty or security, since Israel retained control of the borders, security, land (on which it doubled and even tripled the settlements), water, and air. In other words, the old basis for elections and reform, which had been Oslo, is now null and void. Any attempt to go forward on that kind of platform is simply a wasteful ploy and will produce neither reform nor any real elections. Hence the current confusion, which causes every Palestinian everywhere to feel chagrin and bitter frustration.

What then is to be done if the old basis of Palestinian legitimacy no longer really exists? Certainly there can be no return to Oslo, any more than there can be to Jordanian or Israeli law. As a student of periods of important historical change, I should like to point out that when a major rupture with the past occurs (like the fall of the monarchy because of the French Revolution, or the demise of apartheid in South Africa before the elections of 1994 took place), a new basis of legitimacy has to be created by the only and ultimate source of authority, namely, the people itself. The major interests in Palestinian society, those that have kept life going, from the trade unions, to health workers, teachers, farmers, lawyers, and doctors, in addition to all the many NGOs, must now become the basis on which Palestinian reform—despite Israel's incursions and the occupation—is to be constructed. It seems to me useless to wait for Arafat, or Europe, or the United States, or the Arabs to do this: it must absolutely be done by Palestinians themselves by way of a constituent assembly that contains in it all the major elements of Palestinian society. Only such a group, constructed by the people themselves and not by the remnants of the Oslo dispensation, certainly not by the shabby fragments of Arafat's discredited Authority, can hope to succeed in reorganizing society from the ruinous, indeed catastrophically incoherent condition in which it is to be found. There is one basic job for such an assembly, which is to construct an emergency system of order that has two purposes. One, to keep Palestinian life going in an orderly way with full participation for all concerned. Two, to choose an emergency executive committee whose mandate is to end the occupation, not negotiate with it. It is quite obvious that militarily we are no match for Israel. Kalashnikovs are not effective weapons when the balance of power is so lopsided. What is needed is a creative method of struggle that mobilizes all the human resources at our disposal to highlight, isolate, and gradually make untenable the main aspects of Israeli occupation—that is, settlements, settlement roads, roadblocks, and house demolitions. The present group around Arafat is hopelessly incapable of thinking of, much less actually implementing, such a strategy: it is too bankrupt, too bound up in corrupt, selfish practices, too burdened with the failures of the past.

For such a Palestinian strategy to work, there has to be an Israeli component made up of individuals and groups with whom a common basis of struggle against occupation can and indeed must be established. This is the great lesson of the South African struggle: it proposed the vision of a multiracial society from which neither individuals nor groups and leaders were ever deflected. The only vision coming out of Israel today is violence, forcible separation, and the continued subordination of Palestinians to an idea of Jewish supremacy. Not every Israeli believes in these things, of course, but it must be up to us to project the idea of coexistence in two states that have natural relations with each other on the basis of sovereignty and equality. Mainstream Zionism has still not been able to produce such a vision, so it must come from the Palestinian people and their new leaders, whose new legitimacy has to be constructed now, at a moment when everything is crashing down and everyone is anxious to remake Palestine in his own image and according to his own ideas.

We have never faced a worse or, at the same time, a more seminal moment. The Arab order is in total disarray; the U.S. administration is effectively controlled by the Christian right and the Israeli lobby (within twenty-four hours, everything that George W. Bush seems to have agreed to with Egypt's Hosni Mubarak was reversed by Sharon's visit); and our society has been nearly wrecked by poor leadership and the insanity of thinking that suicide bombing will lead directly to an Islamic Palestinian state. There is always hope for the future, but one has to able to look for it and find it in the right place. It is quite clear that in the absence of any serious Palestinian or Arab information policy in the United States (especially in the Congress), we cannot for a moment delude ourselves that Powell and Bush are about to set a real agenda for Palestinian rehabilitation. That's why I keep saying that the effort must come from us, by us, for us. I'm at least trying to suggest a different avenue of approach. Who else but the Palestinian people can construct the legitimacy they need to rule themselves and fight the occupation with weapons that don't kill innocents and lose us more support than ever before? A just cause can easily be subverted by evil or inadequate or corrupt means. The sooner this is put into practice, the better the chance we have to lead ourselves out of the present impasse.

Al-Ahram, June 13–19, 2002
Al-Hayat, June 16, 2002

CHAPTER THIRTY-ONE

One-Way Street

Even by the terribly low standards of his other speeches, George W. Bush's June 24, 2002, speech to the world about the Middle East was a startling example of how an execrable combination of muddled thought, words with no actual meaning in the real world of living, breathing human beings, preachy and racist injunctions against the Palestinians, and incredible blindness—a delusional blindness, to the realities of an ongoing Israeli invasion and conquest against all the laws of war and peace—all of it wrapped in the smug accents of a moralistic, stiff-necked, and ignorant judge who has arrogated to himself divine privileges, now sits astride U.S. foreign policy. And this, it is important to remember, from a man who virtually stole an election he did not win, and whose record as governor of Texas includes the worst pollution, scandalous corruption, and the highest rates of imprisonment and capital punishment in the world. So this dubiously endowed man of few gifts except the blind pursuit of money and power has the capability to condemn Palestinians not just to the tender mercies of war criminal Sharon but to the dire consequences of his own empty condemnations. Flanked by three of the most venal politicians in the world (Powell, Rumsfeld, and Rice), he pronounced his speech with the halting accents of a mediocre elocution student and thereby allowed Sharon to kill or injure many more Palestinians in a U.S.-endorsed illegal military occupation.

It wasn't only that Bush's speech lacked any historical awareness of what he was proposing, but that its capacity for extended harm was so great. It was as if Sharon had written the speech, amalgamating the disproportionate American obsession with terrorism to Sharon's determination to eliminate Palestinian national life under the rubric of terrorism and Jewish supremacy on "the land of Israel." For the rest, Bush's perfunctory concessions to a "provisional" Palestinian state (whatever that may be, perhaps analogous to a provisional pregnancy?) and his casual remarks about alleviating the difficulties of Palestinian life brought nothing to this new pronouncement that warranted the widespread—I would go so far as to say comically—positive reaction elicited from the Arab leadership, Yasir Arafat leading the pack so far as enthusiasm is concerned.

Over fifty years of Arab and Palestinian dealings with the United States have ended in the rubbish bin, so that Bush and his advisers could convince themselves and much of the electorate that they had a God-given mission to exterminate terrorism, which meant essentially all the enemies of Israel. A quick survey of those fifty years shows dramatically that neither a defiant Arab attitude nor a submissive one has made any changes in U.S. perceptions of American interests in the Middle East, which remain the quick and cheap supply of oil and the protection of Israel as the two main aspects of its regional dominance. From the days of Abdel Nasser to today's Bashar al-Assad, King Abdullah, and Hosni Mubarak, however, Arab policy has undergone a 180-degree turn, with more or less the same results. First there was a defiant Arab alignment in the postindependence years, inspired by the anti-imperialist, anti–cold war philosophy of Bandung and Nasserism. That ended catastrophically in 1967.

Thereafter led by Egypt under Anwar Sadat, the shift took place that brought cooperation between the United States and the Arabs under the totally delusional rubric that the United States controlled 99 percent of the cards. What remained of inter-Arab cooperation slowly withered away from its high point in the 1973 war and the oil embargo to an Arab cold war pitting various states against one another. Sometimes, as in Kuwait and Lebanon, small weak states became the battleground, but for all intents and purposes the official mindset of the Arab state system came to think exclusively in terms of the United States as the pivotal focus for Arab policy. With the first Gulf War (there is soon to be a second) and the end of the cold war, America remained as the only superpower, which instead of prompting a radical reappraisal of Arab policy drove the various states into a deeper individual or rather bilateral embrace of the United States, whose reaction in effect was to take them for granted. Arab summits became occasions less for putting forth credible positions than for expressing derisory contempt. It was soon realized by U.S. policymakers that Arab leaders barely represented their own countries, much less the whole Arab world; and in addition, one didn't have to be a genius to remark that various bilateral agreements between Arab leaders and the United States were more important to their regimes' security than to the United States. This is not even to mention the petty jealousies and animosities that virtually emasculated the Arab people as a power to be reckoned with in the modern world. No wonder then that today's Palestinian, suffering the horrors of Israeli occupation, is just as likely to blame "the Arabs" as he is the Israelis.

By the early 1980s all parts of the Arab world were ready to make peace with Israel as a way of ensuring U.S. good faith toward them, as for example the Fez plan of 1982, which stipulated peace with Israel in return for withdrawal from all the Occupied Territories. The March 2002 Arab summit replayed the same scene for the second time—this time as farce, it should be added—and with equally negligible effect. And it is precisely from that time two decades ago that U.S. policy on Palestine completely changed its bases, for the worse. As former CIA senior analyst Kathleen Christison points out in an excellent study published in the U.S. biweekly *Counterpunch* (May 16–31, 2002), the old land-for-peace formula was given up by the Reagan administration, then more enthusiastically by Clinton's, just ironically at the same time that Arab policy generally and Palestinian policy in particular had concentrated their energies on placating the United States on as many fronts as possible. By November 1988 the PLO had officially abandoned "liberation" and at the Algiers meeting of the Palestinian National Council (PNC), which I attended as a member, voted for partition and coexistence for two states; in December of that year Yasir Arafat publicly renounced terrorism, and a PLO–United States dialogue was begun in Tunis.

The new Arab order that emerged after the Gulf War institutionalized the one-way traffic between the United States and the Arabs: the Arabs gave, and the Americans gave more and more to Israel. The Madrid conference of 1991 was based on the premise for the Palestinians that the United States would recognize them and persuade Israel to do the same. I recall vividly that during the summer of 1991 a group of senior PLO figures and independents, including myself, were asked by Arafat to formulate a series of assurances that we required from the United States in order to enter the about-to-be-convened Madrid conference, which would lead (although none of us knew it) to the Oslo process of 1993. In effect Arafat vetoed all our suggestions for U.S. guarantees. He only wanted assurances that he would remain the main negotiator for the Palestinians; nothing else seemed to matter to him, even though a good West Bank–Gaza delegation headed by Haidar Abdel Shafi was proceeding with its work in Washington facing a tough Israeli team that had been instructed by Yitzhak Shamir to concede nothing and to extend the talk for ten years if necessary. Arafat's idea was to undercut every one of his own people by offering more concessions, which essentially meant that he made no prior demands on either Israel or the United States, just so he could remain in power.

That, and the prevailing post-1967 environment, has solidified the Palestinian-U.S. dynamic into the by-now-permanent distortions of the Oslo and post-Oslo period. To the best of my knowledge, the United States never called on the Palestinian Authority (nor any other Arab regime) to establish democratic procedures. Quite the contrary, Clinton and Gore both publicly approved the Palestinian state security courts while on visits to Gaza and Jericho respectively, and little emphasis, if any, was placed on ending corruption, monopolies, and the like. I myself had been writing about the problems of Arafat's rule since the mid-1990s, with either indifference or open scorn as reactions to what I had to say (most of which proved to be correct). I was accused of a utopian lack of pragmatism and realism. It was clear that for the Israelis and the Americans, as well as the other Arabs, there was a concert of interests that made the Authority what it was and that kept it in place either as an Israeli police force or, later, as the focus of everything that Israelis loved to hate. No serious resistance to occupation was developed under Arafat, and he continued to allow bands of militants, other PLO factions, and security forces to run rampant across the civil landscape. A great deal of illicit money was made, as the general population lost over 50 percent of its pre-Oslo livelihood.

The intifada changed everything, as did Barak's tenure, which prepared the way for Sharon's reentry on to the scene. And still Arab policy was to placate the United States. A small sign of this is the change in Arab discourse here. Abdullah of Jordan stopped criticizing Israel completely on American TV, referring always to the need for "the two sides" to stop "the violence." Similar language was heard from various other Arab spokesmen from major countries, which is to say that Palestine had become a nuisance to be contained rather than an injustice to be righted.

The most significant thing of all is that between them, Israeli propaganda, American contempt for the Arabs, and Arab (as well as Palestinian) incapacity to formulate and represent the interests of their own people has led to a vast dehumanization of the Palestinians, whose enormous suffering on a daily, indeed hourly and minute-by-minute basis has no status at all. It's as if Palestinians have no existence except when someone performs a terrorist act, and then the entire world media apparatus leaps up and smothers their actual existence as breathing and sentient people with a real history and a real society by holding over them an enormous blanket saying "terrorist." I know of no systematic dehumanization in modern history that even approaches this, despite the occasional dissenting voice here and there.

What concerns me finally is Arab and Palestinian cooperation (collaboration is the better word) in the dehumanization. Our tiny number of representatives in the media at best speak competently and dispassionately about the merits of the Bush speech or the Mitchell plan, but in no way do any of them whom I have seen represent the sufferings of their people, or their history, or actuality. I have spoken often about the need for a mass campaign against the occupation in the United States but have finally come to the conclusion that for Palestinians under this dreadful, Kafkaesque Israeli occupation, the chances of mounting one are small. Where I think we have a hope is in trying (as I suggested in my last article, on Palestinian elections) to establish a constituent assembly at the grassroots level. We have so long been passive objects of Israeli and Arab policy that we do not adequately appreciate how important, and indeed how urgent, it is for Palestinians now to take an independent foundational step of their own, to try to establish a new self-making process that creates legitimacy and the possibility of a better polity for ourselves than now exists. All the cabinet shuffles and projected elections that have been announced so far are ridiculous games played with the fragments and ruins of Oslo. Arafat and his assembly planning democracy is like trying to put together the pieces of a shattered glass.

Fortunately, however, the new Palestinian National Initiative announced two weeks ago by its authors, Ibrahim Dakkak, Mustafa Barghuti, and Haidar Abdel Shafi, answers exactly to this need, which springs from the failure both of the PLO and of groups like Hamas to provide a way forward that doesn't depend (ludicrously, in my opinion) on American and Israeli goodwill. The Initiative provides for a vision of peace with justice, coexistence, and, extremely important, secular social democracy for our people that is unique in Palestinian history. Only a group of independent people well grounded in civil society, untainted by collaboration or corruption, can possibly furnish the outlines of the new legitimacy we need. We need a real constitution, not a basic law toyed with by Arafat; we need truly representative democracy that only Palestinians can provide for themselves through a founding assembly. This is the only positive step that can reverse the process of dehumanization that has infected so many sectors of the Arab world. Otherwise we shall sink in our suffering and continue to endure the awful tribulations of Israeli collective punishment, which can only be stopped by a collective political independence, of which we are still very capable. Colin Powell's goodwill and fabled "moderation" will never do it for us. Never.

Al-Ahram, July 11–17, 2002
Al-Hayat, July 22, 2002

CHAPTER THIRTY-TWO

Slow Death: Punishment by Detail

Aside from the obvious physical discomforts, being ill for a long period of time fills the spirit with a terrible feeling of helplessness, but also with periods of analytic lucidity, which, of course, must be treasured. For the past three months now I have been in and out of the hospital, with days marked by lengthy and painful treatments, blood transfusions, endless tests, hours and hours of unproductive time spent staring at the ceiling, draining fatigue and infection, unable to do normal work, and thinking, thinking, thinking. But there are also the intermittent passages of lucidity and reflection that sometimes give the mind a perspective on daily life that allows it to see things (without being able to do much about them) from a different perspective. Reading the news from Palestine and seeing the frightful images of death and destruction on television, I have been utterly amazed and aghast at what I have deduced from those details about Israeli government policy, more particularly about what has been going on in the mind of Ariel Sharon. And when, after the recent Gaza bombing by one of his F-16s in which nine children were massacred, he was quoted as congratulating the pilot and boasting of a great Israeli success, I was able to form a much clearer idea than before of what a pathologically deranged mind is capable of, in terms not only of what it plans and orders but, worse, of how it manages to persuade other minds to think in the same delusional and criminal way. Getting inside the official Israeli mind is a worthwhile, if lurid, experience.

In the West, however, there's been such repetitious and unedifying attention paid to Palestinian suicide bombing that a gross distortion in reality has completely obscured what is much worse: the official Israeli, and perhaps the uniquely Sharonian, evil that has been visited so deliberately and so methodically on the Palestinian people. Suicide bombing is reprehensible, but it is a direct and, in my opinion, a consciously programmed result of years of abuse, powerlessness, and despair. It has as little to do with the Arab or Muslim supposed propensity for violence as the man in the moon. Sharon wants terrorism, not peace, and he does everything in his power to create the conditions for it. But for all its horror, Palestinian violence, the response of a desperate and horribly oppressed people, has been stripped of its context and the terrible suffering from which it arises: a failure to see that is a failure in humanity, which doesn't make it any less terrible but at least situates it in a real history and real geography.

Yet the location of Palestinian terror—of course it is terror—is never allowed a moment's chance to appear, so remorseless has been the focus on it as a phenomenon apart, a pure, gratuitous evil that Israel, supposedly acting on behalf of pure good, has been virtuously battling in its variously appalling acts of disproportionate violence against a population of 3 million Palestinian civilians. I am speaking not only about Israel's manipulation of opinion but about its exploitation of the American equivalent of the campaign against terrorism, without which Israel could not have done what it has done. (In fact, I cannot think of any other country on earth that, in full view of nightly TV audiences, has performed such miracles of detailed sadism against an entire society and gotten away with it.) That this evil has been made consciously part of George W. Bush's campaign against terrorism, irrationally magnifying American fantasies and fixations with extraordinary ease, is no small part of its blind destructiveness. Like the brigades of eager (and in my opinion completely corrupt) American intellectuals who spin enormous structures of falsehoods about the benign purpose and necessity of U.S. imperialism, Israeli society has pressed into service numerous academics, policy intellectuals at think tanks, and ex-military men now in defense-related and public relations business, all to rationalize and make convincing inhuman punitive policies that are supposedly based on the need for Israeli security.

Israeli security is now a fabled beast rather like a unicorn. It is always being hunted or looked for and never found, and yet is everlastingly made the goal of future action. That over time Israel has in fact become less secure and more unacceptable to its neighbors scarcely merits a moment's notice. But then who challenges the view that Israeli security ought to define the moral world we live in? Certainly not the Arab and Palestinian leaderships who for thirty years have conceded everything to Israeli security. Shouldn't that ever be questioned, given that Israel has wreaked more damage on the Palestinians and other Arabs relative to its size than any country in the world, Israel with its nuclear arsenal, its air force, navy, and army limitlessly supplied by the U.S. taxpayer? As a result, the daily, minute occurrences of what Palestinians have to live through are hidden and, more important, covered over by a logic of self-defense and the pursuit of terrorism (terrorist infrastructure, terrorist nests, terrorist bomb factories, terrorist suspects—the list is infinite) that perfectly suits Sharon and the lamentable George W. Bush. Ideas about terrorism have thus taken on a life of their own, legitimized and relegitimized without proof, logic, or rational argument.

Consider for instance the devastation of Afghanistan, on the one hand, and the "targeted" assassinations of almost a hundred Palestinians (to say nothing of many thousands of "suspects" rounded up and still imprisoned by Israeli soldiers) on the other: nobody asks whether all these people killed were in fact terrorists, or proved to be terrorists, or—as was the case with most of them—about to become terrorists. They are all assumed to be dangers by acts of simple, unchallenged affirmation. All you need is an arrogant spokesman or two, like the loutish Ranaan Gissin, Avi Pazner, or Dore Gold, and in Washington a nonstop apologist for ignorance and incoherence like Ari Fleischer, and the targets in question are just as good as dead. Without doubts, questions, or demurral. No need for proof or any such tiresome delicacy. Terrorism and its obsessed pursuit have become an entirely circular, self-fulfilling murder and slow death of enemies who have no choice or say in the matter.

With the exception of reports by a few intrepid journalists and writers such as Amira Hass, Gideon Levy, Amos Elon, Tanya Reinhart, Jeff Halper, Israel Shamir, and a few others, public discourse in the Israeli media has declined terribly in quality and honesty. Patriotism and blind support for the government have replaced skeptical reflection and moral seriousness. Gone are the days of Israel Shahak, Jacob Talmon, and Yehoshua Leibowitch. I can think of few Israeli academics and intellectuals—men like Zeev Sternhell, Uri Avnery, and Ilan Pappe, for instance—who are courageous enough to depart from the imbecilic and debased debate about "security" and "terrorism" that seems to have overtaken the Israeli peace establishment, or even its rapidly dwindling left opposition. Crimes are being committed every day in the name of Israel and the Jewish people, and yet the intellectuals chatter on about strategic withdrawal, or perhaps whether to incorporate settlements or not, or whether to keep building that monstrous fence (has a crazier idea ever been realized in the modern world, that you can put several million people in a cage and say they don't exist?), in a manner befitting a general or a politician, rather than in ways more suited to intellectuals and artists with independent judgment and some sort of moral standard. Where are the Israeli equivalents of Nadine Gordimer, Andre Brink, Athol Fugard, those white writers who spoke out unequivocally and with unambiguous clarity against the evils of South African apartheid? They simply don't exist in Israel, where public discourse by writers and academics has sunk to equivocation and the repetition of official propaganda, and where most really first-class writing and thought has disappeared from even the academic establishment.

But to return to Israeli practices and the mindset that has gripped the country with such obduracy during the past few years, think of Sharon's plan. It entails nothing less than the obliteration of an entire people by slow, systematic methods of suffocation, outright murder, and the stifling of everyday life. Intrinsic to this plan is the unrelenting expropriation of Palestinian land through settlements, military areas, and occupied towns and villages: through the Oslo process, Israel conceded only 18 percent of the West Bank and 60 percent of Gaza, both of which now have been reoccupied and redivided many times. There is a remarkable story by Kafka, "In the Penal Colony," about a crazed official who shows off a fantastically detailed torture machine whose purpose is to write all over the body of the victim, using a complex apparatus of needles to inscribe minute letters that ultimately cause the prisoner to bleed to death. This is what Sharon and his brigades of willing executioners are doing to the Palestinians, with only the most limited and most symbolic of opposition. Every Palestinian has become a prisoner. Gaza is surrounded by an electrified wire fence on three sides; imprisoned like animals, Gazans are unable to move, unable to work, unable to sell their vegetables or fruit, unable to go to school. They are exposed from the air to Israeli planes and helicopters and are gunned down like turkeys on the ground by tanks and machine guns. Impoverished and starved, Gaza is a human nightmare, each of whose little pieces of episodes—like what takes place at Erez, or near the settlements—involves thousands of soldiers in the humiliation, punishment, and intolerable enfeeblement of each Palestinian, without regard for age, gender, or illness. Medical supplies are held up at the border, ambulances are fired upon or detained. Hundreds of houses are demolished, and hundreds of thousands of trees and agricultural land are destroyed in acts of systematic collective punishment against civilians, most of whom are already refugees from Israel's destruction of their society in 1948. Hope has been eliminated from the Palestinian vocabulary so that only raw defiance remains, and still Sharon and his sadistic minions prattle on about eliminating terrorism by an ever-encroaching occupation that has continued now for thirty-five years. That the campaign itself is, like all colonial brutality, futile, or that it has the effect of making Palestinians more, rather than less, defiant, simply does not enter Sharon's closed mind.

The West Bank is occupied by a thousand Israeli tanks whose sole purpose is to fire upon and terrorize civilians. Curfews are imposed for periods of up to two weeks, without respite. Schools and universities are either closed or impossible to get to. No one can travel, not just between the nine main cities but within the cities. Every town today is a wasteland of destroyed buildings, looted offices, purposely ruined water and electrical systems. Commerce is finished. Malnutrition prevails in half the children. Two-thirds of the population lives below the poverty level of two dollars a day. Tanks in Jenin (where the demolition of the refugee camp by Israeli armor, a major war crime, was never investigated because cowardly international bureaucrats such as Kofi Annan back down when Israel threatens) fire upon and kill children, but that is only one drop in an unending stream of Palestinian civilian deaths caused by Israeli soldiers who furnish the illegal Israeli military occupation with loyal, unquestioning service. Palestinians are all "terrorist suspects." The soul of this occupation is that young Israeli conscripts are allowed full rein to subject Palestinians at checkpoints to every known form of private torture and abjection. There is the waiting in the sun for hours; then there is the detention of medical supplies and produce until they rot; there are the insulting words and beatings administered at will; the sudden rampage of jeeps and soldiers against civilians waiting their turn by the thousands at the innumerable checkpoints that have made of Palestinian life a choking hell; making dozens of youths kneel in the sun for hours; forcing men to take off their clothes; insulting and humiliating parents in front of their children; forbidding the sick to pass through for no other reason than personal whim; stopping ambulances and firing on them. And the steady number of Palestinian deaths (quadruple that of Israelis) increases on a daily, mostly untabulated basis. More "terrorist suspects" plus their wives and children, but "we" regret those deaths very much. Thank you.

Israel is frequently referred to as a democracy. If so, then it is a democracy without a conscience, a country whose soul has been captured by a mania for punishing the weak, a democracy that faithfully mirrors the psychopathic mentality of its ruler, General Sharon, whose sole idea—if that is the right word for it—is to kill, reduce, maim, drive away Palestinians until "they break." He provides nothing more concrete as a goal for his campaigns, now or in the past, beyond that, and like the garrulous official in Kafka's story, he is most proud of his machine for abusing defenseless Palestinian civilians, all the while monstrously abetted in his grotesque lies by his court advisers and philosophers and generals, as well as by his chorus of faithful American servants. There is no Palestinian army of occupation, there are no Palestinian tanks, no soldiers, no helicopter gunships, there is no artillery, no government to speak of. But there are the "terrorists" and the "violence" that Israel has invented so that its own neuroses can be inscribed on the bodies of Palestinians, without effective protest from the overwhelming majority of Israel's laggard philosophers, intellectuals, artists, and peace activists. Palestinian schools, libraries, and universities have ceased normal functioning for months now: and we still wait for the Western freedom-to-write groups and the vociferous defenders of academic freedom in America to raise their voices in protest. I have yet to see one academic organization either in Israel or in the West make a declaration about this profound abrogation of the Palestinian right to knowledge, to learning, to attend school.

In sum, Palestinians must die a slow death so that Israel can have its security, which is just around the corner but cannot be realized because of the special Israeli "insecurity." The whole world must sympathize, while the cries of Palestinian orphans, sick old women, bereaved communities, and tortured prisoners simply go unheard and unrecorded. Doubtless, we will be told, these horrors serve a larger purpose than mere sadistic cruelty. After all, "the two sides" are engaged in a "cycle of violence" that has to be stopped, sometime, somewhere. Once in a while we ought to pause and declare indignantly that there is only one side with an army and a country: the other is a stateless disposed population of people without rights or any present way of securing them. The language of suffering and concrete daily life has been either hijacked or so perverted as, in my opinion, to be useless except as pure fiction deployed as a screen for the purpose of more killing and painstaking torture—slowly, fastidiously, inexorably. That is the truth of what Palestinians suffer. But in any case, Israeli policy will ultimately fail.

Al-Ahram, August 8–14, 2002
Al-Hayat, August 10, 2002

CHAPTER THIRTY-THREE

Arab Disunity and Factionalism

U nderlying most of the findings in the much-cited 2002 United Nations Human Development Report is the extraordinary lack of coordination among Arab countries. There is considerable irony in the fact that the Arabs are discussed and referred to, both in this report and elsewhere, as a group, even though they seem rarely to function as one, except negatively. Thus the report correctly says that there is no Arab democracy, Arab women are uniformly an oppressed majority, and in science and technology every Arab state is behind the rest of the world. Certainly there is little strategic cooperation among them and virtually none in the economic sphere. As for more specific issues like policy toward Israel, the United States, and the Palestinians, and despite a common front of embarrassed hand-wringing and disgraceful powerlessness, one senses a frightened determination first of all not to offend the United States, not to engage in war or in a real peace with Israel, not ever to think of a common Arab front even on matters that affect an overall Arab future or security. Yet when it comes to the perpetuation of each regime, the Arab ruling classes are united in purpose and survival skills.

This shambles of inertia and impotence is, I am convinced, an affront to every Arab. This is why so many Egyptians, Syrians, Jordanians, Moroccans, and others have taken to the streets in support of the Palestinian people undergoing the nightmare of Israeli occupation, with the Arab leadership looking on and basically doing nothing. Street demonstrations are not only demonstrations of support for Palestine but also protests at the immobilizing effects of Arab disunity. An even more eloquent sign of the common disenchantment is the frequent, wrenchingly sad television scene of a Palestinian woman surveying the ruins of her house demolished by Israeli bulldozers, wailing to the world at large, "*Ya Arab, ya Arab*" ("oh you Arabs, you Arabs"). There is no more eloquent testimony to the betrayal of the Arab people by their (mostly unelected) leaders than that indictment, which is to say: "Why don't you Arabs ever do anything to help us?" Despite money and oil aplenty, there is only the stony silence of an unmoved spectator.

Even on an individual level, alas, disunity and factionalism have crippled one national effort after the other. Take the saddest of all instances, the case of the Palestinian people. I recall wondering during the Amman and Beirut days why it was necessary for somewhere between eight to twelve Palestinian factions to exist, each fighting over uselessly academic issues of ideology and organization while Israel and the local militias bled us dry. Looking back over the Lebanese days that came to a terrible end in Sabra and Shatila, whose purpose did it serve to have the Popular Front, Fateh, and the Democratic Front—to mention only three factions—fighting among one another, to have leaders within Fateh proclaiming needlessly provocative slogans like "the road to Tel Aviv goes through Jounieh," even as Israel allied itself with the right-wing Lebanese militias to destroy the Palestinian presence for its own purposes? And what cause has been served by Yasir Arafat's tactics of creating factions, subgroups, and security forces to war against one another during the Oslo process and of leaving his people unprotected and unprepared for the Israeli destruction of the infrastructure and reoccupation of Area A?

It's always the same thing, factionalism, disunity, the absence of a common purpose for which in the end ordinary people pay the price in suffering, blood, and endless destruction. Even on the level of social structure, it is almost a commonplace that Arabs as a group fight among themselves more than they do for a common purpose. We are individualists, it is said by way of justification, ignoring the fact that such disunity and internal disorganization in the end damage our very existence as a people. Nothing can be more disheartening than the disputes that corrode Arab expatriate organizations, especially in places like the United States and Europe, where relatively small Arab communities are surrounded by hostile environments and militant opponents who will stop at nothing to discredit the Arab struggle. Still, instead of trying to unite and work together, these communities get torn apart by totally unnecessary ideological and factional struggles that have no immediate relevance, no necessity at all so far as the surrounding field is concerned.

A few days ago I was startled by a discussion program on Al-Jazeera television in which the two participants and a needlessly provocative moderator vehemently discussed Arab American activism during the present crisis. One man, a certain Mr. Dalbah who was identified vaguely as a "political analyst" in Washington (without apparent affiliation or institutional connection), spent all of his time discrediting the one serious national Arab-American group, the American-Arab Anti-Discrimination Committee (ADC), which he accused of ineffectiveness and its leaders of egoism, opportunism, and personal corruption. The other gentleman, whose name I didn't catch, admitted that he has been in the United States for only a very few years and didn't seem to know much about what was going on, except of course to argue that he had better ideas than all the other community leaders. Although I only watched the first and last parts of the program, I was thoroughly disillusioned and even disgraced by the discussion. What was the point? I asked myself. In what way is it useful to tear down an organization that has been doing by far the best work in a country where Arabs are outnumbered and outorganized not only by all the many, much larger and extremely well-financed Zionist organizations, but also where the society itself and its media are so hostile to Arabs, Islam, and their causes in general? It is not at all useful, of course, but this one had an instance of the pernicious factionalism by which with almost Pavlovian regularity Arabs try to hurt and impede one another rather than unite behind a common purpose. For if there is little justification for such behavior in the Arab lands themselves, surely there is less reason for it abroad, where Arab individuals and communities are targeted and threatened as undesirable aliens and terrorists.

The Al-Jazeera program was more offensive by its gratuitous inaccuracy and the needless personal harm it did to the late Hala Salam Maksoud, who literally gave her life to the cause of the ADC, and to its current president, Dr. Ziad Asali, a public-spirited physician who voluntarily gave up his medical practice to run the organization on a pro bono basis. Dalbah kept insinuating that both these activists were motivated by reasons of personal monetary gain, and that whatever the ADC did, it did badly. Aside from the scandalous untruth of such allegations, Dalbah's idle and malicious gossip—it was no more than that—harmed the collective Arab cause, leaving anger and more factionalism in its wake. Moreover, it should be noted that given the extremely inhospitable American political setting to the Arab cause, the ADC has been very successful in Washington and nationally as an organization rebutting charges against Arabs in the media, protecting individuals from government persecution after 9/11, and keeping Arab Americans involved and participating in the national debate. *Because* of this success under Asali, factionalism has infected the organization's employees, who have suddenly embarked on a campaign of personal vilification masked as ideological argument. Of course, everyone has the right to criticize, but why in the face of such threats as those we face in the United States should we splinter and weaken ourselves like this, when it is clear that the only beneficiary is the pro-Israel lobby? Organizations like the ADC are first of all American organizations and cannot function as partisans in struggles of the kind that recall those of Fakahani in the mid-1970s.

Perhaps the main reason for Arab factionalism at every level of our societies, at home and abroad, is the marked absence of ideals and role models. Since Gamal Abdel Nasser's death, whatever one may have thought of some of his more ruinous policies, no figure has captured the Arab imagination or had a role in setting a popular liberation struggle. Look at the disaster of the PLO, which has been reduced from the days of its glory to an old unshaven man, sitting at a broken-down table, in half a house in Ramallah, trying to survive at any cost, whether or not he sells out, whether or not he says foolish things, whether what he says means anything or not. (A couple of weeks ago he was quoted as saying that he now accepts the 2000 Clinton plan; the only problem is that it is now 2002 and Clinton is no longer president.) It has been years since Arafat represented his people, their sufferings and cause, and like his other Arab counterparts, he hangs on like a much-too-ripe fruit without real purpose or position. There is thus no strong moral center in the Arab world today. Cogent analysis and rational discussion have given way to fanatical ranting, concerted action on behalf of liberation has been reduced to suicidal attacks, and the idea if not the practice of integrity and honesty as a model to be followed has simply disappeared. So corrupting has the atmosphere exuded from the Arab world become that one scarcely knows why some people are successful while others are thrown in jail.

As a terribly shocking instance, consider the Egyptian sociologist Saadedin Ibrahim's fate. Released by a civil court a few months ago, he has now been tried, found guilty, and sentenced to a cruelly unjustified sentence by the state security court for exactly those "crimes" for which he was earlier released. Where is the moral justification for such toying with a person's life, career, and reputation? A matter of months ago he was a trusted adviser to the government and on the boards of several Arab institutes and projects. Now he is considered to be a condemned criminal. Whose interests, whether by virtue of national unity, or coherent strategy, or moral imperative, does his gratuitous punishment in this way serve? The result is only more factionalism, more disintegration, more sense of drift and fear, and a pervading sense of frustrated justice.

Arabs have for so long been deprived of a sense of participation and citizenship by their rulers that most of us have lost even the capacity of understanding what personal commitment to a cause bigger than ourselves might mean. The Palestinian struggle is a collective miracle, I think—that a people should endure such unremitting cruelty from Israel and still not give up—but why can't the lessons of living (as opposed to suicidal, nihilistic) resistance be made clearer and more possible to follow? This is the real problem, the absence all over the Arab world and abroad of a leadership that communicates with its people, not via communiqués that express an impersonal, almost disdainful disregard of them as citizens, but through the actual practice of concerted dedication and personal example. Unable to move the United States from its illegal support of Israel's crimes, the Arab leaders simply throw out one "peace" proposal (the same one) after another, each of which is dismissed derisively by both Israel and the United States. Bush and his psychopathic henchman Rumsfeld keep leaking news of their impending invasion for "regime change" in Iraq, and the Arabs still have not communicated a unified deterrent position against this new American insanity. When individuals and organizations like the ADC try to do something on behalf of a cause, they are gunned down by troublemakers who have little else to do but destroy and disturb.

Surely the time has come to start thinking of ourselves as a people with a common history and goals, and not as a collection of cowardly delinquents. But that is up to each one, and it's no good sitting back blaming "the Arabs" since, after all, *we* are the Arabs.

Al-Ahram, August 15–21, 2002
Al-Hayat, August 19, 2002

CHAPTER THIRTY-FOUR

Low Point of Powerlessness

Sixty years ago the Jews of Europe were at the lowest point of their collective existence. Herded like cattle into trains, they were transported from the rest of Europe by Nazi soldiers into death camps, where they were systematically exterminated in gas ovens. They had offered some resistance in Poland, but in most places they first lost their civil status, then they were removed from their jobs, then they were designated official enemies to be destroyed, and then they were. In every significant instance they were the most powerless of people, treated as insidious, potentially overpowering enemies by leaders and armies whose own power was far, far greater; indeed, even the idea of Jews representing a danger to the might of countries like Germany, France, and Italy was preposterous. But it was an accepted idea, since with few exceptions most of Europe turned its back on them during their slaughter. It is only one of the ironies of history that the word used most frequently to describe them in the hideous official jargon of fascism was the word "terrorists," just as Algerians and Vietnamese were later called "terrorists" by their enemies.

Every human calamity is different, so there is no point in trying to look for equivalence between one and the other. But it is certainly true that one universal truth about the Holocaust is not only that it should never again happen to Jews, but that as a cruel and tragic collective punishment, it should not happen to any people at all. But if there is no point in looking for equivalence, there is a value in seeing analogies and perhaps hidden similarities, even as we preserve a sense of proportion. Quite apart from his actual history of mistakes and misrule, Yasir Arafat is now being made to feel like a hunted Jew by the state of the Jews. There is no gainsaying the fact that the greatest irony of his siege by the Israeli army in his ruined Ramallah compound is that his ordeal has been planned and carried out by a psychopathic leader who claims to represent the Jewish people. I do not want to press the analogy too far, but it is true to say that Palestinians under Israeli occupation today are as powerless as Jews were in the 1940s. Israel's army, air force, and navy, heavily subsidized by the United States, have been wreaking havoc on the totally defenseless civilian population of the occupied West Bank and Gaza Strip. For the past half century the Palestinians have been a dispossessed people, millions of them refugees, most of the rest under a thirty-five-year-old military occupation, at the mercy of armed settlers who systematically have been stealing their land and an army that has killed them by the thousands. Thousands more have been imprisoned, thousands have lost their livelihood, made refugees for the second or third time, all of them without civil or human rights.

And still Sharon makes the case that Israel is struggling to survive against Palestinian terrorism. Is there anything more grotesque than this claim, even as this deranged killer of Arabs sends his F-16s, his attack helicopters, and hundreds of tanks against unarmed people without any defenses at all? They are terrorists, he says, and their leader, humiliatingly imprisoned in a crumbling building with Israeli destruction all around him, is characterized as the arch-terrorist of all time. Arafat has the courage and defiance to resist, and he has his people with him on that score. Every Palestinian feels the deliberate humiliation inflicted on him as a cruelty without political or military purpose except punishment, pure and simple. What right does Israel have to do this?

The symbolism is truly awful to register and is made even more so by the knowledge that Sharon and his supporters, to say nothing of his criminal army, intend what the symbolism so starkly illustrates. Israeli Jews are the powerful ones, Palestinians their hunted and despised Others. Luckily for Sharon, he has Shimon Peres, perhaps the greatest coward and hypocrite in world politics today, going around everywhere saying that Israel understands the difficulties of the Palestinian people, and "we" are willing to make the closures slightly less onerous. After which not only does nothing improve, but the curfews, demolitions, and killings intensify. And of course, the Israeli position is to call for massive international humanitarian aid that, as Terje Roed-Larsen correctly says, is in effect to cajole international donors into actually underwriting the Israeli occupation. Sharon must surely feel that he can do anything and not only get away with it completely but somehow even manage a campaign whose purpose is to give Israel the role of victim.

As popular protests grow worldwide, the organized Zionist counter-response has been to complain that anti-Semitism is on the rise. On September 17, 2002, Harvard University president Lawrence Summers issued a statement to the effect that an antidivestment campaign led by professors—an attempt to pressure the university into divesting itself of shares in American firms selling military equipment to Israel—was anti-Semitic. A Jewish president of the country's oldest and richest university complains of anti-Semitism! Criticism of Israeli policy is now routinely equated with anti-Semitism of the kind that brought about the Holocaust, even though in the United States there is no anti-Semitism to speak of. In the United States a group of Israeli and American academics are organizing a McCarthy-style campaign against professors who have spoken up about Israeli human rights abuses; the main purpose of the campaign is to ask students and faculty to inform against their pro-Palestinian colleagues, intimidating the right of free speech and seriously curtailing academic freedom.

A further irony is that protests against Israeli brutality—most recently Arafat's humiliating isolation in Ramallah—have taken place on a mass level. Palestinians by the thousands defied curfews in Gaza and several West Bank towns in order to go out on the streets in support of their embattled leader. For their part, the Arab rulers have been silent or powerless or both together. Every one of them, including Arafat, has for years openly stated a willingness for peace with Israel; two leading Arab countries actually have treaties with it. Yet all Sharon gives in return is a kick to their collective bottoms. Arabs, he says repeatedly, only understand force, and now that we have power, we shall treat them as they deserve (and as we used to be treated).

Uri Avnery is right: Arafat is being murdered. And with him, according to Sharon, will die the aspirations of the Palestinians. This is an exercise short of complete genocide to see how far Israeli power can go in sadistic brutality without being stopped or apprehended. Today Sharon has said that in the event of a war with Iraq, which is definitely coming, he will retaliate against Iraq, thus no doubt causing Bush and Rumsfeld the nightmares they rightly deserve. Sharon's last attempt at regime change was in Lebanon during 1982. He put Bashir Gemayel in as president, then was summarily told by Gemayel that Lebanon would never be an Israeli vassal, then Gemayel was assassinated, then the Sabra and Shatila massacres took place, then after twenty bloody and ignominious years the Israelis sullenly withdrew from Lebanon.

What conclusion is one to draw from all this? That Israeli policy has been a disaster for the entire region. The more powerful it becomes, the more ruin it sows in the countries around it, to say nothing of the catastrophes it has executed against the Palestinian people, and the more hated it becomes. It is power used for evil purposes, not self-defense at all. The Zionist dream of a Jewish state being a normal state like all others has come to the vision of the leader of Palestine's indigenous people hanging on to his life by a thread, while Israeli tanks and bulldozers continue to wreck everything around him. Is this the Zionist goal for which hundreds of thousands have died? Isn't it clear what logic of resentment and violence is at work in all this, and what power will come from the powerlessness that can now only witness but will certainly develop later? Sharon is proud to have defied the entire world, not because the world is anti-Semitic but because what he does in the name of the Jewish people is so outrageous. Isn't it time for those who feel that his appalling actions do not represent them to call a halt to his behavior?

Al-Ahram, September 26–October 2, 2002
Al-Hayat, September 30, 2002

PART THREE

Israel, Iraq, and the United States

CHAPTER THIRTY-FIVE

Israel, Iraq, and the United States

Many parts of Lebanon were bombed heavily by Israeli warplanes on June 4, 1982. Two days later the Israeli army entered Lebanon through the country's southern border. Menachem Begin was prime minister, Ariel Sharon his minister of defense. The immediate reason for the invasion was an attempted assassination in London of the Israeli ambassador, but then as now, Begin and Sharon placed the blame on the "terrorist organization" of the PLO, whose forces in South Lebanon had actually observed a cease-fire for about one full year before the invasion. A few days later, on June 13, Beirut was under Israeli military siege, even though, as the campaign began, Israeli government spokesmen had cited the Awali River, 35 kilometers north of the border, as their goal. Later, it was to emerge without equivocation that Sharon was trying to kill Yasir Arafat, by bombing everything around the defiant Palestinian leader. Accompanying the siege was a blockade of humanitarian aid, the cutting off of water and electricity, and a sustained aerial bombing campaign that destroyed hundreds of Beirut buildings and, by the end of the siege in late August, had killed eighteen thousand Palestinians and Lebanese, most of them civilians.

Lebanon had been racked with a terrible civil war since the spring of 1975, and although Israel had only once sent its army into Lebanon before 1982, it had been sought out as an ally by the Christian right-wing militias early on. With a stronghold in East Beirut, these militias cooperated with Sharon's forces right through the siege, which ended after a horrendous day of indiscriminate bombing on August 12 and of course the massacres of Sabra and Shatila. Sharon's main ally was Bashir Gemayel, the head of the Phalange Party, who was elected Lebanon's president by the parliament on August 23. Gemayel hated the Palestinians who had unwisely entered the civil war on the side of the National Movement, a loose coalition of left-wing and Arab nationalist parties that included

Amal, a forerunner of today's Hizbollah Shi'ite movement that was to play the major role in driving out the Israelis in May 2000. Faced with the prospect of direct Israeli vassalage after Sharon's army had in effect brought about his election, Gemayel seems to have demurred. He was assassinated on September 14. Two days later the camp massacres began inside a security cordon provided by the Israeli army so that Bashir's vengeful fellow Christian extremists could do their hideous work unopposed and undistracted.

Under UN and of course U.S. supervision, French troops had entered Beirut on August 21. They were to be joined by U.S. and other European forces a little later, although PLO fighters began their evacuation from Lebanon on August 21. By the first of September, that evacuation was over, and Arafat plus a small band of advisers and soldiers were lodged in Tunis. Meanwhile the Lebanese civil war continued until about 1990, when a concordat was fashioned together in Taif, more or less restoring the old confessional system, which remains in place today. In mid-1994 Arafat—still head of the PLO—and some of those same advisers and soldiers were able to enter Gaza as part of the so-called Oslo agreements. Earlier this year Sharon was quoted as regretting his failure to kill Arafat in Beirut. Not for want of trying, though, since dozens of hiding places and headquarters were smashed into rubble with great loss of life. Nineteen eighty-two hardened Arabs, I think, to the notion that not only would Israel use advanced technology (planes, missiles, tanks, and helicopters) to attack civilians indiscriminately, but that neither the United States nor the other Arabs would do anything at all to stop the practice, even if meant targeting leaders and capital cities. (For more on this episode, see Rashid Khalidi, *Under Siege,* New York, 1986; Robert Fisk, *Pity the Nation,* London, 1990; more specifically on the Lebanese civil war, Jonathan Randal, *Going All the Way,* New York, 1983.)

Thus ended the first full-scale contemporary attempt at military regime change by one sovereign country against another in the Middle East. I bring it up as a messy backdrop to what is occurring now. Sharon is now Israel's prime minister; his armies and propaganda machine are once again surrounding and dehumanizing Arafat and the Palestinians as "terrorists." It is worth recalling that the word *terrorist* began to be employed systematically by Israel to describe any Palestinian act of resistance beginning in the mid-1970s. That has been the rule ever since, especially during the first intifada of 1987–93, eliminating the distinction between resistance and pure terror and effectively depoliticizing the reasons for armed struggle. During the 1950s and 1960s Ariel Sharon earned his spurs, so to speak, by heading the infamous Unit 101, which killed Arab civilians and razed their houses with the approval of Ben-Gurion. He was in charge of the pacification of Gaza in 1970–71. None of this, including the 1982 campaign, ever resulted in getting rid of the Palestinian people, or in changing the map or the regime enough by military means to ensure a total Israeli victory.

The main difference between 1982 and 2002 is that the Palestinians now being victimized and besieged are in Palestinian territories that were occupied in 1967, and they have remained there despite the ravages of the occupation and the destruction of the economy and the whole civilian infrastructure of collective life. The main similarity is, of course, the disproportional means used to do it, for example the hundreds of tanks and bulldozers used to enter towns and villages like Jenin or refugee camps like Jenin's and Deheisheh, to kill, vandalize, prevent ambulances and first-aid workers from helping, cut off water and electricity, and so on. All with the support of the United States, whose president actually went so far as to call Sharon a man of peace during the worst rampages of March and April 2002. It is significant of how Sharon's intention went far beyond "rooting out terror" that his soldiers destroyed every computer and then carried off the files and hard drives from the Central Bureau of Statistics, the Ministries of Education, of Finance, and of Health, cultural centers, vandalizing officers and libraries, all as a way of reducing Palestinian collective life to a premodern level.

I don't want to rehearse my criticisms of Arafat's tactics or the failures of his deplorable regime during the Oslo negotiations and thereafter. I have done so at length here and elsewhere. Besides, as I write the man is quite literally hanging on to life by his teeth; his crumbling quarters in Ramallah are also still besieged, while Sharon does everything possible to injure him short of actually having him killed. What concerns me is the whole idea of regime change as an attractive prospect for individuals, ideologies, and institutions that are asymmetrically more powerful than their adversaries. What kind of thinking makes it relatively easy to conceive of great military power as licensing political and social change on a scale not imagined before, and doing so with little concern for the damage on a vast scale that such change necessarily entails? And how do the prospects of not incurring much risk of casualties for one's own side stimulate more and still more fantasies about surgical strikes, clean war, high-technology battlefields, changing the entire map, creating democracy, and the like, all of it giving rise to ideas of omnipotence, wiping the slate clean, and being in ultimate control of what matters to "our" side?

During the current American campaign for regime change in Iraq, it is the people of Iraq, the vast majority of whom have paid a terrible price in poverty, malnutrition, and illness as a result of ten years of sanctions, who have dropped out of sight. This is completely in keeping with U.S. Middle East policy, built as it is on two mighty pillars, the security of Israel and plentiful supplies of inexpensive oil. The complex mosaic of traditions, religions, cultures, ethnicities, and histories that make up the Arab world—especially in Iraq—despite the existence of nation-states with sullenly despotic rulers, is lost to U.S. and Israeli strategic planners. With a five-thousand-year-old history, Iraq is mainly now thought of either as a "threat" to its neighbors, which, in its currently weakened and besieged condition, is rank nonsense, or as a "threat" to the freedom and security of the United States, which is more nonsense. I am not even going to bother here to add my condemnations of Saddam Hussein as a dreadful person: I shall take it for granted that he certainly deserves by almost every standard to be ousted and punished. Worst of all, he is a threat to his own people.

Yet since the period before the first Gulf War, the image of Iraq as in fact a large, prosperous, and diverse Arab country has disappeared; the image that has circulated both in media and policy discourse is of a desert land peopled by brutal gangs headed by Saddam. That Iraq's debasement now has, for example, nearly ruined the Arab book-publishing industry, given that Iraq provided the largest number of readers in the Arab world; that it was one of the few Arab countries with a large, educated, and competent professional middle class; that it has oil, water, and fertile land; that it has always been the cultural center of the Arab world (the Abbasid Empire, with its great literature, philosophy, architecture, science, and medicine was an Iraqi contribution that is still the basis for

Arab culture); that the bleeding wound of Iraqi suffering has, like the Palestinian calvary, been a source of continuing sorrow for Arabs and Muslims alike—all this is literally never mentioned. Its vast oil reserves, however, are, and as the argument goes, if "we" took them away from Saddam and got hold of them, we wouldn't be so dependent on Saudi oil. That too is rarely cited as a factor in the various debates racking the U.S. Congress and the media. But it is worth mentioning that second to Saudi Arabia, Iraq has the largest oil reserves on earth, and the roughly $1.1 trillion worth of oil—much of it already committed by Saddam to Russia, France, and a few other countries—that have been available to Iraq are a crucial aim of U.S. strategy, something that the Iraqi National Congress has used as a trump card with non-U.S. oil consumers. (For more details on all this, see Michael Klare, "Oiling the Wheels of War," *The Nation*, October 7.) A good deal of the bargaining between Putin and Bush concerns how much of a share of that oil U.S. companies are willing to promise Russia. It is eerily reminiscent of the $3 billion offered by Bush Senior to Russia. Both Bushes are oil businessmen, after all, and they care more about that sort of calculation than they do about the delicate points of Middle Eastern politics, like rewrecking Iraq's civilian infrastructure.

Thus the first step in the dehumanization of the hated Other is to reduce his existence to a few insistently repeated simple phrases, images, and concepts. This makes it much easier to bomb the enemy without qualm. After September 11, this has been quite easy for Israel and the United States to do with respectively the Palestinians and the Iraqis as people. The important thing to note is that by an overwhelming preponderance the same policy and the same severe one-, two-, or three-stage plan is put forward principally by the same Americans and Israelis. In the United States, as Jason Vest has written in *The Nation* (September 2/9), men from the very right-wing Jewish Institute for National Security (JINSA) and the Center for Security Policy (CSP) populate Pentagon and State Department committees, including the one run by Richard Perle (appointed by Wolfowitz and Rumsfeld). Israeli and American security are equated, and JINSA spends the "bulk of its budget taking a bevy of retired US generals and admirals to Israel." When they come back, they write op-eds and appear on TV hawking the Likud line. *Time* magazine ran a piece on the Pentagon's Defense Policy Board, many of whose members are drawn from JINSA and CSP, in its August 23 issue entitled "Inside the Secret War Council."

For his part, Sharon has numbingly repeated that his campaign against Palestinian terrorism is identical with the American war on terrorism generally, Usama bin Laden and al-Qaeda in particular. And they, he claims, are in turn part of the same terrorist international that includes many Muslims all over Asia, Africa, Europe, and North America, even if Bush's axis of evil seems for the moment to be concentrated on Iraq, Iran, and North Korea. There are now 132 countries with some sort of American military presence, all of it linked to the war on terror, which remains undefined and floating so as to whip up more patriotic frenzy and fear and support for military action on the domestic front, where things go from bad to worse. Every major West Bank and Gaza area is occupied by Israeli troops who routinely kill and/or detain Palestinians on the grounds that they are "suspected" terrorists and militants; similarly, houses and shops are often demolished with the excuse that they shelter bomb factories, terrorist cells, and militant meeting places. No proof is given, none asked for by reporters who accept the unilateral Israeli designation without a murmur.

An immense carpet of mystification and abstraction has therefore been laid down all over the Arab world by this effort at systematic dehumanization. What the eye and ear perceive are terror, fanaticism, violence, hatred of freedom, insecurity, and the ultimate, weapons of mass destruction (WMD), which are to be found not where we know they are and are never looked for (in Israel, Pakistan, India, and obviously the United States among others) but in the hypothetical spaces of the terrorist ranks, Saddam's hands, a fanatical gang, and so on. A constant figure in the carpet is that Arabs hate Israel and Jews for no other reason except that they hate America, too. Potentially Iraq is the most fearsome enemy of Israel because of that country's economic and human resources; Palestinians are formidable because they stand in the way of complete Israeli hegemony and land occupation. Right-wing Israelis like Sharon who represent the Greater Israel ideology claiming all of historical Palestine as a Jewish homeland have been especially successful at making their view of the region the dominant one among U.S. supporters of Israel. Uzi Landau, Israeli internal security minister (and member of the Likud Party), commented on U.S. TV this summer that all this talk of "occupation" was nonsense. We are a people coming home. He was not even quizzed about this extraordinary concept by Mort Zuckerman, host of the program, also owner of *U.S. News & World Report* and president of the Council of Presidents of Major Jewish Organizations. But Israeli journalist Alex Fishman, in *Yediot Aharonot* of September 6, describes the "revolutionary ideas" of Condoleezza Rice, Donald Rumsfeld (who now also refers to "so-called occupied territories"), Dick Cheney, Paul Wolfowitz, Douglas Feith, and Richard Perle (who commissioned the notorious Rand study designating Saudi Arabia as the enemy and Egypt as the prize for America in the Arab world) as being terrifyingly hawkish because they advocate regime change in every Arab country. Fishman quotes Sharon as saying that this group, many of them members of JINSA and CSP and connected to the AIPAC affiliate the Washington Institute of Near East Affairs, dominates Bush's thinking (if that's the right word for it); he says, "next to our American friends Effi Eitam [one of the Israeli cabinet's most remorseless hard-liners] is a total dove."

The other, scarier side of this is the unchallenged proposition that if "we" don't preempt terrorism (or any other potential enemy), we will be destroyed. This premise is now the core of U.S. security strategy that is regularly drummed out in interviews and talk shows by Rice, Rumsfeld, and Bush himself. The formal statement of this view appeared a short time ago in "The National Security Strategy of the United States of America," an official paper prepared as an overall manifesto for the administration's new, post–cold war foreign policy. The working presumption is that we live in an exceptionally dangerous world with a network of enemies that does in fact exist, that it has factories, offices, and endless numbers of members, and that its entire existence is given up to destroying "us," unless we get them first. This is what frames and gives legitimacy to the wars on terrorism and on Iraq, for which the Congress and the UN are now being asked to give endorsement.

Fanatical individuals and groups do exist, of course, and many of them are generally in favor of somehow harming either Israel or the United States. On the other hand, Israel and the United States are widely perceived in the Islamic and Arab worlds first of having created the so-called *jihadi* extremists of whom Bin Laden is the most famous, and second of blithely overriding international law and UN resolutions in the pursuit of their own hostile and destructive policies in those worlds. David Hirst writes in a *Guardian* column datelined Cairo that even Arabs who oppose their own despotic regimes "will see it [the U.S. attack on Iraq] as an act of aggression aimed not just at Iraq, but at the whole Arab world; and what will make it supremely intolerable is that it will be done on behalf of Israel, whose acquisition of a large arsenal of weapons of mass destruction seems to be as permissible as theirs is an abomination" (September 6).

I am also saying that there is a specific Palestinian narrative and, at least since the mid-1980s, a formal willingness to make peace with Israel that is quite contrary to the more recent terrorist threat represented by al-Qaeda or the spurious threat supposedly embodied by Saddam Hussein, who is a terrible man, of course, but is scarcely able to wage intercontinental war; only occasionally is it admitted by the administration that he might be a threat to Israel, but that seems to be one of his grievous sins. None of his neighbors perceives him as a threat. The Palestinians and Iraq get mixed up in this scarcely perceptible way so as to constitute a menace that the media reinforces time and time again. Most stories about the Palestinians that appear in genteel and influential mass-circulation publications like *The New Yorker* and *The New York Times Magazine* show Palestinians as bomb-makers, collaborators, and suicide bombers, and only that. Neither of these publications has published anything from the Arab viewpoint since 9/11. Nothing at all.

So that when an administration flack like Dennis Ross (in charge of Clinton's side of the Oslo negotiations, but both before and after his stint in that job a member of an Israeli lobby affiliate) keeps saying that the Palestinians turned down a generous Israeli offer at Camp David, he is flagrantly distorting the facts, which as several authoritative sources have shown were that Israel conceded noncontiguous Palestinian areas with Israeli security posts and settlements surrounding them all and with no common border between Palestine and any Arab state (e.g., Egypt in the south, Jordan in the east). Why words like *generous* and *offer* should apply to territory illegally held by an occupying power in contravention of international law and UN resolutions, no one has bothered to ask. But given the power of the media to repeat, re-repeat, and underline simple assertions, plus the untiring efforts of the Israeli lobby to repeat the same idea—Dennis Ross himself has been singularly obdurate in his insistence on this falsehood—it is now locked into place that the Palestinians chose "terror instead of peace." Hamas and Islamic Jihad are seen not as (a perhaps misguided) part of the Palestinian struggle to be rid of Israeli military occupation but as part of the general Palestinian desire to terrorize, threaten, and be a menace. Like Iraq.

In any event, with the U.S. administration's newest and rather improbable claim that secular Iraq has been giving haven and training to the madly theocratic al-Qaeda, the case against Saddam seems to have been closed. The prevailing (but by no means uncontested) government consensus is that since UN inspectors cannot ascertain what he has of WMD, what he has hidden, and what he might still do, he should be attacked and removed. The whole point of going to the UN for authorization, from the U.S. point of view, is to get a resolution so stiff and so punitive that no matter whether or not Saddam Hussein complies, he will be so incriminated with having violated "international law" that his mere existence will warrant military regime change. In late September, on the other hand, in a Security Council resolution passed unanimously (with U.S. abstention), Israel was enjoined to end its siege of Arafat's Ramallah compound and to withdraw from Palestinian territory illegally occupied since March (for which Israel's excuse has been "self-defense"). Israel has refused to comply, and the underlying U.S. rationale for the United States not doing much to enforce even its own stated position is that "we" understand that Israel must defend its citizens. Why the UN is to be sought after in one instance, ignored in another is one of those inconsistencies that the United States simply indulges in.

A small group of unexamined and self-invented phrases such as "anticipatory preemption" and "preventive self-defense" are bandied about by Donald Rumsfeld and his colleagues to persuade the public that the preparations for war against Iraq or any other state in need of "regime change" (or in the other somewhat rarer euphemism, "constructive destruction") are buttressed by the notion of self-defense. The public is kept on tenterhooks by repeated red or orange alerts, people are encouraged to inform law enforcement authorities of "suspicious" behavior, and thousands of Muslims, Arabs, and South Asians have been detained and in some cases arrested on suspicion. All of this is carried out at the president's behest as a facet of patriotism and love of America. I still have not been able to understand what it means to love a country (in U.S. political discourse, love of Israel is also a current phrase), but it seems to mean unquestioning blind loyalty to the powers that be, whose secrecy, evasiveness, and willful refusal to engage with an alert public, which for the time being doesn't seem to be awakened into coherent or systematic responsiveness, has concealed the ugliness and destructiveness of the whole Iraq and Middle East policy of the Bush administration.

So powerful is the United States in comparison with most other major countries combined that it can't really be constrained or compelled to obey any international system of conduct, not even one its secretary of state may wish to. Along with the abstractness of whether "we" should go to war against Iraq seven thousand miles away, discussion of foreign policy denudes other people of any thick or real human identity; Iraq and Afghanistan, seen from the bombsight of a smart missile or on television, are at best chessboards that "we" decide to enter, destroy, reconstruct, or not, at will. The word *terrorism*, as well as the war on it, serves nicely to further this sentiment, since in comparison with many Europeans, the great majority of Americans have had no contact or lived experience with the Muslim lands and peoples and therefore feel no sense of the fabric of life that a sustained bombing campaign (as in Afghanistan) would tear to shreds. And seen as it is, like an emanation from nowhere except from well-financed *madrasas* on the basis of a "decision" by people who hate our freedoms and who are jealous of our democracy, terrorism engages polemicists in the most extravagant, if unsituated and nonpolitical, debates. History and politics have disappeared, all because memory, truth, and actual human existence have effectively been downgraded. You cannot speak about Palestinian suffering or Arab frustration because Israel's presence in the United States prevents it. At a fervently pro-Israel demonstration in May, Paul Wolfowitz mentioned Palestinian suffering in passing, but he was loudly booed and never could refer to it again.

Moreover, a coherent human rights or free trade policy that consistently stuck to the endlessly underlined virtues of human rights, democracy, and free economies that we are constitutively believed to stand for would likely be undermined domestically by special interest groups (as witness the influence of the ethnic lobbies, the steel and defense industries, the oil cartel, the farming industry, retired people, and the gun lobby, to mention only a few). Every one of the 435 congressional districts represented in Washington, for instance, has a defense or defense-related industry in it; so as Secretary of State James Baker said just before the first Gulf War, the real issue in that war against Iraq was "jobs." When it comes to foreign affairs, it is worth remembering that only something like 25 or 30 percent (compare that with the 15 percent of Americans who have actually traveled abroad) of members of Congress even have passports, and what they say or think has less to do with history, philosophy, or ideals than with who influences the member's campaign, sends money, and so on. Two incumbent House members, Earl Hilliard of Alabama and Cynthia McKinney of Georgia, supportive of the Palestinian right to self-determination and critical of Israel, were recently defeated by relatively obscure candidates who were well financed by what was openly cited as New York (i.e., Jewish) money from outside their states. The defeated pair were berated by the press as extremist and unpatriotic.

As far as U.S. Middle East policy is concerned, the Israeli lobby has no peer and has turned the legislative branch of the U.S. government into what former senator Jim Abourezk once called Israeli-occupied territory. No comparable Arab lobby even exists, much less functions effectively. As a case in point, the Senate will periodically issue forth unsolicited resolutions sent to the president that stress, underline, and reiterate American support for Israel. There was such a resolution in May 2002, just at the time when Israeli forces were occupying and in effect destroying all the major West Bank towns. One of the drawbacks of this wall-to-wall endorsement of Israel's most extreme policies is that in the long run it is simply bad for Israel's future as a Middle East country. Tony Judt has well argued that case, suggesting that Israel's dead-end ideas about staying on in Palestinian land will lead nowhere and simply put off the inevitable withdrawal.

The whole theme of the war against terrorism has permitted Israel and its supporters to commit war crimes against the entire Palestinian population of the West Bank and Gaza, 3.4 million people, who have become (as the going phrase has it) noncombatant collateral damage. Terje Roed-

Larsen, who is the UN's special administrator for the Occupied Territories, has just issued a report charging Israel with inducing a humanitarian catastrophe: unemployment has reached 65 percent, 50 percent of the population lives on less than two dollars a day, and the economy, to say nothing of people's lives, has been shattered. In comparison with this, Israeli suffering and insecurity are considerably less: there aren't Palestinian tanks occupying any part of Israel, or even challenging Israeli settlements. During the past two weeks Israel has killed seventy-five Palestinians, many of them children; it has demolished houses, deported people, razed valuable agricultural land, kept everyone indoors under eighty-hour curfews at a stretch, not permitted civilians through roadblocks or allowed ambulances and medical aid through, and as usual cut off water and electricity. Schools and universities simply cannot function. While these are daily occurrences that, like the occupation itself and the dozens of UN Security Council resolutions, have been in effect for at least thirty-five years, they are mentioned in the U.S. media only occasionally, as endnotes for long articles about Israeli government debates or the disastrous suicide bombings that have occurred. The tiny phrase "suspected of terrorism" is both the justification and the epitaph for whomever Sharon chooses to have killed. The United States doesn't object except in the mildest terms—for example, it says, "This is not helpful"—but this does little to deter the next brace of killings.

We are now closer to the heart of the matter. Because of Israeli interests in this country, U.S. Middle East policy is therefore Israelo-centric. A post-9/11 chilling conjuncture has occurred in which the Christian right, the Israeli lobby, and the Bush administration's semireligious belligerency is theoretically rationalized by neoconservative hawks whose view of the Middle East is committed to the destruction of Israel's enemies, which is sometimes given the euphemistic label of redrawing the map by bringing regime change and "democracy" to the Arab countries that most threaten Israel. (See Ibrahim Warde, "The Dynamics of World Disorder: Which God Is on Whose Side?" *Le Monde Diplomatique*, September 2002, and Ken Silverstein and Michael Scherer, "Born-Again Zionists," *Mother Jones,* October 2002.) Sharon's campaign for Palestinian reform is simply the other side of his effort to destroy the Palestinians politically, his lifelong ambition. Egypt, Saudi Arabia, Syria, even Jordan have been variously threatened, even though, dreadful regimes though they may be, they were protected and supported by the United States since World War II, as indeed was Iraq.

In fact, it seems obvious to anyone who knows anything about the Arab world that its parlous state is likely to get a whole lot worse once the United States begins its assault on Iraq. Supporters of the administration's policy occasionally say vague things like how exciting it will be when we bring democracy to Iraq and the other Arab states, without much consideration for what exactly, in terms of lived experience, that will mean for the people who actually live there, especially after B-52 strikes tear their land and homes apart relentlessly. I can't imagine that there is a single Arab or Iraqi who would not like to see Saddam Hussein removed. All the indications are that U.S./Israeli military action has made things a lot worse on a daily basis for ordinary people, but this is nothing in comparison with the terrible anxiety, psychological distortions, and political malformations imposed on their societies.

Today neither the expatriate Iraqi opposition that has been intermittently courted by at least two U.S. administrations nor the various U.S. generals such as Tommy Franks has much credibility as a postwar ruler of Iraq. Nor does there seem to have been much thought given to what Iraq will need once the regime is changed, once the internal actors get moving again, once even the Ba'ath is detoxified. It may be the case that not even the Iraqi army will lift a finger in battle on behalf of Saddam. Interestingly, though, in a recent congressional hearing three former generals from the U.S. Central Command have expressed serious and, I would say, crippling reservations about the hazards of this whole adventure as it is being planned militarily. But even those doubts do not sufficiently address the country's seething internal factionalism and ethnoreligious dynamic, particularly after thirty debilitating years under the Ba'ath Party, UN sanctions, and two major wars (three if and when the United States attacks). No one in the United States, no one at all, has any real idea of what might happen in Iraq, or Saudi Arabia, or Egypt if a major military intervention took place. It is enough to know, and then to shudder, that Fouad Ajami and Bernard Lewis are the administration's two major expert advisers. Both are virulently and ideologically anti-Arab as well as discredited by the majority of their colleagues in the field. Lewis has never lived in the Arab world, and what he has to say about it is reactionary rubbish; Ajami is from South Lebanon, a man who was once a progressive supporter of the Palestinian struggle who has now converted to the far right and has espoused Zionism and American imperialism without reservation.

September 11 might have provided a period of national reflection and the pondering of U.S. foreign policy after the shock of that unconscionable atrocity. Such terrorism as that most certainly needs to be confronted and forcefully dealt with, but in my opinion it is always the aftermath of a forceful response that has to be considered first, not just the immediate, reflexive, and violent response. No one would argue today, even after the rout of the Taliban, that Afghanistan is now a much better and more secure place from the standpoint of the country's still-suffering citizens. Nation-building is clearly not the United States' priority there since other wars in different places draw attention away from the last battlefield. Besides, what does it mean for Americans to build a nation with a culture and history as different from theirs as Iraq's? Both the Arab world and the United States are far more complex and dynamic places than the platitudes of war and the resonant phrases about reconstruction would allow. That is obvious in post-U.S. attacks on Afghanistan.

To make matters more complicated, there are dissenting voices of considerable weight in Arab culture today, and there are movements of reform across a wide front. The same is true of the United States where, to judge from my recent experiences lecturing at various campuses, most citizens are anxious about the war, anxious to know more, and above all, anxious not to go to war with such messianic bellicosity and vague aims in mind. Meanwhile, as *The Nation* put it in its last editorial, the country marches toward war as if in a trance, while, with an increasing number of exceptions, Congress has simply abdicated its role of representing the people's interest. As someone who has lived within the two cultures all my life, it is appalling that the "clash of civilizations," that reductive and vulgar notion so much in vogue now, has taken over thought and action. What we need to put in place is a universalist framework for comprehending and dealing with Saddam Hussein as well as Sharon and the rulers of Myanmar, Syria, Turkey, and a whole host of those countries where depredations are endured without sufficient resistance. Demolition of houses, torture, the denial of a right to education are to be opposed wherever they occur. I know no other way of re-creating or restoring the framework but through education and the fostering of open discussion, exchange, and intellectual honesty that will have no truck with concealed special pleading or the jargons of war, religious extremism, and preemptive "defense." But that, alas, takes a long time and, to judge from the governments of the United States and the United Kingdom, its little partner, wins no votes. We must do everything in our power to provoke discussion and ask embarrassing questions, thereby slowing down and finally stopping the recourse to war that has now become a theory and not just a practice.

Al-Ahram, October 10–16, 2002
Al-Hayat, October 14, 15, 2002
London Review of Books, October 17, 2002

CHAPTER THIRTY-SIX

Europe Versus America

Although I have visited England dozens of times, I have never spent more than one or two weeks there at a single stretch. This year, for the first time, I am in residence for almost two months at Cambridge University, where I am the guest of a college and giving a series of lectures on humanism at the university.

The first thing to be said is that life here is far less stressed and hectic than it is in New York, at my university, Columbia. Perhaps this slightly relaxed pace is due in part to the fact that Great Britain is no longer a world power, but also to the salutary idea that the ancient universities here are places of reflection and study rather than economic centers for producing experts and technocrats who will serve the corporations and the state. So the postimperial setting is a welcome environment for me, especially since the United States is now in the middle of a war fever that is absolutely repellent as well as overwhelming. If you sit in Washington and have some connection to the country's power elites, the rest of the world is spread out before you like a map, inviting intervention anywhere and at any time. The tone in Europe is not only more moderate and thoughtful: it is also less abstract, more human, more complex and subtle. Certainly Europe generally and Britain in particular have a much larger and more demographically significant Muslim population, whose views are part of the debate about war in the Middle East and against terrorism. So discussion of the upcoming war against Iraq tends to reflect their opinions and their reservations a great deal more than in America, where Muslims and Arabs are already considered to be on the "other side," whatever that may mean. And being on the other side means no less than supporting Saddam Hussein and being "un-American." Both of these ideas are abhorrent to Arab and Muslim Americans, but the idea that to be an Arab or Muslim means to blindly support Saddam and al-Qaeda persists nonetheless. (Incidentally, I know no other country where the adjective *un* is used with the nationality as a way of designating the common enemy. No one says un-Spanish or un-Chinese: these are uniquely American confections that claim to prove that we all "love" our country. How can one actually "love" something so abstract and imponderable as a country anyway?)

The second major difference I have noticed between America and Europe is that religion and ideology play a far greater role in the former than in the latter. A recent poll taken in the United States reveals that 86 percent of the American population believes that God loves them. There's been a lot of ranting and complaining about fanatical Islam and violent jihadists, who are thought to be a universal scourge. Of course they are, as are any fanatics who claim to do God's will and to fight his battles in his name. But what is most odd is the vast number of Christian fanatics in the United States, who form the core of George W. Bush's support and at 60 million strong represent the single most powerful voting bloc in U.S. history. Whereas church attendance is down dramatically in England, it has never been higher in the United States, whose strange fundamentalist Christian sects are, in my opinion, a menace to the world and furnish Bush's government with its rationale for punishing evil while righteously condemning whole populations to submission and poverty.

It is the coincidence between the Christian right and the so-called neoconservatives in America that fuels the drive toward unilateralism, bullying, and a sense of divine mission. The neoconservative movement began in the 1970s as an anticommunist formation whose ideology was undying enmity to communism, and American supremacy. The phrase "American values," now so casually trotted out as a phrase to hector the world, was invented then by people like Irving Kristol, Norman Podhoretz, Midge Decter, and others who had once been Marxists and had converted completely (and religiously) to the other side. For all of them the unquestioning defense of Israel as a bulwark of Western democracy and civilization against Islam and communism was a central article of faith. Many though not all the major neocons (as they are called) are Jewish, but under the Bush presidency they have welcomed the extra support of the Christian right, which, while it is rabidly pro-Israel, is also deeply anti-Semitic. (These Christians—many of them Southern Baptists—believe that all the Jews of the world must gather in Israel so that the Messiah can come again; those Jews who convert to Christianity will be saved, the rest will be doomed to eternal perdition.) It is the next generation of neoconservatives, such as Richard Perle, Dick Cheney, Paul Wolfowitz, Condoleezza Rice, and Donald Rumsfeld, who are behind the push to go to war against Iraq, a cause from which I very much doubt that Bush can ever be deterred. Colin Powell is too cautious a figure, too interested in saving his career, too little a man of principle, to represent much of a threat to this group, which is supported by the editorial pages of the *Washington Post* and dozens of columnists and media pundits on CNN, CBS, and NBC, as well as the national weeklies, who repeat the same clichés about the need to spread American democracy and fight the good fight, no matter how many wars have to be fought all over the world.

There is no trace of this sort of thing in Europe that I can detect. Nor is there that lethal combination of money and power on a vast scale that can control elections and national policy at will. Remember that George W. Bush spent over $200 million to get himself elected two years ago, and even Mayor Michael Bloomberg of New York spent $60 million for his election: this scarcely seems like the democracy to which other nations might aspire, much less emulate. But it is accepted uncritically by what seems to be an enormous majority of Americans, who equate all this with freedom and democracy, despite its obvious drawbacks. More than any other country today, the United States is controlled at a distance from most citizens; the great corporations and lobbying groups do their will with "the people's" sovereignty, leaving little opportunity for real dissent or political change. Democrats and Republicans, for example, voted to give Bush a blank check for war with such enthusiasm and unquestioning loyalty as to make one doubt that there was any thought in the decision. The ideological position common to nearly everyone in the system is that America is best, its ideals perfect, its history spotless, its actions and society at the highest levels of human achievement and greatness. To argue with that—if that is at all possible—is to be "un-American" and guilty of the cardinal sin of anti-Americanism, which derives not from honest criticism but from hatred of the good and the pure.

No wonder then that America has never had an organized left or a real opposition party, as has been the case in every European country. The substance of American discourse is that it is divided into black and white, evil and good, ours and theirs. It is the task of a lifetime to make a change in that Manichean duality that seems to be set forever in an unchanging ideological dimension. And so it is for most Europeans, who see America as having been their savior and as now their protector, yet whose embrace is both encumbering and annoying at the same time. Tony Blair's whole-heartedly pro-American position therefore seems even more puzzling to an outsider like myself. I am comforted that even to his own people, he seems like a humorless aberration, a European who has decided in effect to obliterate his own identity in favor of this other one, represented by the lamentable Mr. Bush. I still have time to learn when Europe will come to its senses and assume the countervailing role to America that its size and history entitle it to play. Until then, the war approaches inexorably.

Al-Ahram, November 14–20, 2002
Al-Hayat, November 11, 2002

CHAPTER THIRTY-SEVEN

Misinformation About Iraq

The flurry of reports, leaks, and misinformation about the looming U.S. war against Saddam Hussein's dictatorship in Iraq continues with increasing density. It is impossible to know, however, how much of this is a brilliantly managed campaign of psychological war against Iraq, and how much the public floundering of a government uncertain about its next step. In any event, I find it equally possible to believe that there will be a war or, on the other hand, that there won't be one. Certainly the sheer belligerency of the verbal assaults on the average citizen are unprecedented in their ferocity, with the result that very little is totally certain about what is actually taking place. No one can independently confirm the various troop and navy movements reported on a daily basis, and given the lurching opacity of his thinking, George W. Bush's real intentions are difficult to read. But that the whole world is concerned—indeed, deeply anxious—about the catastrophic chaos that will ensue after another Afghanistan-like air campaign against the people of Iraq, of that there is little doubt.

And yet one aspect of the deluge of opinion and fact that is most disturbing quite on its own and without reference to its actual intention is the spate of articles concerning post-Saddam Iraq. One that I'd like to discuss in particular is obviously part of a continuing effort by an Iraqi expatriate, Kanan Makiya, to promote himself as the father of what he calls a "non-Arab" and decentralized post-Ba'ath country. Now it is quite clear to anyone with the slightest concern about the travails of this rich and once-flourishing country that the years of Ba'ath rule have been disastrous, despite the regime's early program of development and building. So there can be little quarrel with trying to imagine what Iraq might look like if Saddam is toppled either by American intervention or by internal coup. Makiya's contribution to this effort has been a steady one, both on the airwaves and in quality journals, where he is given a platform to air his views, about which I shall speak in a moment. What has been made less clear, however, is who he is and from what background he emerges. I think it is important to know these things, if only to judge the value of his contribution and to understand more precisely the special quality of his thoughts and ideas.

Usually identified as having a research connection with Harvard and as a professor at Brandeis University (both in the Boston area), Makiya when I knew him first in the early 1970s was closely affiliated with the Popular Democratic Front for the Liberation of Palestine. As I recall, he was then an architecture student at MIT, but he hardly said anything during the occasions I saw him. Then he disappeared from view, or rather from my view. He surfaced in 1990 as Samir Khalil, the author of a vaunted book called *The Republic of Fear* that described Saddam Hussein's rule with considerable dread and drama. One of the media-rousing works of the first Gulf War, *The Republic of Fear* seemed to have been written—according to a fawning interview with Makiya that appeared in *The New Yorker*—while Makiya took time off from working as an associate of his father's architectural firm in Iraq itself. He admitted in the interview that, in a sense, Saddam had financed the writing of his book indirectly, although no one accused Makiya of collaborating with a regime he obviously detested.

In his next book, *Cruelty and Silence,* Makiya attacked Arab intellectuals whom he accused of opportunism and immorality because they either praised various Arab regimes or remained silent about the various governments' abuses against their own people. Of course, Makiya said nothing about his own history of silence and complicity as a beneficiary of the Iraqi regime's munificence, even though, of course, he was entitled to work for whomever he pleased. But he said the vilest things about people like Mahmoud Darwish and myself for being nationalists, allegedly supporting extremism and, in Darwish's case, for having written an ode to Saddam. Most of what Makiya wrote in the book was, in my opinion, revolting, based on cowardly innuendo and false interpretation, but the book, of course, enjoyed a popular moment or two since it confirmed the view in the West that Arabs were villainous and shabby conformists. It seemed not to matter that Makiya himself had worked for Saddam or that he had never written anything about the Arab regimes until his

Republic of Fear, until, that is, he was out of Iraq and finished with his employment there. He was hailed here and there in America for being a brave man of conscience and for having defied the self-censoring practice of Arab intellectuals, but this praise was usually heaped on him by people who had no knowledge of the fact that Makiya himself never wrote in an Arab country and that whatever meager writing he produced had been written behind a pseudonym and a prosperous, risk-free life in the West.

Except for his two books and an article urging the U.S. administration to occupy Baghdad during the first Gulf War, Makiya wasn't much heard from after that. Then last year he produced an unreadable novel proving somehow that the Dome of the Rock was really built by a Jew; it was sent to me by the publisher, so I happened to have skimmed it before it appeared officially, but I was nevertheless aghast at how badly written it was, and how, unable to resist showing off how many books its author had read, it was peppered with footnotes, surely an unusual thing for what purported to be a work of fiction. It died a merciful death, however, and Makiya lapsed back into silence.

Until the government-inspired campaign against Iraq broke out a few months ago, Makiya had said little about the war against terror, the events of 9/11, and the war in Afghanistan. It is true that he did a kind of commentary for a popular American biweekly on Mohamed Atta's supposed Islamic terrorist handbook, but even by his standards, it was a negligible performance. I vividly recall, however, that late last summer I happened by chance to hear a radio interview with him in which he was identified for the first time as heading a U.S. State Department group planning for a postwar, post-Saddam Iraq. His name had not appeared among those mentioned as being part of the U.S.-funded Iraqi opposition groups; nor had he written anything that could be read by a member of the general public about the Palestinian-Israeli conflict or any other Middle Eastern issues, although I had heard that he had visited Israel a number of times.

The most complete version of his plans for Iraq after an American invasion, which derive from his current employment as a resident employee of the U.S. Department of State, appears in the November 2002 issue of *Prospect,* a good liberal British monthly to which I subscribe. Makiya begins his "proposal" by enumerating the extraordinary assumptions behind his arguments, two of which almost by definition are unimaginable. The first is that "the unseating" of Saddam should not occur after a bombing campaign. Makiya must have been living on Mars to imagine that, in the event of a war, a massive bombing attack would not occur, even though every single plan circulated for regime change in Iraq has stated explicitly that Iraq would be bombed mercilessly. The second assumption is equally imaginative, since Makiya seems to believe against all evidence that the United States is committed to democracy and nation-building in Iraq. Why he thinks that Iraq is like Germany and Japan after World War II (both of which were rebuilt because of the cold war) is beyond me; besides, he doesn't once mention the fact that the United States is determined to bring down the Iraqi regime because of the country's oil reserves and because Iraq is an enemy of Israel. So he starts out by making preposterous assumptions that simply fly in the face of all the evidence.

Undeterred by such unimportant considerations, he presses on. Iraqis are committed to federalism, he says, rather than to a centralized government. The proof that he offers is pretty negligible. As in all his other attempts to convince his reader that he makes telling points, his logic here is weak because it is based equally on fictional supposition and on his own highly dubious personal affirmations. He is committed to federalism, and so he says are the Kurds. Where federalism as a system is supposed to come from (other than from his desk in the State Department), he doesn't bother to say. Clearly, he plans to have it imposed from the outside, although he makes the largely unsubstantiated claim that "everyone" is agreed that federalism in Iraq should be the outcome. This "means devolving power away from Baghdad to the provinces," presumably by a stroke of General Tommy Franks's pen. One would have thought that post-Tito Yugoslavia never existed and that that tragic country's federalism was a total success. But Makiya is so committed to his views as a kinglike theoretician of government that he simply ignores consequences, history, people, communities, and reality altogether so that he can make his ludicrously improbable case. This of course is exactly what the U.S. government likes, that is, to have miscellaneous Arab intellectuals who are responsible to no constituency urge the U.S. military on to war while pretending to be bringing "democracy" to the place, in full contradiction of America's real aims and its actual historical practices. Makiya seems not to have heard about ruinous U.S. interventions in Indochina, Afghanistan, Central America, Somalia, Sudan, Lebanon, and the Philippines, or that the United States is currently involved militarily with about eighty countries.

The grand climax of Makiya's justification for the invasion of Iraq by the United States is his proposal that the new Iraq should be non-Arab. (Along the way, he speaks contemptuously of Arab opinion, which, he says, will never amount to anything. This obviously clears the board for his airy speculations about both the future and the past.) How this magical de-Arabizing solution is to come about, Makiya doesn't say, any more than he shows us how Iraq is to be relieved of its Islamic identity and its military capabilities. He refers to a mysterious alchemical quality he calls "territoriality" and proceeds to build another sand castle on that as the basis for a future state of Iraq. In the end, however, he volunteers that all this is going to be guaranteed "from the outside" by the United States. Where this has ever taken place before is not an issue that troubles Makiya, any more than he seems concerned about U.S. unilateralism and needless destructiveness.

One scarcely knows whether to laugh or cry at Makiya's posturings. Clearly this is a man with no recorded experience of government or even of citizenship. Between countries and cultures and with no visible commitment to anyone (except to his upwardly mobile career), he has now found a haven deep inside the U.S. government that he uses to fuel his amazingly speculative flights of fancy. For someone who has lectured his peers about intellectual responsibility and independent judgment, he provides examples of neither one nor the other. Exactly the opposite. Perched on a pulpit that has freed him from any accountability, he seems now to be serving a master who has paid him well for his services—as Saddam employed him in the past—and his versatile conscience. I find it incredible that Makiya allows himself such sanctimony and vanity, but then why shouldn't he? He has never engaged in a public debate with any of his fellow Iraqis, never written for an Arab audience, never put himself forward for an office or for any political role requiring personal courage and commitment. He has either written pseudonymously or attacked people who have had no chance to respond to his defamations.

It is sad that Makiya implicitly suggests that his is the voice and the example of the future Iraq. And to think that thousands of lives have already been lost to his patron's cruel sanctions, and that many more lives and livelihoods are about to be destroyed by electronic warfare wreaked on his country by George W. Bush's government. But this man is untroubled by any of this. Devoid of either compassion or real understanding, he prattles on for Anglo American audiences who seem satisfied that here at last is an Arab who exhibits the proper respect for their power and civilization, regardless of what role Britain played in the imperialist partition of the Arab world or what mischief the United States dealt the Arabs through its support for Israel and the collective Arab dictatorships.

In and of himself, Makiya is a passing phenomenon. He is, however, a symptom of several things at once. He represents the intellectual who serves power unquestioningly; the greater the power, the fewer doubts he has. He is a man of vanity who has no compassion, no demonstrable awareness of human suffering. With no stable principles or values, he is typical of the cynical anti-Arab hawks (like Richard Perle, Paul Wolfowitz, and Donald Rumsfeld) who dot the Bush administration like flies on a cake. British imperialism, Israel's brutal occupation policies, or American arrogance do not detain him for a moment. Worst of all, he is a man of pretension and superficiality, flattering himself on his reasonableness even as he condemns his own people to more travail and more dislocation. Woe to Iraq!

Al-Ahram, November 28–December 4, 2002
Al-Hayat, December 3, 2002

CHAPTER THIRTY-EIGHT

Immediate Imperatives

The daily hemorrhage of Palestinian lives and property accelerates without respite. Both the Arab and Western media report horrifically sensational suicide bombings, complete with pictures and names of the victims as well as gut-wrenching details. I do not hesitate now to say again that these efforts are morally repugnant and politically disastrous on all sorts of grounds. But what I find just as awful is the fact that Israel kills a far larger number of mostly unarmed Palestinian civilians—a ninety-year-old man here, a whole family there, a mentally disabled youth today, a nurse yesterday, and so on—and refuses to stop or in any way place restrictions on its troops who have visited mayhem on the Palestinians unremittingly for far too many recent months. Most of the time, however, these dreadful slaughters are reported on the back pages on newspapers and are never mentioned on TV. As for the continued practice of extralegal assassinations, Israel is allowed to get away with phrases from journalists who use words like "alleged" or "officials say" to cover their own irresponsibility as reporters. The *New York Times* in particular is now so clotted with such phrases in reporting on the Middle East (Iraq included) that it might as well be renamed *Officials Said*.

In other words, the fact that illegal Israeli practices continue to deliberately bleed the Palestinian civilian population is obscured, hidden from view, though it continues steadily all the time. Sixty-five percent unemployment, 50 percent poverty (people living on less than two dollars a day), schools, hospitals, universities, businesses under constant military pressure: these are only the outward manifestations of Israeli crimes against humanity. Over 40 percent of the Palestinian population is malnourished, and famine is now a genuine threat to the entire society. Nonstop curfews, the endless expropriation of land, the building of settlements (now numbering almost two hundred), and the destruction of crops, trees, houses have made life for ordinary Palestinians intolerable.

Many are leaving or, like the inhabitants of Yanun village, must leave because settlers' terror against them, the burning of their houses, and threats against their lives make it impossible to stay. Ethnic cleansing is what this is all about, although Sharon's demonic plan is to do it in tiny daily increments that won't properly be reported and that are never seen cumulatively as part of a general pattern. With the Bush administration backing his policies unconditionally, no wonder Sharon can afford to say "we are placing no restriction on our operations. Israel is under no pressure. No one is criticizing us or has the right to do so. We are talking here about Israel's right to protect its citizens" (Reuters, November 15, 2002). Why this kind of arrogance goes unanswered or isn't immediately associated with the kind of thing for which Slobodan Milosevic is now being tried in The Hague is a sign of how mendacious the international community has become. With U.S. cover, Sharon kills Palestinians at will under the guise of fighting terrorism.

Were this not bad enough, there is in addition the sorry state of Palestinian and Arab politics, many of its leaders and elites never more corrupt, rarely more injurious to their people than now. Neither collectively nor individually have these people put up any systematic strategy, much less even a systematic protest, against the United States' announced plans to redraw the map of the Middle East after the invasion of Iraq. All these regimes can do now seems to be either to market themselves as indispensable to the United States or to suppress any sign of dissent in their midst. Or both together. The unseemly bickering and disorderliness of the Iraqi opposition in London—under the watchful eye of the United States' Zalmay Khalilzad, an American University of Beirut graduate, once a neighbor of mine in New York, now a neoconservative protégé of Cheney and Wolfowitz—gives an excellent idea of where we are as a people. Representatives who represent only themselves, the condescending imperial patronage of a power that is about to destroy a country in order to grab its resources, the tyrannical, discredited local regimes (of which Saddam's is the worst) ruling by terror, the absence of any semblance of democracy within and without such regimes—these are not reassuring prospects for the future. What is especially, indeed glaringly, noticeable about the general situation is the powerlessness and silence of the overwhelming majority of the people, who suffer their humiliation within an envelope of overall indifference and repression. Everything in the Arab world is done either from above by basically unelected rulers or behind a curtain by undesignated albeit resourceful middlemen. Resources are bartered or sold without accountability; political futures are designed for the convenience of the powerful and their local subcontractors; human compassion and care for the citizens' well-being have few institutions to nurture them.

The Palestinian situation embodies all this with startling drama. As the culmination of its thirty-five-year-old military occupation, the Israeli army has spent the last nine months destroying the rudimentary infrastructure of civilian life on the West Bank and in Gaza: people there, in effect, live in cages, with electrical and concrete fences or Israeli troops to guard and interdict their free movement. Yasir Arafat and his men, who are at least as responsible for the current paralysis and devastation because of what they signed away in Oslo, and because they gave legitimacy to the Israeli occupation, seem to be hanging on anyway, even as extraordinary stories of their corruption and illegally acquired wealth dribble out all over the Israeli, Arab, and international media. It is deeply troubling that many of these men have recently been involved in secret negotiations with the European Union, with the CIA, with the Scandinavian countries on the basis of their former credibility as surrogates and servants of Arafat. In the meantime Mr. Palestine himself continues to issue orders and ludicrous denunciations, all of them either futile or years out of date; his recent attack on Usama bin Laden is one example, as is his retrospective acceptance of the Clinton plan of 2000. Still, he and his henchmen, like the sinister Mohammed Rashid (aka Khalid Salam), continue to employ large sums of money to bribe, to corrupt, and to prolong their rule past all decency. No one seems to be paying attention as the infamous Quartet (the United States, the UN, the European Union, and Russia) announces a peace conference and reform with one voice on one day, then withdraws the plan the next, while encouraging Israel in its repression on the third day.

What could be more preposterous than the call for Palestinian elections, which Mr. Arafat of all people, imprisoned in an Israeli vise, announces, retracts, postpones, and reannounces? Everyone speaks of reform except the very people whose future depends on it—the citizens of Palestine, who have endured and sacrificed so much even as their impoverishment and misery increase all the time. Isn't it ironic, not to say grotesque, that in the name of that long-suffering people, schemes of rule are being hatched everywhere, except by those people themselves? Surely the Swedes, the Spanish, the British, the Americans, and even the Israelis know perfectly well that the symbolic key to the future of the Middle East is Palestine, and that is why they do everything within their power to make sure that the Palestinian people are kept as far away from decisions about the future as possible. And this during a heated campaign for war against Iraq, for which numerous Americans, Europeans, and Israelis have openly stated that this is the time to redraw the map of the Middle East and bring in "democracy."

The time has come for the emperor who claims to be wearing new clothes, which he calls democracy, to be exposed for the charlatan he really is. Democracy cannot be imported or imposed: it is the prerogative of citizens who can make it and desire to live under it. Ever since the end of World War II, the Arab countries have been living in various states of "emergency," which has been a license for their rulers to do what they want in the name of security. Even the Palestinians under Oslo had a regime imposed on them that existed first of all to serve Israel's security and second to serve (and help) itself.

For all sorts of reasons, among them that the cause of Palestine (like the liberation of apartheid South Africa) has always served as a model for Arabs and fair-minded idealistic people everywhere, it is today imperative that Palestinians take steps to restore the fashioning of their destiny to their own hands. The political stage in Palestine is now divided between two unattractive and unviable alternatives. On the one side, there is what's left of the Palestinian Authority and Arafat. On the other, the Islamic parties. Neither one nor the other can possibly secure a decent future for the citizens of Palestine. The Authority is so discredited, its failure to build institutions so basic, and its corrupt and cynical history so compromised in every way that it is incapable of being entrusted with the future. Only rogues will pretend otherwise, as some of its security chiefs and prominent negotiators are now pretending. As for the Islamic parties, they lead desperate individuals into a negative space of endless religious strife and antimodern decline. If we speak of Zionism as having failed politically and socially, how can it be acceptable to turn passively to another religion and look there for worldly salvation? Impossible. Human beings make their own history, not gods or magic or miracles. Purifying the land of "aliens," whether it is spoken of by Muslims, Christians, or Jews, is a defilement of human life as it is lived by billions of people who are mixed by race, history, ethnic identity, religion, or nationality.

But a large majority of Palestinians and, I think, Israelis know these things. And fortunately a political alternative already exists that is neither Hamas nor Arafat's Authority. I am speaking here of an impressive formation of Palestinians in the Occupied Territories who in June of this year announced a new Palestinian National Initiative (al-moubadara al-wataniya, al-filastiniya). Among its leaders are Dr. Mustafa Barghuti and Dr. Haidar Abdel Shafi, Rawia al-Shawa, and many more independents who understand that in its weakened state Palestinian society is being targeted for "reform" by parties whose real interest is to liquidate Palestine as a political and moral force for years to come. Idle talk of elections by Arafat and his lieutenants is meant to reassure outsiders that democracy is on the way. Far from it, since these people simply want to continue their corrupt and bankrupt ways by any means possible, including outright fraud. The 1996 elections, it should be remembered, were conducted on the basis of the Oslo process, whose main aim was to continue Israeli occupation under a different title. The Legislative Council (al-majlis al-tashriei) was in reality powerless before both Arafat's edict and the Israeli veto. What Sharon and the Quartet now propose is an extension of the same unacceptable regime. This is why the National Initiative has become the inevitable choice for Palestinians everywhere. In the first place, unlike the Authority, it proposes liberation from, rather than cooperation with, the Israeli occupation. Second, it is representative of a broad base in civil society and therefore includes no military or security people and no hangers-on of Arafat's court. Third, it argues for liberation and not a readjustment of the occupation to suit elites and VIPs.

Most important, the Initiative—which I am happy to endorse enthusiastically—puts forward the idea of a national unified authority, elected to serve the people and its need for liberation, for democratic freedoms, and for public debate and accountability. These things have been put off for far too long. The old divisions between Fateh, the Popular Front, Hamas, and all the others are meaningless today. We cannot afford such ridiculous posturing since as a people under occupation, we need a leadership whose main goal is to rid us of Israeli depredations and occupations and to provide us with an order that can fulfill our needs for honesty, national scope, transparency, and direct speech. Arafat has a history of double-talk. Barghuti, on the other hand—I use him as an example here—takes a principled line, whether he addresses Palestinians, Israelis, or the foreign media. He has the respect of his people because of his medical services in the villages, and his honesty and leadership have inspired everyone who has had contact with him. I also think it is very important that the Palestinian people should be led now by modern, well-educated people for whom the values of citizenship are central to their vision. Our rulers today have never been citizens, they have never stood in line to buy bread, they have never paid their own medical or school bills, they have never endured the uncertainty and cruelty of arbitrary arrest, tribal bullying, conspiratorial power grabs. Barghuti's and Abdel Shafi's examples, as indeed those of all the main figures in the Initiative, speak to our need for independence of mind and responsible, modern citizenship. The old days are over and should be buried as expeditiously as possible.

I conclude by saying that real change can come about only when people actively *will* that change, make it possible themselves. The Iraqi opposition is making a terrible mistake by throwing its fate into American hands and in so doing is paying insufficient attention to the needs of the actual people of Iraq, who now suffer the terrible persecutions of autocracy and are about to submit to an equally terrible bombing by the United States. In Palestine it should be possible to have elections now, not to reinstall Arafat's ragged crew, but rather to choose delegates for a constitutional and truly representative assembly. It is a lamentable reality that during his ten years of misrule Arafat actively prevented the creation of a constitution, despite all his ridiculous jibberish about "Palestinian democracy." His legacy is neither a constitution nor even a basic law, but only a decrepit mafia. Despite that, and despite Sharon's frantic wish to bring an end to Palestinian national life, our popular and civil institutions still function under extreme hardship and duress. Somehow teachers teach, nurses nurse, doctors doctor, and so on. These everyday activities have never stopped, if only because necessity dictates unstinting effort. Now those institutions and those people who have truly served their society must bring themselves forward and provide a moral and intellectual framework for liberation and democracy, by peaceful means and with genuine national intent. In this effort, Palestinians under occupation and those in the *shatat* or diaspora have an equal obligation to make the effort. Perhaps this national initiative may provide a democratic example for other Arabs as well.

Al-Ahram, December 19–25, 2002
Al-Hayat, December 31, 2002

CHAPTER THIRTY-NINE

An Unacceptable Helplessness

One opens the *New York Times* on a daily basis to read the most recent article about the preparations for war that are taking place in the United States. Another battalion, one more set of aircraft carriers and cruisers, an ever-increasing number of aircraft, new contingents of officers are being moved to the Persian Gulf area. Sixty-two thousand more soldiers were transferred to the Gulf last weekend. An enormous, deliberately intimidating force is being built up by America overseas, while inside the country economic and social bad news multiplies with a joint relentlessness. The huge capitalist machine seems to be faltering, even as it grinds down the vast majority of citizens. Nonetheless, George Bush proposes another large tax cut for the 1 percent of the population that is comparatively rich. The public education system is in a major crisis, and health insurance for 50 million Americans simply does not exist. Israel asks for $15 billion in additional loan guarantees and military aid. And the unemployment rates in the United States mount inexorably, as more jobs are lost every day.

Nevertheless, preparations for an unimaginably costly war continue and continue without either public approval or dramatically noticeable disapproval. A generalized indifference (which may conceal great overall fear, ignorance, and apprehension) has greeted the administration's war-mongering and its strangely ineffective response to the challenge forced on it recently by North Korea. In the case of Iraq, with no weapons of mass destruction to speak of, the United States plans a war; in the case of North Korea, it offers that country economic and energy aid. What a humiliating difference between contempt for the Arabs and respect for the North Koreans, an equally grim and cruel dictatorship.

In the Arab and Muslim worlds, the situation appears more peculiar. For almost a year American politicians, regional experts, administration officials, and journalists have repeated the charges that have become standard fare so far as Islam and the Arabs are concerned. Most of this chorus predates September 11, as I have shown in my books *Orientalism* and *Covering Islam*. To today's practically unanimous chorus has been added the authority of the United Nations Human Development Report on the Arab world, which certified that Arabs dramatically lag behind the rest of the world in democracy, knowledge, and women's rights. Everyone says (with some justification, of course) that Islam needs reform and that the Arab educational system is a disaster, in effect, a school for religious fanatics and suicide bombers funded not just by crazy imams and their wealthy followers (like Usama bin Laden) but also by governments who are supposed allies of the United States. The only "good" Arabs are those who appear in the media decrying modern Arab culture and society without reservation. I recall the lifeless cadences of their sentences for, with nothing positive to say about themselves or their people and language, they simply regurgitate the tired American formulas already flooding the airwaves and pages of print. We lack democracy, they say, we haven't challenged Islam enough, we need to do more about driving away the specter of Arab nationalism and the credo of Arab unity. That is all discredited, ideological rubbish. Only what we, and our American instructors, say about the Arabs and Islam—vague recycled Orientalist clichés of the kind repeated by a tireless mediocrity like Bernard Lewis—is true. The rest isn't realistic or pragmatic enough. "We" need to join modernity, modernity in effect being Western, globalized, free-marketed, and democratic—whatever those words might be taken to mean. (If I had the time, there would be an essay written about the prose style of people like Fouad Ajami, Fawaz Gerges, Kanan Makiya, Ghada Talhami, Mamom Fandy, et al., academics whose very language reeks of subservience, inauthenticity, and a hopelessly stilted mimicry that has been thrust upon them.)

The clash of civilizations that George W. Bush and his minions are trying to fabricate as a cover for a preemptive oil and hegemony war against Iraq is supposed to result in a triumph of democratic nation-building, regime change, and forcible modernization à l'américain. Never mind the bombs and the ravages of the sanctions, which are unmentioned. This will be a purifying war whose goal is to throw out Saddam and his men and replace them with a redrawn map of the whole region. New Sykes-Picot. New Balfour. New Wilsonian Fourteen Points. New world altogether. Iraqis, we are told by the Iraqi dissidents, will welcome their liberation and perhaps forget entirely about their past sufferings. Perhaps.

Meanwhile, the soul- and body-destroying situation in Palestine worsens all the time. There seems no force capable of stopping Sharon and Shaul Mofaz, who bellow their defiance to the whole world. We forbid, we punish, we ban, we break, we destroy. The torrent of unbroken violence against an entire people continues. As I write these lines, I am sent an announcement that the entire village of Al-Daba' in the Qalqilya area of the West Bank is about to be wiped out by sixty-ton American-made Israeli bulldozers: 250 Palestinians will lose their 42 houses, 700 dunams of agricultural land, a mosque, and an elementary school for 132 children. The United Nations stands by, looking on as its resolutions are flouted on an hourly basis. Typically, alas, George W. Bush identifies with Sharon, not with the sixteen-year-old Palestinian kid who is used as a human shield by Israeli soldiers.

Meanwhile, the Palestinian Authority offers a return to peacemaking and, presumably, to Oslo. Having been burned for ten years the first time, Arafat seems inexplicably to want to have another go at it. His faithful lieutenants make declarations and write opinion pieces for the press, suggesting their willingness to accept anything, more or less. Remarkably, though, the great mass of these heroic people seem willing to go on, without peace and without respite, bleeding, going hungry, dying day by day. They have too much dignity and confidence in the justice of their cause to submit shamefully to Israel, as their leaders have done. What could be more discouraging for the average Gazan who goes on resisting Israeli occupation than to see his or her leaders kneel as supplicants before the Americans?

In this entire panorama of desolation, what catches the eye is the utter passivity and helplessness of the Arab world as a whole. The American government and its servants issue statement after statement of purpose, they move troops and material, they transport tanks and destroyers, but the Arabs individually and collectively can barely muster a bland refusal (at most they say, no, you cannot use military bases in our territory), only to reverse themselves a few days later.

Why is there such silence and such astounding helplessness?

The largest power in history is about to launch, and is unremittingly reiterating its intention to launch, a war against a sovereign Arab country now ruled by a dreadful regime, a war the clear purpose of which is not only to destroy the Ba'ath regime but to redesign the entire region. The Pentagon has made no secret that its plans are to redraw the map of the whole Arab world, perhaps changing other regimes and many borders in the process. No one can be shielded from the cataclysm when it comes (if it comes, which is not yet a complete certainty). And yet there is only long silence, followed by a few vague bleats of polite demurral, in response. After all, millions of people will be affected. America contemptuously plans for their future without consulting them. Do we deserve such racist derision?

This is not only unacceptable: it is impossible to believe. How can a region of almost 300 million Arabs wait passively for the blows to fall without issuing a collective roar of resistance and a loud proclamation of an alternative view? Has the Arab will been completely dissolved? Even a prisoner about to be executed usually has some last words to pronounce. Why is there now no last testimonial to an era of history, to a civilization about to be crushed and transformed utterly, to a society that despite its drawbacks and weaknesses nevertheless goes on functioning. Arab babies are born every hour, children go to school, men and women marry and work and have children, they play and laugh and eat, they are sad, they suffer illness and death. There is love and companionship, friendship and excitement. Yes, Arabs are repressed and misruled, terribly misruled, but they manage to go on with the business of living despite everything. This is the fact that both the Arab leaders and the United States simply ignore when they fling empty gestures at the so-called "Arab street" invented by mediocre Orientalists.

But who is now asking the existential questions about our future as a people? The task cannot be left to a cacophony of religious fanatics and submissive, fatalistic sheep. But that seems to be the case. The Arab governments—no, most of the Arab countries from top to bottom—sit back in their seats and just wait as America postures, lines up, threatens, and ships out more soldiers and F-16s to deliver the punch. The silence is deafening.

Years of sacrifice and struggle, of bones broken in hundreds of prisons and torture chambers from the Atlantic to the Gulf, families destroyed, endless poverty and suffering. Huge, expensive armies. For what?

This is not a matter of party or ideology or faction: it's a matter of what the great theologian Paul Tillich used to call ultimate seriousness. Technology, modernization, and certainly globalization are not the answer for what threatens us as a people now. We have in our tradition an entire body of secular and religious discourse that treats of beginnings and endings, of life and death, of love and anger, of society and history. This is there, but no voice, no individual with great vision and moral authority, seems able now to tap into that and bring it to attention. We are on the eve of a catastrophe that our political, moral, and religious leaders can only just denounce a little bit while, behind whispers and winks and closed doors, they make plans somehow to ride out the storm. They think of survival and perhaps of heaven. But who is in charge of the present, the worldly, the land, the water, the air, and the lives dependent on one another for existence? No one seems to be in charge. There is a wonderful colloquial expression in English that very precisely and ironically catches our unacceptable helplessness, our passivity and inability to help ourselves, now when our strength is most needed. The expression is: will the last person to leave please turn out the lights? We are that close to a kind of upheaval that will leave very little standing and perilously little left even to record, except for the last injunction that begs for extinction.

Hasn't the time come for us collectively to demand and try to formulate a genuinely Arab alternative to the wreckage about to engulf our world? This is not only a trivial matter of regime change, although God knows that we can do with quite a bit of that. Surely it can't be a return to Oslo, another offer to Israel to please accept our existence and let us live in peace, another cringing, crawling, inaudible plea for mercy? Will no one come out into the light of day to express a vision for our future that isn't based on a script written by Donald Rumsfeld and Paul Wolfowitz, those two symbols of vacant power and overweening arrogance? I hope someone is listening.

Al-Ahram, January 16–22, 2003
Al-Hayat, January 23, 2003
The Guardian, January 25, 2003

CHAPTER FORTY

A Monument to Hypocrisy

It has finally become intolerable to listen to or look at news in this country. I've told myself over and over again that one ought to leaf through the daily papers and turn on the TV for the national news every evening, just to find out what "the country" is thinking and planning, but patience and masochism have their limits. Colin Powell's UN speech, designed obviously to outrage the American people and bludgeon the United Nations into going to war, seems to me a new low point in moral hypocrisy and political manipulation. But Donald Rumsfeld's lectures in Munich this past weekend went the bumbling Powell one further, in unctuous sermonizing and bullying derision. For the moment I shall discount George W. Bush and his coterie of advisers, spiritual mentors, and political managers, like Pat Robertson, Franklin Graham, and Karl Rove: they seem to me slaves of power perfectly embodied in the repetitive monotone of their collective spokesman, Ari Fleischer. Bush is, he has said, in direct contact with God or, if not God, then at least Providence. Perhaps only Israeli settlers can converse with him. But the secretaries of state and defense seem to have emanated from the secular world of real women and men, so it may be somewhat more opportune to linger for a time over their words and activities.

First, a few preliminaries. The United States has clearly decided on war: there seem to be no two ways about it. Yet whether the war will actually take place (given all the activity started, not by the Arab states—which as usual seem to dither and be paralyzed at the same time—but by France, Russia, and Germany) is something else again. Nevertheless, to have transported 200,000 troops to Kuwait, Saudi Arabia, and Qatar, leaving aside smaller deployments in Jordan, Turkey, and Israel, can mean only one thing.

Second, the planners of this war, as Ralph Nader has forcefully said, are chicken hawks—that is, hawks who are too cowardly to do any fighting themselves. Wolfowitz, Perle, Bush, Cheney, and others of that entirely civilian group were to a man in strong favor of the Vietnam War, yet each of them got a deferment based on privilege and therefore never fought or so much as even served in the armed forces. Their belligerence is therefore morally repugnant and, in the literal sense, antidemocratic in the extreme. What this unrepresentative cabal seeks in a war with Iraq has nothing to do with actual military considerations. Iraq, whatever the disgusting qualities of its deplorable regime, is simply not an imminent and credible threat to its neighbors like Turkey, or Israel, or even Jordan (each of which could easily handle it militarily), or certainly to the United States. Any argument to the contrary is simply a preposterous, entirely frivolous proposition. With a few outdated Scuds and a small amount of chemical and biological material, most of it supplied by the United States in earlier days (as Nader has said, we know that because we have the receipts for what was sold to Iraq by U.S. companies), Iraq is, and has easily been, containable, though at unconscionable immoral cost to the long-suffering civilian population. For this terrible state of affairs, I think it is absolutely true to say that there has been collusion between the Iraqi regime and the Western enforcers of the sanctions.

Third, once big powers start to dream of regime change—a process already begun by the Perles and Wolfowitzes of this country—there is simply no end in sight. Isn't it outrageous that people of such a dubious caliber actually go on blathering about bringing democracy, moderniza-tion, and liberalization to the Middle East? God knows that the area needs it, as so many Arab and Muslim intellectuals and ordinary people have said over and over. But who appointed these characters as agents of progress anyway? And what entitles them to pontificate in so shame-less a way when there are already so many injustices and abuses in their own country to be remedied? It's particularly galling that Perle, about as unqualified a person as it is imaginable to be on any subject touching on democracy and justice, should have been an election adviser to Benjamin Netanyahu's extreme right-wing government during the period 1996–99, in which he counseled the renegade Israeli to scrap any and all peace attempts, to annex the West Bank and Gaza, and to try to get rid of as many Palestinians as possible. This man now talks about bringing democ-racy to the Middle East and does so without provoking the slightest objection from any of the media pundits who politely (abjectly) quiz him on national television.

Fourth, Colin Powell's speech, despite its many weaknesses, its plagiarized and manufactured evidence, its confected audiotapes, and its doctored pictures, was correct in one thing. Saddam Hussein's regime has violated numerous human rights and UN resolutions. There can be no arguing with that and no excuses can be allowed. But what is so monumentally hypocritical about the official U.S. position is that literally everything Powell has accused the Ba'athis of doing has been the stock in trade of every Israeli government since 1948, and at no time more flagrantly than since the occupation of 1967. Torture, illegal detention, assassination, assaults against civilians with missiles, helicopters, and jet fighters, annexation of territory, transportation of civilians from one place to another for the purpose of imprisonment, mass killing (as in Qana, Jenin, Sabra, and Shatila to mention only the most obvious), denial of rights to free passage and unimpeded civilian movement, education, medical aid, use of civilians for human shields, humiliation, punishment of families, house demolitions on a mass scale, destruction of agricultural land, expropriation of water, illegal settlement, economic pauperization, attacks on hospitals, medical workers, and ambulances, killing of UN personnel, to name only the most outrageous abuses: all these, it should be noted with emphasis, have been carried on with the total, unconditional support of the United States, which has not only supplied Israel with the weapons for such practices and every kind of military and intelligence aid but has also given the country upward of $135 billion in economic aid on a scale that beggars the relative amount per capita spent by the U.S. government on its own citizens.

This is an unconscionable record to hold against the United States and Mr. Powell as its human symbol in particular. As the person in charge of U.S. foreign policy, it is his specific responsibility to uphold the laws of this country and to make sure that the enforcement of human rights and the promotion of freedom—the proclaimed central plank in American foreign policy since at least 1976—is applied uniformly, without exception or condition. How he and his bosses and coworkers can stand up before the world and righteously sermonize against Iraq while at the same time completely ignoring the ongoing American partnership in human

rights abuses with Israel defies credibility. And yet no one, in all the justified critiques of the U.S. position that have appeared since Powell made
his great UN speech, has focused on this point, not even the ever-so-
upright French and Germans. The Palestinian territories today are witnessing the onset of a mass famine; there is a health crisis of catastrophic
proportions; there is a civilian death toll that totals at least a dozen to
twenty people a week; the economy has collapsed; hundreds of thousands
of innocent civilians are unable to work, study, or move about as curfews
and at least three hundred barricades impede their daily lives; and houses
are blown up or bulldozed on a mass basis (sixty just yesterday). And all
of it with U.S. equipment, U.S. political support, U.S. finances. Bush
declares that Sharon, who is a war criminal by any standard, is a man of
peace, as if to spit on the innocent Palestinian lives that have been lost
and ravaged by Sharon and his criminal army. And he has the gall to say
that he acts in God's name, and that he (and his administration) act to
serve "a just and faithful God." And more astounding yet, he lectures the
world on Saddam's flouting of UN resolutions even as he supports a
country, Israel, that has flouted at least sixty-four of them on a daily basis
for more than half a century.

But so craven and so ineffective are the Arab regimes today that they
don't dare state any of these things publicly. Many of them need U.S. economic aid. Many of them fear their own people and need U.S. support to
prop up their regimes. Many of them could be accused of some of the
same crimes against humanity. So they say nothing and just hope and
pray that the war will pass, allowing them to stay in power as they are.

But it is also a great and noble fact that for the first time since World
War II, there are mass protests against the war taking place *before* rather
than during the war itself. This is unprecedented and should become the
central political fact of the new globalized era into which our world has
been thrust by the United States and its superpower status. What this
demonstrates is that despite the awesome power wielded by autocrats
and tyrants like Saddam and his American antagonists, despite the complicity of a mass media that has (willingly or unwillingly) hastened the
rush to war, and despite the indifference and ignorance of a great many
people, mass action and mass protest on the basis of human community
and sustainability are still formidable tools of human resistance. Call

them weapons of the weak, if you wish. But that they have at least tampered with the plans of the Washington chicken hawks and their corporate backers, as well as the millions of religious monotheistic extremists (Christian, Jewish, Muslim) who believe in wars of religion, is a great beacon of hope for our time. Wherever I go to lecture or speak out against these injustices, I haven't found anyone in support of the war. Our job as Arabs is to link our opposition to U.S. action in Iraq to our support for human rights in Iraq, Palestine, Israel, Kurdistan, and everywhere in the Arab world—and also to ask others to force the same linkage on everyone, Arab, American, African, European, Australian, and Asian. These are world issues, human issues, not simply strategic matters for the United States or the other major powers.

We cannot in any way lend our silence to a policy of war that the White House has openly announced will include 300 to 500 Cruise missiles a day (800 of them during the first forty-eight hours of the war) raining down on the civilian population of Baghdad in order to produce "shock and awe," or even a human cataclysm that will produce, as its boastful planner a certain Mr. (or is it Dr.?) Harlan Ullman has said, a Hiroshima-style effect on the Iraqi people. Note that during the 1991 Gulf War, after forty-one days of bombing Iraq, this scale of human devastation was not even approached. And the United States has six thousand "smart" missiles ready to do the job. What sort of God would want this to be a formulated and announced policy for His people? And what sort of God would claim that this was going to bring democracy and freedom to the people not only of Iraq but to the rest of the Middle East?

These are questions I won't even try to answer. But I do know that if anything like this is going to be visited on any population on earth, it will be a criminal act, and its perpetrators and planners war criminals according to the Nuremberg laws that the United States itself was crucial in formulating. Not for nothing do General Sharon and Shaul Mofaz welcome the war and praise George W. Bush. Who knows what more evil will be done in the name of Good? Every one of us must raise our voices, and march in protest, now and again and again. We need creative thinking and bold action to stave off the nightmares planned by a docile, professionalized staff in places like Washington and Tel Aviv and Baghdad. For if what they have in mind is what they call "greater security," then words have no meaning at all in the ordinary sense. That Bush and Sharon have contempt for the nonwhite people of this world is clear. The question is, how long can they keep getting away with it?

Al-Ahram, February 13–19, 2003
Al-Hayat, February 25, 2003

CHAPTER FORTY-ONE

Who Is in Charge?

The Bush administration's relentless unilateral march toward war is profoundly disturbing for many reasons, but so far as American citizens are concerned, the whole grotesque show is a tremendous failure in democracy. An immensely wealthy and powerful republic has been hijacked by a small cabal of individuals, all of them unelected and therefore unresponsive to public pressure, and simply turned on its head. It is no exaggeration to say that this war is the most unpopular on a world scale of any war in modern history. Before the war has even begun, more people have protested it in this country alone than did so at the height of the anti–Vietnam War demonstrations during the 1960s and 1970s. Note also that those rallies took place well after the war had been going on for several years: this one has yet to begin, even though of course a large number of overtly aggressive and belligerent steps have already been taken by the United States and its loyal puppy, the UK government of the increasingly ridiculous Tony Blair.

I have been criticized recently for my antiwar position by illiterates who claim that what I say is an implied defense of Saddam Hussein and his appalling regime. To my Kuwaiti critics, do I need to remind them that I publicly opposed Ba'ath Iraq during the only visit I made to Kuwait, in 1985, when in an open conversation with the then minister of education Hassan el-Ibrahim I accused him and his regime of aiding and abetting Arab fascism in their financial support of Saddam Hussein? I was told then that Kuwait was proud to have committed literally billions of dollars to Saddam's war against "the Persians," as they were then contemptuously called, and that it was a more important struggle than someone like me could comprehend. I remember clearly warning those Kuwaiti acolytes of Saddam Hussein about him and his ill will against Kuwait, but all to no avail. I have been a public opponent of the Iraqi regime since it came to power in the 1970s: I never visited the place, never was fooled by its claims to secularism and modernization (even when many of my contemporaries either worked for or celebrated Iraq as the main gun in the Arab arsenal against Zionism, a stupid idea, I thought), never concealed my contempt for its methods of rule and its dreadful fascist behavior. And now when I speak my mind about the ridiculous posturing of certain members of the Iraqi opposition as hapless strutting tools of U.S. imperialism, I am told that I know nothing about life without democracy (about which more later) and am therefore unable to appreciate their nobility of soul! Little notice is taken of the fact that barely a week after extolling President Bush's commitment to democracy, Kanan Makiya is now denouncing the United States and its plans for a post-Saddam military-Ba'ath government in Iraq. When individuals get in the habit of switching gods whom they worship politically, there's no end to the number of changes they make before they finally come to rest in utter disgrace and well-deserved oblivion.

But to return to the United States and its current actions, in all my encounters and travels, I have yet to meet a person who is for the war. Even worse, most Americans now feel that this mobilization has already gone too far to stop, and that we are on the verge of a disaster for the country. Consider first of all that, such as it is, the Democratic Party with few exceptions has simply gone over to the president's side, in a gutless display of false patriotism. Wherever one looks in the Congress, there are tell-tale signs of either the Zionist lobby, the right-wing Christians, or the military-industrial complex, three inordinately influential minority groups who share an interest in their hostility to the Arab world, their unbridled support for extremist Zionism, and an insensate conviction that they are on the side of the angels. Every one of the 435 congressional districts in this country has a defense industry in it, so that war has been turned into a matter of jobs, not of security. But one might well ask, how does running an unbelievably expensive war provide a remedy, for instance, for economic recession, the almost-certain bankruptcy of the Social Security system, a mounting national debt, and a massive failure in the public education system of this country? None whatsoever, of course, but still the party of war goes its own, unimpeded way. Demonstrations are looked at simply as a kind of degraded mob action, while the most hypocritical lies pass for absolute truth, without criticism and without objection.

The media has simply become a branch of the war effort. What has entirely disappeared from television is anything remotely resembling a consistently dissenting voice. Every major channel now employs retired generals, former CIA agents, terrorism experts, and known neoconservatives as "consultants" who speak a revolting jargon that is designed to sound authoritative but in effect supports everything done by the United States, from the UN to the sands of Arabia. Only one major daily newspaper (in Baltimore) has published anything about U.S. eavesdropping, telephone tapping, and message intercepting of the six small countries who are members of the Security Council and whose votes are undecided about a war resolution. There are no antiwar voices to read or hear in any of the major medias of this country, no Arabs or Muslims (who have been consigned en masse to the ranks of the fanatics and terrorists of this world), no critics of Israel, not on public broadcasting, not in the *New York Times, The New Yorker, U.S. News & World Report,* CNN, and the rest. When all these organizations mention Iraq's flouting of seventeen UN resolutions as a pretext for war, the sixty-four resolutions flouted by Israel (with U.S. support) are never mentioned, any more than the enormous human suffering of the Iraqi people during the past twelve years is mentioned. Whatever the dreaded Saddam has done, Israel and Sharon have also done with American support, yet no one says anything about the latter while fulminating about the former. This makes a total mockery of taunts by Bush and others that the UN should abide by its own resolutions.

The American people have thus been deliberately lied to, their interests cynically misrepresented and misreported, the real aims and intentions of this private war of Bush the son and his junta concealed with complete arrogance. Never mind that Wolfowitz, Feith, and Perle, all of them unelected officials who work for unelected Donald Rumsfeld at the Pentagon, for instance, have for some time openly advocated Israeli annexation of the West Bank and Gaza and the cessation of the Oslo process and have called for war against Iraq (and later Iran) and the building of more illegal Israeli settlements in their capacity (during Netanyahu's successful campaign for prime minister in 1996) as private consultants to him, and that that has become U.S. policy now.

Never mind that Israel's iniquitous policies against Palestinians, which are reported only at the ends of articles (when they are reported at all) as so many miscellaneous civilian deaths, are never compared with Saddam's crimes, which they match or in some cases exceed, all of them in the final analysis paid for by the U.S. taxpayer without consultation or approval. Over 40,000 Palestinians have been wounded seriously in the last two years, and about 2,500 killed wantonly by Israeli soldiers who are instructed to humiliate and punish an entire people during what has become the longest military occupation in modern history.

Never mind that not a single critical Arab or Muslim voice has been seen or heard on the major American media—liberal, moderate, or reactionary—with any regularity at all since the preparations for war have gone into their final phase. Consider also that none of the major planners of this war—certainly not the so-called experts, such as Bernard Lewis and Fouad Ajami, neither of whom has so much as lived in or come near the Arab world in decades; nor the military and political people such as Powell, Rice, Cheney, and the great god Bush himself, who know next to nothing about the Muslim or Arab world directly except through Israeli or oil company or military lenses—have any idea what a war of this magnitude against Iraq can produce by way of awful consequences for the people actually living there.

And consider, too, that the sheer unadorned hubris of men like Wolfowitz and his assistants, who are asked to testify to the largely somnolent Congress about the war's consequences and costs, has allowed them to get away without so much as the slightest concrete answer—thereby overruling or derisively dismissing the evidence of the army chief of staff, who has spoken of a military occupation force of 400,000 troops for ten years at a cost of almost $1 trillion—to such questions, thus further misleading a public that never asked for their presence in the first place.

Democracy traduced and betrayed, democracy celebrated but in fact humiliated and trampled on by a tiny group of men who have simply taken charge of this republic as if it were nothing more than, what, an Arab country? It is right to ask who is in charge, since clearly the people of the United States are not properly represented by the war this administration is about to unleash on a world already beleaguered by too much misery and poverty to endure any more. And Americans have been badly served by a media controlled essentially by a tiny group of men who edit out anything that might cause the government the slightest concern or worry. As for the demagogues and servile intellectuals who talk about war as from the privacy of their fantasy worlds, who has given them the right to connive in the immiseration of millions of people whose major crime seems to be that they are Muslims and Arabs? Which American except for this small unrepresentative group is seriously interested in increasing the world's already ample anti-Americanism? Hardly any, I would suppose.

Jonathan Swift, thou shouldst be living at this hour.

Al-Ahram, March 6–12, 2003
Al-Hayat, March 10, 2003

CHAPTER FORTY-TWO

A Stupid War

Full of contradictions, flat-out lies, groundless affirmations, the clotted media torrent of reporting and commentary on the war against Iraq (which is still being waged by something called "the coalition," whereas it is an American war with some British help) has obscured what has been so criminally stupid about its planning, propaganda, and justifying discourse by military and policy experts. For the past two weeks, I have been traveling in Egypt and Lebanon trying to keep up with the unending stream of information and misinformation coming out of Iraq, Kuwait, Qatar, and Jordan, a lot of it misleadingly upbeat but some of it horrifyingly dramatic in its import as well of course as its immediacy. The Arab satellite channels, Al-Jazeera being by now the most notorious and efficient, have given on the whole a totally opposed view of the war than the standard stuff served up by "embedded" reporters—including speculations about Iraqis being killed for not fighting, mass uprisings in Basra, four or five "falls" of Um Kasr and Fao—who have supplied grimy pictures of themselves as lost as the English-speaking soldiers they have been living with. Al-Jazeera has had reporters inside Mosul, Baghdad, Basra, and Nasiriya—one of them, the impressible Taysir Aloni, a fluent journalistic veteran of the Afghanistan war—and they have presented a much more detailed, on-the-spot account of the shattering realities of the heavy bombardment that has devastated Baghdad and Basra, as well as the extraordinary resistance and anger of the Iraqi population, which was supposedly to have been only a sullen bunch of people waiting to be liberated and throw flowers at Clint Eastwood look-alikes.

Let's get straight to what is so unwise and substandard about this war, leaving aside for the moment its illegality and vast unpopularity, to say nothing about the way American wars of the past half century have been lumbering, humanly unacceptable, and so utterly destructive. In the first place, no one has satisfactorily proved that Iraq possesses the weapons of mass destruction that furnish an imminent threat to the United States.

No one. Iraq is a hugely weakened and subpar Third World state ruled by a hated despotic regime: there is no disagreement about that anywhere, least of all in the Arab and Islamic world. But that it is any kind of threat to anyone in its current state of siege is a laughable notion, one that no journalist of the overpaid legions who swarm around the Pentagon, State Department, and White House has ever bothered to pursue.

In theory Iraq might have been a challenge to Israel sometime in the future, since it is the only Arab country that has the human, natural, and infrastructural resources to take on not so much America's but rather Israel's arrogant brutality. This is why Menachem Begin's air force bombed Iraq preemptively in 1981. Note therefore the creeping replication of Israeli assumptions and tactics (all of them, as I shall be showing, remarkably flawed) in what the United States has been planning and implementing in its current post–9/11 campaign or preemptive war. How regrettable that the media have been so timorous in not investigating the Likud's slow taking-over of U.S. military and political thinking about the Arab world. So fearful has everyone been of the charge of anti-Semitism—bandied about recklessly, even by Harvard's president—that the neoconservative–cum–Christian right–cum–Pentagon civilian hawks' stranglehold on American policy has become a sort of reality forcing on the entire country an attitude of total belligerency and free-floating hostility. One would have thought that but for America's global dominance, we were headed for another Holocaust.

Nor, second, could it have been true by any normal human standard that Iraq's population would have welcomed the American forces that entered the country after a terrifying aerial bombardment. But that that preposterous notion became one of the linchpins of U.S. policy is testament to the outright rubbish fed the administration by the Iraqi opposition (many of whom were out of touch with their country as well as keen on promoting their postwar careers by persuading the Americans of how easy an invasion would be) and by the two accredited Orientalist experts identified long ago as having the most influence over American Middle East policy, Bernard Lewis and Fouad Ajami.

Now in his late eighties, Lewis came to the United States about thirty-five years or so ago to teach at Princeton, where his fervent anticommunism and sarcastic disapproval of everything (except modern Turkey) about the modern Arabs and Islam pushed him to the forefront in the pro-Israel battles of the last years of the twentieth century. An old-fashioned Orientalist, he was quickly bypassed by advances in the social sciences and humanities that formed a new generation of scholars, who treated the Arabs and Islam as living subjects rather than as backward natives. For Lewis, vast generalizations about the whole of Islam and the civilizational backwardness of "the Arabs" were viable routes to the truth, which was available only to an expert like him. Common sense about human experience was out, whereas resounding pronouncements about the clash of civilizations were in. (Huntington found his lucrative concept in one of Lewis's more strident essays about the "return of Islam.") A generalist and ideologue who resorted to etymology to make his points about Islam and the Arabs, Lewis found a new audience within the American Zionist lobby to whom, in journals such as *Commentary* and later *The New York Review of Books,* he addressed his tendentious pontifications that basically reinforced the prevailing negative stereotypes of Arabs and Muslims.

What made Lewis's work so appalling in its effects was the fact that without any other views to counter his, American policy-makers in particular fell for them. That plus the icy distance and superciliousness of his manner made Lewis an "authority," even though he hadn't entered, much less lived in, the Arab world in decades. His last book, *What Went Wrong?*, became a post–9/11 best seller and, I am told, required reading for the U.S. military, despite its vacuousness and unsupported, usually factually incorrect, statements about the Arabs during the past five hundred years. Reading the book, you get an idea that the Arabs are a useless bunch of backward primitives, easier to attack and destroy than ever before.

Lewis also formulated the equally fraudulent thesis that there are three concentric circles in the Middle East—countries with pro-American people and governments (Jordan, Egypt, and Morocco), those with pro-American people and anti-American governments (Iraq and Iran), and those with anti-American governments and people (Syria and Libya). All of this gradually crept its way into Pentagon planning, especially as Lewis kept spewing out his simplistic formulae on television and in articles for the right-wing press. Hence Arabs wouldn't fight, they didn't know how, they would welcome us, and above all, they were totally susceptible to whatever power America could bring to bear.

Ajami is a Lebanese Shi'a educated in the United States who first made his name as a pro-Palestinian commentator. By the mid-1980s he had become a professor at Johns Hopkins and a fervent anti–Arab nationalist ideologue, who was quickly adopted by the right-wing Zionist lobby (he now works for people like Martin Peretz and Mort Zuckerman) and groups like the Council on Foreign Relations. He is fond of describing himself as a nonfiction V. S. Naipaul and quotes Joseph Conrad while actually sounding as hokey as Khalil Gibran. In addition, Ajami has a penchant for catchy one-liners, ideally suited for television if not for reflective thought. The author of two or three ill-informed and tendentious books, he has become influential because as a "native informant" he can harangue TV viewers with his venom while demoting the Arabs to the status of subhuman creatures whose world and actuality don't matter to anyone. Ten years ago he started deploying "we" as a righteous imperial collectivity that, along with Israel, never does anything wrong. Arabs are to blame for everything and therefore deserve "our" contempt and hostility.

Iraq has drawn out his special venom. He was an early advocate of the 1991 war and has, I think, deliberately misled the basically ignorant American strategic mind into believing that "our" power can set things straight. Dick Cheney quoted him in a major speech last August as saying that Iraqis would welcome "us" as liberators in "the streets of Basra," which still fights on as I write. Like Lewis, Ajami hasn't been a resident of the Arab world for years, although he is rumored to be close to the Saudis, of whom he has reasonably spoken as models for the Arab world's future governance.

If Ajami and Lewis are the leading intellectual figures in U.S. Middle East planning, one can only wince at how even more banal and weak-minded policy hacks in the Pentagon and White House have spun out such "ideas" into the scenario for a quick romp in a friendly Iraq. The State Department, after a long Zionist campaign against its so-called "Arabists," is purged of any countervailing views, and Colin Powell, it should be remembered, is little more than a dutiful servant of power. So because of its potential for anti-Israel troublemaking, Saddam's Iraq was targeted for military and political termination, quite irrespective of its history, its complicated society, its internal dynamics, and its contradictions. Paul Wolfowitz and Richard Perle said exactly that when they were consultants to Benjamin Netanyahu's 1996 election campaign. Saddam Hussein is of course an awful tyrant, but it isn't as if, for instance, most Iraqis haven't suffered terribly due to the U.S. sanctions and are willing to accept more punishment on the off chance that they will be "liberated." After such liberation, what forgiveness? After all, look at the war against Afghanistan, which also featured bombing and peanut butter sandwiches. Yes, Hamid Karzai is now in power of a very iffy kind, but the Taliban, the Pakistani secret services, and the poppy fields are all back, as are the warlords. Hardly a brilliant blueprint to follow in Iraq, which doesn't resemble Afghanistan very much anyway.

The expatriate Iraqi opposition has always been a motley bunch. Its leader, Ahmad Chalabi, is a brilliant man now wanted for embezzlement in Jordan and without a real constituency beyond Paul Wolfowitz's Pentagon office. He and his helpers (e.g., the thoroughly shabby Kanan Makiya, who has said that the merciless high-altitude U.S. bombing of his native land is "music to my ears"), plus a few ex-Ba'athists, Shi'a clerics, and others have also sold the U.S. administration a bill of goods about quick wars, deserting soldiers, and cheering crowds, equally unsupported by evidence or lived experience. One can't, of course, fault these people for wanting to rid the world of Saddam Hussein: we'd all be better off without him. The problem has been the falsifying of reality and the creation of either ideological or metaphysical scenarios that basically ignorant and unchecked American policy planners would foist undemocratically on a fundamentalist president and a largely misinformed public. In all, this Iraq might as well have been the moon and the Pentagon and White House Swift's Academy of Lagado.

Other racist premises underlying the campaign in Iraq are such thought-stopping propositions as redrawing the Middle East map and setting in motion a "domino effect" in bringing democracy there, as well as the assumption that the Iraqi people constitute a kind of tabula rasa on which to inscribe the ideas of William Kristol, Robert Kagan, and other far-right deep thinkers. As I have said in an earlier article, such ideas were first tried out by Ariel Sharon in Lebanon during the 1982 invasion, and then again in Palestine since he took office two years ago. There's been lots of destruction but little else in security and peace and subaltern compliance to show for it. Never mind: well-trained U.S. special forces have practiced and perfected the storming of civilian homes with Israeli soldiers in Jenin. It is hard to believe, as the ill-conceived Iraq war advances, that things will be much different than that bloody episode, but with other countries like Syria and Iran involved, shaky regimes shaken more, and general Arab outrage inflamed to the boiling point, one cannot imagine that victory in Iraq will resemble any of the simple-minded myths posited by Bush and his little clique.

But what is truly puzzling is that the regnant American ideology is still undergirded by the view that U.S. power is fundamentally benign and altruistic. This surely accounts for the outrage expressed by U.S. pundits and officials that Iraqis had the gall to undertake resistance at all, or that when captured, U.S. soldiers were exhibited on Iraqi TV. The practice is much worse than (a) bombing markets and whole cities, and (b) showing rows of Iraqi prisoners made to kneel or lie spread-eagled facedown in the sand. All of a sudden the Geneva conventions are involved not for Camp X-Ray but for Saddam, and when his forces hide inside cities, that is cheating, whereas carpet bombing from thirty thousand feet is playing fair.

This is the stupidest and most recklessly undertaken war in modern times. It is all about imperial arrogance unschooled in worldliness, unfettered either by competence or experience, undeterred by history or human complexity, unrepentant in brutal violence and cruel electronic gadgetry. To call it "faith-based" is to give faith an even worse name than it already has. With its too-long and vulnerable supply lines, its lurching from illiterate glibness to blind military pounding, its poorly planned logistical inadequacy, and its slick wordy self-explanations, the U.S. war against Iraq is almost perfectly embodied by poor George W. Bush's groping to stay on cue and on top of the texts they've prepared for him, which he can scarcely read, and Rummy Rumsfeld's wordy petulance, sending out lots of young soldiers either to die or to kill as many people as possible. What winning, or for that matter losing, such a war will ultimately entail is almost literally unthinkable. But pity the Iraqi civilians who must still suffer a great deal more before they are finally "liberated."

Al-Hayat, April 14, 2003
London Review of Books, April 17, 2003

CHAPTER FORTY-THREE

What Is Happening to the United States?

In a scarcely reported speech given on the Senate floor on March 19, 2003, the day the war was launched against Iraq, Robert Byrd, Democrat of West Virginia and the most eloquent speaker in that chamber, asked, "What is happening to this country? When did we become a nation which ignores and berates our friends? When did we decide to risk undermining international order by adopting a radical and doctrinaire approach to using our awesome military might? How can we abandon diplomacy when the turmoil in the world cries out for diplomacy?" No one bothered to answer him, but as the vast American military machine now planted in Iraq begins to stir restlessly in other directions in the name of the American people, their love of freedom, and their deep-seated values, these questions give urgency to the failure, if not the corruption, of democracy that we are living through.

Let's examine first what U.S. Middle East policy has wrought since George W. Bush came to power almost three years ago in an election decided finally by the Supreme Court, not by the popular vote. Even before the atrocities of September 11, Bush's team had given Ariel Sharon's government a free hand to colonize the West Bank and Gaza, to kill, detain, and expel people at will, to demolish their homes, expropriate their land, imprison them by curfew and hundreds of military blockades, and make life for them generally speaking impossible; after 9/11, Sharon simply hitched his wagon to the "war on terrorism" and intensified his unilateral depredations against a defenseless civilian population, now under occupation for thirty-six years, despite literally tens of UN Security Council resolutions enjoining Israel to withdraw and otherwise desist from its war crimes and human rights abuses. Bush called Sharon a man of peace last June and kept the $5 billion subsidy coming without even the vaguest hint that it was at risk because of Israel's lawless brutality.

On October 7, 2001, Bush launched the invasion of Afghanistan, which opened with concentrated high-altitude bombing (increasingly an "antiterrorist" military tactic, bearing in its effects and structure a strong resemblance to ordinary, garden-variety terrorism) and by December had installed in that devastated country a client regime with no effective power beyond a few streets in Kabul. There has been no significant U.S. effort at reconstruction, and it would seem the country has returned to its former abjection, albeit with a noticeable return of elements of the Taliban, as well as a thriving drug based economy.

Since the summer of 2002, the Bush administration has conducted an all-front campaign against the despotic government of Iraq and, having unsuccessfully tried to push the Security Council into compliance, began its war along with the United Kingdom against the country. I would say that from about last November on, dissent disappeared from a mainstream media swollen with a surfeit of ex-generals and ex-intelligence agents, sprinkled with recent terrorism and security experts drawn from the Washington right-wing think tanks. Anyone who spoke up against the war and actually managed to appear was labeled anti-American by failed academics who mounted Web sites to list "enemy" scholars who didn't toe the line. E-mails of the few visible public figures who struggled to say something were swamped, their lives threatened, their ideas trashed and mocked by media news readers who had just become the self-appointed, all-too-embedded sentinels of America's war.

An overwhelming torrent of crude as well as sophisticated material appeared everywhere equating the tyranny of Saddam Hussein not only with evil but with every known crime: much of this in part was factually correct, but it eliminated from mention the extraordinarily important role played by the United States and Europe in fostering the man's rise, fueling his ruinous wars, and maintaining his power. No less a personage than the egregious Donald Rumsfeld visited Saddam in the early 1980s as a way of assuring him of U.S. approval for his catastrophic war against Iran. The various U.S. corporations who supplied Iraq with nuclear, chemical, and biological material for the weapons that we supposedly went to war for were simply erased from the public record.

But all this and more was deliberately obscured by both government and media in manufacturing the case for the further destruction of Iraq, which has been taking place for the past month. The demonization of the country and its strutting leader turned it into a simulacrum of a formidable quasi-metaphysical threat, whereas—and this bears repeating—its demoralized and basically useless armed forces were a threat to no one at all. What *was* formidable about Iraq was its rich culture, its complex society, its long-suffering people: these were all made invisible, the better to smash the country as if it were only a den of thieves and murderers. Either without proof or with fraudulent information, Saddam was accused of harboring weapons of mass destruction that were a direct threat to the United States, seven thousand miles away. He was identical with the whole of Iraq, a desert place "out there" (to this day most Americans have no idea where Iraq is, what its history consists of, and what besides Saddam it contains), destined for the exercise of U.S. power unleashed illegally as a way of cowing the entire world in its Captain Ahab–like quest for reshaping reality and imparting democracy to everyone. At home the Patriot and Anti-Terrorism Acts have given the government an unseemly grip over civil life. A dispiritingly quiescent population for the most part accepts the bilge, passed off as fact, about imminent security threats, with the result that preventive detention, illegal eavesdropping, and a menacing sense of a heavily policed public space have made even the university a cold, hard place to be for anyone who tries to think and speak independently.

The appalling consequences of the U.S. and British intervention in Iraq are only just beginning to unfold, first with the coldly calculated destruction of its modern infrastructure, then with the looting and burning of one of the world's richest civilizations, and finally with the totally cynical American attempt to engage a band of motley "exiles" plus various large corporations in the supposed rebuilding of the country and the appropriation not only of its oil but also of its modern destiny. In response to the dreadful scenes of looting and burning that in the end are the occupying power's responsibility, Rumsfeld managed to put himself in a class beyond even Hulagu, the thirteenth-century Mongol ruler who sacked Baghdad and destroyed its library, throwing its contents into the Tigris. "Freedom is untidy," he said on one occasion, and, "Stuff happens," on another. Remorse or sorrow were nowhere in evidence.

General Jay Garner, hand-picked for the job, seems like a person straight out of the TV series *Dallas*. The Pentagon's favorite exile, Ahmad Chalabi, for example, has intimated openly that he plans to sign a peace treaty with Israel, hardly an Iraqi idea. Bechtel has already been awarded a huge contract. This too in the name of the American people. The whole business smacks of nothing so much as Israel's 1982 invasion of Lebanon.

This is an almost total failure in democracy—ours as Americans, not Iraq's. Seventy percent of the American people are supposed to be for all this, but nothing is more manipulative and fraudulent than polls of random numbers of Americans who are asked whether they "support our president and troops in time of war." As Senator Byrd said in his speech, "There is a pervasive sense of rush and risk and too many questions unanswered. . . . A pall has fallen over the Senate Chamber. We avoid our solemn duty to debate the one topic on the minds of all Americans, even while scores of our sons and daughters faithfully do their duty in Iraq." Who is going to ask questions now that that midwestern farm boy General Tommy Franks sits triumphantly with his staff around one of Saddam's tables in a Baghdad palace?

I am convinced that in nearly every way this was a rigged, and neither a necessary nor a popular, war. The deeply reactionary Washington "research" institutions that spawned Wolfowitz, Perle, Abrams, Feith, and the rest provide an unhealthy intellectual and moral atmosphere. Policy papers circulate without real peer review, adopted by a government requiring what seems to be rational (even moral) justification for a dubious, basically illicit policy of global domination. Hence the doctrine of military preemption, which was never voted on either by the people of this country or by their half-asleep representatives. How can citizens stand up against the blandishments offered the government by companies like Halliburton, Boeing, and Lockheed? And as for planning and charting a strategic course for what is by far the most lavishly endowed military establishment in history, one that is fully capable of dragging us into unending conflicts, that task is left to the various ideologically based pressure groups, such as the fundamentalist Christian leaders like Franklin Graham, who have been unleashed with their Bibles on destitute Iraqis, the wealthy private foundations, and such lobbies as AIPAC, the American Israel Public Affairs Committee, along with *its* associated think tanks and research centers.

What seems so monumentally criminal is that good, useful words like *democracy* and *freedom* have been hijacked, pressed into service as a mask for pillaging, muscling in on territory, and settling scores. The American program for the Arab world is the same as Israel's. Along with Syria, Iraq theoretically represents the only serious long-term military threat to Israel, and therefore it had to be put out of commission for decades. What does it mean to liberate and democratize a country when no one asked you to do it, and when in the process you occupy it militarily and, at the same time, fail miserably to preserve public law and order? The mix of resentment and relief at Saddam's cowardly disappearance that most Iraqis feel has brought with it little understanding or compassion either from the United States or from the other Arab states, who have stood by idly quarreling over minor points of procedure while Baghdad has burned. What a travesty of strategic planning when you assume that "natives" will welcome your presence after you've bombed and quarantined them for thirteen years. The truly preposterous mindset about American beneficence, and with it that patronizing Puritanism about what is right and wrong, has infiltrated the minutest levels of the media coverage. In a story about a seventy-year-old Baghdad widow who ran a cultural center from her house—wrecked in the U.S. raids—and is now beside herself with rage, *New York Times* reporter Dexter Filkins implicitly chastises her for having had "a comfortable life under Saddam Hussein" and then piously disapproves of her tirade against the Americans, "and this from a graduate of London University."

Adding to the fraudulence of the weapons that weren't there, the Stalingrads that didn't occur, the formidable artillery defenses that never happened, I wouldn't be surprised if Saddam disappeared suddenly because a deal was made in Moscow to let him out with his family and money in return for the country. The war had gone badly for the United States in the south, and Bush couldn't risk more of the same in Baghdad. On April 6 a Russian convoy left Baghdad. U.S. National Security adviser Condoleezza Rice appeared in Russia on April 7. Two days later, on April 9, Baghdad fell. Draw your own conclusions, but isn't it possible that as a result of discussions with the Republican Guard mentioned by Rumsfeld, Saddam bought himself out in return for abandoning the whole thing to the Americans and their British allies, who could then proclaim a brilliant victory?

Americans have been cheated, Iraqis have suffered impossibly, and

Bush looks like the moral equivalent of a cowboy sheriff who has just led his righteous posse to a victorious showdown against an evil enemy. On matters of the gravest importance to millions of people, constitutional principles have been violated and the electorate lied to unconscionably. We are the ones who must have our democracy back. Enough of smoke and mirrors and smooth-talking hustlers.

Al-Ahram, April 24–30, 2003
Al-Hayat, April 28, 2003
The Observer, April 20, 2003

CHAPTER FORTY-FOUR

The Arab Condition

My impression is that many Arabs today feel that what has been taking place in Iraq over the last two months is little short of a catastrophe. True, Saddam Hussein's regime was a despicable one in every way and deserved to be removed. Also true is the sense of anger many feel at how outlandishly cruel and despotic that regime was, and how dreadful has been the suffering of Iraq's people. There seems little doubt that far too many other governments and individuals connived at keeping Saddam Hussein in power, looking the other way as they went about their business as usual. Nevertheless, the only thing that gave the United States the license to bomb the country and destroy its government was neither a moral right nor a rational argument but rather sheer military power. Having for years supported Ba'athist Iraq and Saddam Hussein himself, the United States and Britain arrogated to themselves the right to negate their own complicity in his despotism, then to state that they were liberating Iraq from his hated tyranny. And what now seems to be emerging in the country, both during and after the illegal Anglo American war against the people and civilization that are the essence of Iraq, represents a very grave threat to the Arab people as a whole.

It is therefore of the utmost importance that we recall in the first instance that, despite their many divisions and disputes, the Arabs are in fact a people, not a collection of random countries passively available for outside intervention and rule. There is a clear line of imperial continuity that begins with Ottoman rule over the Arabs in the sixteenth century until our own time. After the Ottomans in World War I came the British and the French, and after them, in the period following World War II, came America and Israel. One of the most insidiously influential strands of thought in recent American and Israeli Orientalism, evident in American and Israeli policy since the late 1940s, is a virulent, extremely deep-seated hostility to Arab nationalism and a political will to oppose and fight it in every possible way. The basic premise of Arab nationalism in the broad sense is that, with all their diversity and pluralism of substance and style, the people whose language and culture are Arab and Muslim (call them the Arab-speaking peoples, as Albert Hourani did in his last book) constitute a nation and not just a collection of states scattered between North Africa and the western boundaries of Iran. Any independent articulation of that premise was openly attacked, as in the 1956 Suez War, the French colonial war against Algeria, the Israeli wars of occupation and dispossession, and the campaign against Iraq, a war whose stated purpose was to topple a specific regime but whose real goal was the devastation of the most powerful Arab country. And just as the French, British, Israeli, and American campaign against Gamal Abdel Nasser was designed to bring down a force that openly stated as its ambition the unification of the Arabs into a very powerful independent political force, the American goal today is to redraw the map of the Arab world to suit American, and not Arab, interests. U.S. policy thrives on Arab fragmentation, collective inaction, and military and economic weakness.

One would have to be foolish to argue that the nationalism and doctrinaire separateness of individual Arab states, whether the state is Egypt, Syria, Kuwait, or Jordan, is a better thing, a more useful political actuality, than some scheme of inter-Arab cooperation in economic, political, and cultural spheres. Certainly I see no need for total integration, but any form of useful cooperation and planning would be better than the disgraceful summits that have disfigured our national life, say, during the Iraq crisis. Every Arab asks the question, as does every foreigner: why do the Arabs never pool their resources to fight for the causes that officially, at least, they claim to support, and that, in the case of the Palestinians, their people actively, indeed passionately, believe in?

I will not spend time arguing that everything that has been done to promote Arab nationalism can be excused for its abuses, its shortsightedness, its wastefulness, repression, and folly. The record is not a good one. But I do want to state categorically that, since the early twentieth century, the Arabs have never been able to achieve their collective independence as a whole or in part exactly because of the designs on the strategic and cultural importance of their lands by outside powers. Today no Arab state is free to dispose of its resources as it wishes, or to take positions that represent that individual state's interests, especially if those interests seem to threaten U.S. policies. In the fifty-plus years since America assumed world dominance, and more so after the end of the cold war, it has run its Middle East policy based on two principles, and two principles alone: the defense of Israel and the free flow of Arab oil, both of which involved direct opposition to Arab nationalism. In all significant ways, with few exceptions, American policy has been contemptuous of and openly hostile to the aspirations of the Arab people, and with surprising success: since Nasser's demise it has had few challengers among Arab rulers, who have gone along with everything required of them.

During periods of the most extreme pressure on one or other of them (e.g., the Israeli invasion of Lebanon in 1982, the sanctions against Iraq that were designed to weaken the people and the state as a whole, the bombings of Libya and Sudan, the threats against Syria, the pressure on Saudi Arabia), the collective weakness of the Arab states has been little short of stunning. Neither their enormous collective economic power nor the will of their people has moved the Arab states to make even the slightest gesture of defiance. The imperial policy of divide and rule has reigned supreme, since each government seems to fear the possibility that it might damage its bilateral relationship with America. That consideration has taken precedence over any contingency, no matter how urgent. Some countries rely on American economic aid, others on American military protection. All, however, have decided that they do not trust one another any more than they care strongly for the welfare of their own people (which is to say, they care very little), preferring the hauteur and contempt of the Americans, who have gotten progressively worse in their dealings with the Arab states as the only superpower's arrogance has developed over time. Indeed, it is remarkable that the Arab countries have fought one another far more readily than they have fought the real aggressors from the outside.

The result today, after the invasion of Iraq, is an Arab nation that is badly demoralized, crushed, and beaten down, less able to do anything except acquiesce in announced American plans to gesture and posture in all sorts of efforts to redraw the Middle East map to suit American and obviously Israeli interests. Even that extraordinarily grandiose scheme has yet to receive the vaguest collective answer from the Arab states, who seem to be hanging around waiting for something new to happen, as Bush, Rumsfeld, Powell, and the others lurch from threat to plan to visit to snub to bombing to unilateral announcement. What makes the whole business especially galling is that whereas the Arabs have totally accepted the American (or Quartet) road map that seems to have emerged from George W. Bush's waking dream, the Israelis have coolly withheld any such acceptance. How does it feel for a Palestinian to watch a second-rank leader like Abu Mazen, who has always been Arafat's faithful subordinate, embrace Colin Powell and the Americans when it is clear to the youngest child that the road map is designed (a) to stimulate a Palestinian civil war and (b) to offer Palestinian compliance with Israeli-American demands for "reform" in return for nothing much at all? How much further do we sink?

And as for American plans in Iraq, it is now absolutely clear that what is going to happen is nothing less than an old-fashioned colonial occupation, rather like Israel's since 1967. Bringing in American-style democracy to Iraq means basically aligning the country with U.S. policy, that is, a peace treaty with Israel, oil markets for American profit, and civil order kept to a minimum that permits neither real opposition nor real institution-building. Perhaps even the idea is to turn Iraq into civil-war Lebanon. I am not certain. But take one small example of the kind of planning that is being undertaken. It was recently announced in the U.S. press that a thirty-two-year-old assistant professor of law, Noah Feldman, at New York University, would be responsible for producing a new Iraqi constitution. It was mentioned in all the media accounts of this major appointment that Feldman was an extraordinarily brilliant expert in Islamic law, had studied Arabic since he was fifteen, and grew up as an Orthodox Jew. But he has never practiced law in the Arab world, has never been to Iraq, and seems to have no real practical background in the problems of postwar Iraq. What an open-faced snub, not only to Iraq itself, but also to the legions of Arab and Muslim legal minds who could have done a perfectly acceptable job in the service of Iraq's future. But no, America wants it done by a fresh young fellow, so as to be able to say, "We have given Iraq its new democracy." The contempt is thick enough to cut with a knife.

The seeming powerlessness of the Arabs in the face of all this is what is so discouraging, and not only because no real effort has been expended on fashioning a collective response to it. To someone who reflects on the situation from the outside, as I do, I find it amazing that in this moment of crisis, there has been no evidence of any sort of appeal from the rulers to their people for support in what needs to be seen as a collective national threat. American military planners have made no secret of the fact that what they plan is radical change for the Arab world, a change that they can impose by force of arms and because there is little that opposes them. Moreover, the idea behind the effort seems to be nothing less than to destroy the underlying unity of the Arab people once and for all, changing the bases of their lives and aspirations irremediably.

To such a display of power, I would have thought that an unprecedented alliance between Arab rulers and people represented the only possible deterrence. But that, clearly, would require an undertaking by every Arab government to open its society to its people, bring them in so to speak, remove all the repressive security measures in order to provide an organized opposition to the new imperialism. A people coerced into war, or a people silenced and repressed, will never rise to such an occasion. What we must have are Arab societies released finally from their self-imposed state of siege between ruler and ruled. Why not instead welcome democracy in the defense of freedom and self-determination? Why not say, we want each and every citizen willing to be mobilized in a common front against a common enemy? We need every intellectual and every political force to pull together with us against the imperial scheme to redesign our lives without our consent. Why must resistance be left to extremism and desperate suicide bombers?

As a digression, I might mention here that when I read the 2002 United Nations Human Development Report on the Arab world, I was struck by how little appreciation there was in it for imperialist intervention in the Arab world, and how deep and long-standing its effect has been. I certainly don't think that all our problems come from the outside, but I wouldn't want to say that all our problems are of our own making. Historical context and the problems of political fragmentation play a very great role, to which the report itself pays little attention. The absence of democracy is partially the result of alliances made between Western powers on the one hand, and minority ruling regimes or parties on the other, not because the Arabs have no interest in democracy but because democracy has been seen as a threat by several actors in the drama. Besides, why adopt the American formula for democracy (usually a euphemism for the free market, with little attention paid to human entitlement and social services) as the only one? This is a subject that needs considerably more debate than I have time for here. So let me return to my main point.

Consider how much more effective today the Palestinian position might have been under the U.S.-Israeli onslaught had there been a common show of unity instead of an unseemly scramble for positions on the delegation to see Colin Powell. I have not understood over the years why it is that Palestinian leaders have been unable to develop a common unified strategy for opposing the occupation and for avoiding getting diverted into one or another Mitchell, Tenet, or Quartet plan. Why not say to all Palestinians, we face one enemy whose design on our lands and lives is well known and must be fought by us all together? The root problem everywhere, and not just in Palestine, is the fundamental rift between ruler and ruled that is one of the distorted offshoots of imperialism, this basic fear of democratic participation, as if too much freedom might lose the governing colonial elite some favor with the imperial authority. The result, of course, is not only the absence of real mobilization of everyone in the common struggle, but the perpetuation of fragmentation and petty factionalism. As things now stand, there are too many uninvolved, non-participating Arab citizens in the world today.

Whether they want to or not, the Arab people today face a wholesale attack on their future by an imperial power, America, that acts in concert with Israel to pacify, subdue, and finally reduce us to a bunch of warring fiefdoms whose first loyalty is not to their people but to the great super-power (and its local surrogate) itself. Not to understand that this is the conflict that will shape our area for decades to come is willingly to blind oneself. What is now needed is a breaking of the iron bands that tie Arab societies into sullen knots of disaffected people, insecure leaders, and alienated intellectuals. This is an unprecedented crisis. Unprecedented means are therefore required to confront it. The first step then is to realize the scope of the problem, and then go on to overcome what reduces us to helpless rage and marginalized reaction, a condition by no means to be accepted willingly. The alternative to such an unattractive condition promises a great deal more hope.

Al-Ahram, May 22–28, 2003
Al-Hayat, May 26, 2003

CHAPTER FORTY-FIVE

Archaeology of the Road Map

Early in May, while Colin Powell was on his visit to Israel and the Occupied Territories, he met with Mahmoud Abbas, the new Palestinian prime minister, and separately with a small group of civil society activists, including Hanan Ashrawi and Mustafa Barghuti. According to Barghuti, Powell expressed surprise and mild consternation at the computerized maps of the settlements, the eight-meter-high fence, and the dozens of Israeli army checkpoints that have made life so difficult and the future so bleak for Palestinians. Powell's view of Palestinian reality is, to say the least, defective, despite his august position, but he did ask for materials to take away with him, and more important, he reassured the Palestinians that the same effort put in by Bush on Iraq was now going into implementing the road map. Much the same point was made in the last days of May by Bush himself in the course of interviews he gave to the Arab media, although as usual he stressed generalities rather than anything specific. He met with the Palestinian and Israeli leaders in Jordan and, earlier, with the major Arab rulers, excluding Syria's Bashar Al-Assad, of course. All this is part of what now looks like a major American push forward. That Ariel Sharon has accepted the road map (with enough reservations to undercut his acceptance) seems to augur well for a viable Palestinian state.

Bush's vision (the word strikes a weird dreamy note in what is meant to be a hard-headed, definitive, and three-phased peace plan) is supposed to be achieved by a restructured Palestinian Authority, the elimination of all violence and incitement against Israelis, and the installation of a government that meets the requirements of Israel and the so-called Quartet that authored the plan. Israel for its part undertakes to improve the humanitarian situation, easing restrictions and lifting curfews, though where and when are not specified. By June 2003 Phase One is also supposed to see the dismantling of the last sixty hilltop settlements (so-called "illegal outposts" established since March 2001), though nothing is said about removing the others, which account for the 200,000 settlers on the West Bank and Gaza, to say nothing of the 200,000 more in annexed East Jerusalem. Phase Two, described as a transition to run from June to December 2003, is to be focused, rather oddly, on the "option of creating an independent Palestinian state with provisional borders and attributes of sovereignty"—none are specified—culminating in an international conference to approve and then "create" a Palestinian state, once again with "provisional borders." Phase Three is to end the conflict completely, also by way of an international conference, whose job it will be to settle the thorniest issues of all: refugees, settlements, Jerusalem, borders. Israel's role in all this is to cooperate; the real onus is placed on the Palestinians, who must keep coming up with the goods in rapid succession, while the military occupation remains more or less in place, though eased in the main areas invaded during the spring of 2002. No monitoring element is envisioned, and the misleading symmetry of the plan's structure leaves Israel very much in charge of what—if anything—will happen next. As for Palestinian human rights, at present not so much ignored as suppressed, no specific rectification is written into the plan: apparently it is up to Israel whether to continue as before or not.

For once, say all the usual commentators, Bush is offering real hope for a Middle East settlement. Calculated leaks from the White House have suggested a list of possible sanctions against Israel if Sharon gets too intransigent, but this was quickly denied and then disappeared. An emerging media consensus presents the document's contents—many of them from earlier peace plans—as the result of Bush's new-found confidence after his triumph in Iraq. As with most discussions of the Palestinian-Israeli conflict, manipulated clichés and far-fetched suppositions, rather than the realities of power and lived history, shape the flow of discourse. Skeptics and critics are brushed aside as anti-American, while a sizable portion of the organized Jewish leadership has denounced the road map as requiring far too many Israeli concessions. But the establishment press keeps reminding us that Sharon has spoken of an "occupation," which he never conceded until now, and has actually announced his intention to end Israeli rule over 3.5 million Palestinians. But is he even aware of what he proposes to end? The *Ha'aretz* commentator Gideon Levy wrote on June 1, 2003, that, like most Israelis, Sharon knows nothing "about life under curfew in communities that have been under siege for years. What does he know about the humiliation of check-points, or about people being forced to travel on gravel and mud roads, at risk to their lives, in order to get a woman in labor to a hospital? About life on the brink of starvation? About a demolished home? About children who see their parents beaten and humiliated in the middle of the night?"

Another chilling omission from the road map is the gigantic "separa-tion wall" now being built in the West Bank by Israel: 347 kilometers of concrete running north to south, of which 120 have already been erected. It is twenty-five feet high and ten feet thick; its cost is put at $1.6 million per kilometer. The wall doesn't simply divide Israel from a putative Pales-tinian state on the basis of the 1967 borders: it actually takes in new tracts of Palestinian land, sometimes five or six kilometers at a stretch. It is surrounded by trenches, electric wire, and moats; there are watchtow-ers at regular intervals. Almost a decade after the end of South African apartheid, this ghastly racist wall is going up with scarcely a peep from the majority of Israelis or their American allies who, whether they like it or not, are going to pay most of its cost. The forty thousand Palestinian inhabitants of the town of Qalqilya in their homes are on one side of the wall; the land they farm and actually live off of is on the other. It is esti-mated that when the wall is finished—presumably as the United States, Israel, and the Palestinians argue about procedure for months on end—almost 300,000 Palestinians will be separated from their land. The road map is silent about all this, as it is about Sharon's recent approval of a wall on the eastern side of the West Bank, which will, if built, reduce the amount of Palestinian territory available for Bush's dream state to roughly 40 percent of the area. This is what Sharon has had in mind all along.

An unstated premise underlies Israel's heavily modified acceptance of the road map and the United States' evident commitment to it: the rela-tive success of Palestinian resistance. This is true whether or not one deplores some of its methods, its exorbitant cost, and the heavy toll it has taken on yet another generation of Palestinians who have not wholly given up in the face of the overwhelming superiority of Israeli-U.S. power. All sorts of reasons have been given for the emergence of the road map: that 56 percent of Israelis back it, that Sharon has finally bowed to inter-national reality, that Bush needs an Arab-Israeli cover for his military adventures elsewhere, that the Palestinians have finally come to their senses and brought forth Abu Mazen (Abbas's much more familiar nom de guerre, as it were), and so on. Some of this is true, but I still contend that were it not for the fact of the stubborn Palestinian refusal to accept that they are "a defeated people," as the Israeli chief of staff recently described them, there would be no peace plan. Yet anyone who believes that the road map actually offers anything resembling a settlement or that it tackles the basic issues is wrong. Like so much of the prevailing peace discourse, it places the need for restraint and renunciation and sacrifice squarely on Palestinian shoulders, thus denying the density and sheer gravity of Palestinian history. To read through the road map is to confront an unsituated document, oblivious of its time and place.

The road map, in other words, is not about a plan for peace so much as a plan for pacification: it is about putting an end to Palestine as a problem. Hence the repetition of the term "performance" in the document's wooden prose—in other words, how the Palestinians are expected to behave, almost in the social sense of the word. No violence, no protest, more democracy, better leaders and institutions, all based on the notion that the underlying problem has been the ferocity of Palestinian resistance rather than the occupation that has given rise to it. Nothing comparable is expected of Israel, except that the small settlements I spoke of earlier, known as "illegal outposts" (an entirely new classification that suggests that some Israeli implantations on Palestinian land are legal), must be given up and, yes, the major settlements "frozen" but certainly not removed or dismantled. Not a word is said about what since 1948, and then again since 1967, Palestinians have endured at the hands of Israel and the United States. Nothing about the de-development of the Palestinian economy, as described by the American researcher Sara Roy in a forthcoming book.* House demolitions, the uprooting of trees, the five thousand prisoners or more, the policy of targeted assassinations, the closures since 1993, the wholesale ruin of the infrastructure, the incredible number of deaths and maimings—all that and more pass without a word.

The truculent aggression and stiff-necked unilateralism of the Ameri-

---

*Scholarship and Politics: The Israeli Occupation, the Palestinians, and the Failure of Peace, Selected Works of Sara Roy (London: Pluto Press, forthcoming).

can and Israeli teams are already well known. The Palestinian team inspires scarcely any confidence, made up as it is of recycled and aging Arafat cohorts. Indeed, the road map seems to have given Yasir Arafat another lease on life, for all the studied efforts by Powell and his assistants to avoid visiting him. Despite the stupid Israeli policy of trying to humble him by shutting him up in a badly bombed compound, he is still in control of things. He remains Palestine's elected president, he has the Palestinian purse strings in his hands (the purse is far from bulging), and as for his status, none of the present "reform" team (who with two or three significant new additions are reshuffled members of the old team) can match the old man for charisma and power.

Take Abu Mazen for a start. I first met him in March 1977 at my first Palestine National Council meeting in Cairo. He gave by far the longest speech, in the didactic manner that he must have perfected as a secondary school teacher in Qatar, and explained to the assembled Palestinian parliamentarians the differences between Zionism and Zionist dissidence. It was a noteworthy intervention, since most Palestinians had no real notion in those days that Israel was made up not only of fundamentalist Zionists, who were anathema to every Arab, but of various kinds of peaceniks and activists as well. In retrospect, Abu Mazen's speech launched the PLO's campaign of meetings, most of them secret, between Palestinians and Israelis who had long dialogues in Europe about peace and some considerable effect in their respective societies in shaping the constituencies that made Oslo possible.

Nevertheless, no one doubted that Arafat had authorized Abu Mazen's speech and the subsequent campaign, which cost brave men like Issam Sartawi and Said Hammami their lives. And while the Palestinian participants emerged from the center of Palestinian politics (i.e., Fateh), the Israelis were a small marginalized group of reviled peace supporters whose courage was commendable for that very reason. During the PLO's Beirut years between 1971 and 1982, Abu Mazen was stationed in Damascus, but he joined the exiled Arafat and his staff in Tunis for the next decade or so. I saw him there several times and was struck by his well-organized office, his quiet bureaucratic manner, and his evident interest in Europe and the United States as arenas where Palestinians could do useful work promoting peace with Israelis. After the Madrid conference in 1991, he was said to have brought together PLO employees and independent intellectuals in Europe and turned them into teams to prepare negotiating files on subjects such as water, refugees, demography, and boundaries in advance of what were to become the secret Oslo meetings of 1992 and 1993, although to the best of my knowledge none of the files were used, none of the Palestinian experts were directly involved in the talks, and none of the results of this research influenced the final documents that emerged.

In Oslo, the Israelis fielded an array of experts supported by maps, documents, statistics, and at least seventeen prior drafts of what the Palestinians would end up signing, while the Palestinians unfortunately restricted their negotiators to three completely different PLO men, not one of whom knew English or had a background in international (or any other kind of) negotiation. Arafat's idea seems to have been that he was fielding a team mainly to keep himself in the process, especially after his exit from Beirut and his disastrous decision to side with Iraq during the 1991 Gulf War. If he had other objectives in mind, then he didn't prepare for them effectively, as has always been his style. In Abu Mazen's memoir* and in other anecdotal accounts of the Oslo discussions, Arafat's subordinate is credited as the "architect" of the accords, though he never left Tunis; Abu Mazen goes so far as to say that it took him a year after the Washington ceremonies (where he appeared alongside Arafat, Rabin, Peres, and Clinton) to convince Arafat that he hadn't gotten a state from Oslo! Yet most accounts of the peace talks stress the fact that Arafat was pulling all the strings just the same. No wonder then that the Oslo negotiations made the overall situation of the Palestinians a good deal worse. The American team led by Dennis Ross, a former Israeli lobby employee—a job to which he has now returned—routinely supported the Israeli position, which, after a full decade of negotiation, consisted in handing back 18 percent of the Occupied Territories to the Palestinians on highly unfavorable terms, with the Israeli Defense Force left in charge of security, borders, and water. Naturally enough, the number of settlements more than doubled.

Through Secret Channels: The Road to Oslo: Senior PLO Leader Abu Mazen's Revealing Story of the Negotiations with Israel (Reading, England: Garnet, 1995). See also As'ad Abu-Khalil's review of the book in *Journal of Palestine Studies* (Summer 1996), 103–4.

Since the PLO's return to the Occupied Territories in 1994, Abu Mazen has remained a second-rank figure, known universally for his "flexibility" with Israel, his subservience to Arafat, and his total lack of any organized political base, although he is one of Fateh's original founders and a long-standing member and secretary general of its central committee. So far as I know, he has never been elected to anything, and certainly not to the Palestinian Legislative Council. The PLO and the Palestinian Authority under Arafat are anything but transparent. Little is known about the way decisions are made or how money gets spent, where it is, and who besides Arafat has any say in the matter. Everyone agrees, however, that Arafat, a fiendish micromanager and control freak, remains the central figure in every significant way. That is why Abu Mazen's elevation to the status of reforming prime minister, which so pleases the Americans and Israelis, is thought of by most Palestinians as, well, a kind of joke, the old man's way of holding on to power by inventing a new gimmick, so to speak. Abu Mazen is thought of generally as colorless, moderately corrupt, and without any clear ideas of his own, except that he wants to please the white man.

Like Arafat, Abu Mazen has never lived anywhere except the Gulf, Syria, Lebanon, Tunisia, and now occupied Palestine; he knows no languages other than Arabic, and he isn't much of an orator or public presence. By contrast, Mohammed Dahlan, the new security chief from Gaza—the other much-heralded figure in whom the Israelis and Americans place great hope—is younger, cleverer, and quite ruthless. During the eight years that he ran one of Arafat's fourteen or fifteen security organizations, Gaza was known as Dahlanistan. He resigned last year, only to be re-recruited for the job of "unified security chief" by the Europeans, the Americans, and the Israelis, even though of course he too has always been one of Arafat's men. Now he is expected to crack down on Hamas and Islamic Jihad—one of the reiterated Israeli demands behind which lies the hope that there will be something resembling a Palestinian civil war, a gleam in the eyes of the Israeli military.

In any event, it seems clear to me that, no matter how assiduously and flexibly Abu Mazen "performs," he is going to be limited by three factors. One, of course, is Arafat himself, who still controls Fateh, which in theory is also Abu Mazen's power base. Another is Sharon (who will presumably have the United States behind him all the way). In a list of fourteen "remarks" about the road map published in *Ha'aretz* on May 27, Sharon signaled the very narrow limits on anything that might be construed as flexibility on Israel's part. The third is Bush and his entourage; to judge by their handling of postwar Afghanistan and Iraq, they have neither the stomach nor the competence for the nation-building that surely will be required. Already Bush's right-wing Christian base in the South has remonstrated noisily against putting pressure on Israel, and already the high-powered American pro-Israel lobby, with its docile adjunct, the Israeli-occupied U.S. Congress, have swung into action against any hint of coercion against Israel, even though it will be crucial now that a final phase has begun.

It may seem quixotic for me to say, but even if the immediate prospects are grim from a Palestinian perspective, they are not all dark. I return to the stubbornness I mentioned above, and the fact that Palestinian society—devastated, nearly ruined, desolate in so many ways—is, like Hardy's thrush in its blast-beruffled plume, still capable of flinging its soul upon the growing gloom. No other Arab society is as rambunctious and healthily unruly, and none is fuller of civic and social initiatives and functioning institutions (including a miraculously vital musical conservatory). Even though they are mostly unorganized and in some cases lead miserable lives of exile and statelessness, diaspora Palestinians are still energetically engaged by the problems of their collective destiny, and everyone I know is always trying somehow to advance the cause. Only a minuscule fraction of this energy has ever found its way into the Palestinian Authority, which except for the highly ambivalent figure of Arafat has remained strangely marginal to the common fate. According to recent polls, Fateh and Hamas between them have the support of roughly 45 percent of the Palestinian electorate, with the remaining 55 percent evolving quite different, much more hopeful-looking political formations.

One in particular has struck me as significant (and I have attached myself to it), inasmuch as it now provides the only genuine grassroots formation that steers clear both of the religious parties and their fundamentally sectarian politics, and of the traditional nationalism offered up by Arafat's old (rather than young) Fateh activists. It's been called the Palestinian National Initiative (PNI), and its main figure is Mustafa Barghuti, a Moscow-trained physician whose main work has been as director of the impressive Village Medical Relief Committee, which has brought health care to more than 100,000 rural Palestinians. A former Communist Party stalwart, Barghuti is a quiet-spoken organizer and leader who has overcome the hundreds of physical obstacles impeding Palestinian movement or travel abroad to rally nearly every independent individual and organization of note behind a political program that promises social reform as well as liberation across doctrinal lines. Singularly free of conventional rhetoric, Barghuti has worked with Israelis, Europeans, Americans, Africans, Asians, and Arabs to build an enviably well-run solidarity movement that practices the pluralism and coexistence it preaches. The PNI does not throw up its hands at the directionless militarization of the intifada. It offers training programs for the unemployed and social services for the destitute on the grounds that this answers to present circumstances and Israeli pressure. Above all, the PNI, which is about to become a recognized political party, seeks to mobilize Palestinian society at home and in exile for free elections—authentic elections that will represent Palestinian, rather than Israeli or U.S., interests. This sense of authenticity is what seems so lacking in the path cut out for Abu Mazen.

The vision here isn't a manufactured provisional state on 40 percent of the land, with the refugees abandoned and Jerusalem kept by Israel, but a sovereign territory liberated from military occupation by mass action involving Arabs and Jews wherever possible. Because the PNI is an authentic Palestinian movement, reform and democracy have become part of its everyday practice. Many hundreds of Palestine's most notable activists and independents have already signed up, and organizational meetings have already been held, with many more planned abroad and in Palestine, despite the terrible difficulties of getting around Israel's restrictions on freedom of movement. It is some solace to think that, while formal negotiations and discussions go on, a host of informal, uncoopted alternatives exist, of which the PNI and a growing international solidarity campaign are now the main components.

Al-Ahram, June 12–18, 2003
Al-Hayat, June 15, 2003
London Review of Books, June 19, 2003

CHAPTER FORTY-SIX

Dignity and Solidarity

I n early May I was in Seattle lecturing for a few days. While there, I had dinner one night with Rachel Corrie's parents and sister, who were still reeling from the shock of Rachel's murder on March 16 in Gaza by an Israeli bulldozer. Mr. Corrie told me that he had himself driven bulldozers, although the one that killed his daughter deliberately because she was trying valiantly to protect a Palestinian home in Rafah from demolition was a sixty-ton behemoth especially designed by Caterpillar for house demolitions, a far bigger machine than anything he had ever seen or driven. Two things struck me about my brief visit with the Corries. One was the story they told about their return to the United States with their daughter's body. They had immediately sought out their U.S. senators, Patty Murray and Maria Cantwell, both Democrats, told them their story, and received the expected expressions of shock, outrage, and anger and promises of investigations. After both women returned to Washington, the Corries never heard from them again, and the promised investigation simply didn't materialize. As expected, the Israeli lobby had explained the realities to them, and both women simply begged off. An American citizen willfully murdered by the soldiers of a client state of the United States without so much as an official peep or even the de rigueur investigation that had been promised her family.

But the second and far more important aspect of the Rachel Corrie story for me was the young woman's action itself, heroic and dignified at the same time. Born and brought up in Olympia, a small city sixty miles south of Seattle, she had joined the International Solidarity Movement and gone to Gaza to stand with suffering human beings with whom she had never had any contact before. Her letters back to her family are truly remarkable documents of her ordinary humanity that make for very difficult and moving reading, especially when she describes the kindness and concern shown her by all the Palestinians she encounters who clearly welcome her as one of their own, because she lives with them exactly as they do, sharing their lives and worries, as well as the horrors of the Israeli occupation and its terrible effects on even the smallest child. She understands the fate of refugees, and what she calls the Israeli government's insidious attempt at a kind of genocide by making it almost impossible for this particular group of people to survive. So moving is her solidarity that it inspires an Israeli reservist named Danny who has refused service to write her and tell her, "You are doing a good thing. I thank you for it."

What shines through all the letters she wrote home, which were subsequently published in the London *Guardian,* is the amazing resistance put up by the Palestinian people themselves, average human beings stuck in the most terrible position of suffering and despair but continuing to survive just the same. We have heard so much recently about the road map and the prospects for peace that we have overlooked the most basic fact of all, which is that Palestinians have refused to capitulate or surrender even under the collective punishment meted out to them by the combined might of the United States and Israel. It is that extraordinary fact that is the reason for the existence of a road map and all the numerous so-called peace plans before them, not at all because the United States and Israel and the international community have been convinced for humanitarian reasons that the killing and the violence must stop. If we miss that truth about the power of Palestinian resistance (by which I do not at all mean suicide bombing, which does much more harm than good), despite all its failings and all its mistakes, we miss everything. Palestinians have always been a problem for the Zionist project, and so-called solutions have perennially been proposed that minimize, rather than solve, the problem. The official Israeli policy, no matter whether Ariel Sharon uses the word "occupation" or whether he dismantles a rusty, unused tower or two, has always been not to accept the reality of the Palestinian people as equals nor ever to admit that their rights were scandalously violated all along by Israel. Whereas a few courageous Israelis over the years have tried to deal with this other concealed history, most Israelis and what seems like the majority of American Jews have made every effort to deny, avoid, or negate the Palestinian reality. This is why there is no peace.

Moreover, the road map says nothing about justice or about the historical punishment meted out to the Palestinian people for too many decades to count. What Rachel Corrie's work in Gaza recognized, however, was precisely the gravity and the density of the living history of the Palestinian people as a national community, not merely as a collection of deprived refugees. That is what she was in solidarity with. And we need to remember that that kind of solidarity is no longer confined to a small number of intrepid souls here and there but is recognized the world over. In the past six months I have lectured on four continents to many thousands of people. What brings them together is Palestine and the struggle of the Palestinian people, which is now a byword for emancipation and enlightenment, regardless of all the vilification heaped on them by their enemies.

Whenever the facts are made known, there is immediate recognition and an expression of the most profound solidarity with the justice of the Palestinian cause and the valiant struggle by the Palestinian people on its behalf. It is an extraordinary thing that Palestine was a central issue this year both during the Pôrto Alegre antiglobalization meetings and during the Davos and Amman meetings, both poles of the worldwide political spectrum. Just because our fellow citizens in the United States are fed an atrociously biased diet of ignorance and misrepresentation by the media—the occupation is never referred to in lurid descriptions of suicide attacks, the apartheid wall twenty-five feet high, five feet thick, and 350 kilometers long that Israel is building is never even shown on CNN or the networks (or is so much as referred to in passing throughout the lifeless prose of the road map), and the crimes of war, the gratuitous destruction and humiliation, maiming, house demolitions, agricultural destruction, and death imposed on Palestinian civilians are never shown for the daily, completely routine ordeal that they are—one shouldn't be surprised that Americans in the main have a very low opinion of Arabs and Palestinians. After all, please remember that all the main organs of the establishment media, from left liberal all the way over to fringe right, are unanimously anti-Arab, anti-Muslim, and anti-Palestinian. Look at the pusillanimity of the media during the buildup to an illegal and unjust war against Iraq, and look at how little coverage there was of the immense damage against Iraqi society done by the sanctions, and how relatively few accounts there were of the immense worldwide outpouring of opinion against the war. Hardly a single journalist except Helen Thomas has taken the administration to task for the outrageous lies and confected "facts" that were spun out about Iraq as an imminent military threat to the United States before the war, just as now the same government propagandists, whose cynically invented and manipulated "facts" about WMD are now more or less forgotten or shrugged off as irrelevant, are let off the hook by media heavies in discussing the awful, the literally inexcusable, situation for the people of Iraq that the United States has now single-handedly and irresponsibly created there. However else one blames Saddam Hussein as a vicious tyrant, which he was, he provided the people of Iraq with the best infrastructure of services like water, electricity, health, and education of any Arab country. None of this is any longer in place.

It is no wonder, then—with the extraordinary fear of seeming anti-Semitic by criticizing Israel for its daily crimes of war against innocent unarmed Palestinian civilians or criticizing the U.S. government and being called "anti-American" for its illegal war and its dreadfully run military occupation—that the vicious media and government campaign against Arab society, culture, history, and mentality that has been led by Neanderthal publicists and Orientalists like Bernard Lewis and Daniel Pipes has cowed far too many of us into believing that Arabs really are an underdeveloped, incompetent, and doomed people, and that with all the failures in democracy and development, Arabs are alone in this world in being retarded, behind the times, unmodernized, and deeply reactionary. Here is where dignity and critical historical thinking must be mobilized to see what is what and to disentangle truth from propaganda.

No one would deny that most Arab countries today are ruled by unpopular regimes and that vast numbers of poor, disadvantaged young Arabs are exposed to ruthless forms of fundamentalist religion. Yet it is simply a lie to say, as the *New York Times* regularly does, that Arab societies are totally controlled, and that there is no freedom of opinion, that there are no civil institutions, no functioning social movements for and by the people. Press laws notwithstanding, you can go to downtown Amman today and buy a Communist Party newspaper as well as an Islamist one; Egypt and Lebanon are full of papers and journals that suggest much more debate and discussion than these societies are given credit for; the satellite channels are bursting with diverse opinions in a dizzying variety; civil institutions are, on many levels having to do with social services, human rights, syndicates, and research institutes, very lively all over the Arab world. A great deal more must be done before we have the appropriate level of democracy, but we are on the way.

In Palestine alone there are more than a thousand NGOs, and it is this vitality and this kind of activity that has kept society going, despite every American and Israeli effort made to vilify, stop, or mutilate it on a daily basis. Under the worst possible circumstances, Palestinian society has neither been defeated nor crumbled completely. Kids still go to school, doctors and nurses still take care of their patients, men and women go to work, organizations have their meetings, and people continue to live, which seems to be an offense to Sharon and the other extremists who simply want Palestinians either imprisoned or driven away altogether. The military solution hasn't worked at all and never will work. Why is that so hard for Israelis to see? We must help them to understand this, not by suicide bombs but by rational argument, mass civil disobedience, and organized protest, here and everywhere.

The point I am trying to make is that we have to see the Arab world generally and Palestine in particular in more comparative and critical ways than superficial and dismissive books like Lewis's *What Went Wrong?* and Paul Wolfowitz's ignorant statements about bringing democracy to the Arab and Islamic world even begin to suggest. Whatever else is true about the Arabs, there is an active dynamic at work because as real people they live in a real society with all sorts of currents and crosscurrents that can't be easily caricatured as just one seething mass of violent fanaticism. The Palestinian struggle for justice is especially something with which one expresses solidarity rather than endless criticism, exasperated, frustrating discouragement, and crippling divisiveness. Remember the solidarity here and everywhere in Latin America, Africa, Europe, Asia, and Australia, and remember also that there is a cause to which many people have committed themselves, difficulties and terrible obstacles notwithstanding. Why? Because it is a just cause, a noble ideal, a moral quest for equality and human rights.

I want now to speak about dignity, which of course has a special place in every culture known to historians, anthropologists, sociologists, and humanists. I shall begin by saying immediately that it is a radically wrong Orientalist and indeed racist proposition to accept that, unlike Europeans and Americans, Arabs have no sense of individuality, no regard for individual life, no values that express love, intimacy, and understanding, which are supposed to be the property exclusively of cultures such as those of Europe and America, which had a Renaissance, a Reformation, and an Enlightenment. Among many others, it is the vulgar and jejune Thomas Friedman who has been peddling this rubbish, which has, alas, been picked up by equally ignorant and self-deceiving Arab intellectuals—I don't need to mention any names here—who have seen in the atrocities of 9/11 a sign that the Arab and Islamic worlds are somehow more diseased and more dysfunctional than any other, and that terrorism is a sign of a wider distortion than has occurred in any other culture.

We can leave to one side that, between them, Europe and the United States account for by far the largest number of violent deaths during the twentieth century, the Islamic world hardly a fraction of it. And behind all of that specious, unscientific nonsense about wrong and right civilizations is the grotesque shadow of the great false prophet Samuel Huntington, who has led a lot of people to believe that the world can be divided into distinct civilizations battling against each other forever. On the contrary, Huntington is dead wrong on every point he makes. No culture or civilization exists by itself; none is made up of things like individuality and enlightenment that are completely exclusive to it; and none exists without the basic human attributes of community, love, value for life, and all the others. To suggest otherwise, as he does, is the purest invidious racism of the same stripe as people who argue that Africans have naturally inferior brains, or that Asians are really born for servitude, or that Europeans are a naturally superior race. This is a sort of parody of Hitlerian science directed uniquely today against Arabs and Muslims, and we must be very firm so as not even to go through the motions of arguing against it. It is the purest drivel. On the other hand, there is the much more credible and serious stipulation that, like every other instance of humanity, Arab and Muslim life has an inherent value and dignity, which are expressed by Arabs and Muslims in their unique cultural style, and those expressions needn't resemble or be a copy of one approved model suitable for everyone to follow.

The whole point about human diversity is that it is in the end a form of deep coexistence between very different styles of individuality and experience that can't all be reduced to one superior form: this is the spurious argument foisted on us by pundits who bewail the lack of development and knowledge in the Arab world. All one has to do is to look at the huge variety of literature, cinema, theater, painting, music, and popular culture produced by and for Arabs from Morocco to the Gulf. Surely that needs to be assessed as an indication of whether Arabs are developed, and not just how on any given day statistical tables of industrial production either indicate an appropriate level of development or show failure.

The more important point I want to make, though, is that there is a very wide discrepancy today between our cultures and societies and the small group of people who now rule these societies. Rarely in history has such power been so concentrated in so tiny a group as the various kings, generals, sultans, and presidents who preside today over the Arabs. The worst thing about them as a group, almost without exception, is that they do not represent the best of their people. This is not just a matter of the absence of democracy. It is that they seem to radically underestimate themselves and their people in ways that close them off, that make them intolerant and fearful of change, frightened of opening up their societies to their people, terrified most of all that they might anger big brother, that is, the United States. Instead of seeing their citizens as the potential wealth of the nation, they regard them all as guilty conspirators vying for the ruler's power.

This is the real failure, how during the terrible war against the Iraqi people, no Arab leader had the self-dignity and confidence to say something about the pillaging and military occupation of one of the most important Arab countries. Fine, it is an excellent thing that Saddam Hussein's appalling regime is no more, but who appointed the United States to be the Arab mentor? Who asked the United States to take over the Arab world allegedly on behalf of its citizens and bring it something called "democracy," especially at a time when the school system, the health care system, and the whole economy in America are degenerating into the worst levels since the 1929 Depression? Why was the collective Arab voice *not* raised against the flagrantly illegal U.S. intervention, which did so much harm and inflicted so much humiliation upon the entire Arab nation? This is truly a colossal failure in nerve, in dignity, in self-solidarity.

With all the Bush administration's talk about guidance from the Almighty, doesn't one Arab leader have the courage just to say that, as a great people, we are guided by our own lights and traditions and religion? But nothing, not a word, as the poor citizens of Iraq live through the most terrible ordeals and the rest of the region quakes in its collective boots, each one petrified that his country may be next. How unfortunate the embrace of George W. Bush, the man whose war destroyed an Arab country gratuitously, by the combined leadership of the major Arab countries last week. Was there no one there who had the guts to remind George W. what he has done to humiliate and bring more suffering to the Arab people than anyone before him, and must he always be greeted with hugs, smiles, kisses, and low bows? Where is the diplomatic and political and economic support necessary to sustain an antioccupation movement on the West Bank and Gaza? Instead all one hears is that foreign ministers preach to the Palestinians to mind their ways, avoid violence, and keep at the peace negotiations, even though it has been so obvious that Sharon's interest in peace is just about zero. There has been no concerted Arab response to the separation wall, or to the assassinations, or to collective punishment, only a bunch of tired clichés repeating the well-worn formulas authorized by the State Department.

Perhaps the one thing that strikes me as the low point in Arab inability to grasp the dignity of the Palestinian cause is expressed by the current state of the Palestinian Authority. Abu Mazen, a subordinate figure with little political support among his own people, was picked for the job by Arafat, Israel, and the United States precisely because he has no constituency, because he is not an orator or a great organizer or anything really except a dutiful aide to Yasir Arafat, and because, I am afraid, they see in him a man who will do Israel's bidding. But how could even Abu Mazen stand there in Aqaba to pronounce words written for him, like a ventriloquist's puppet, by some State Department functionary, in which he commendably speaks about Jewish suffering but then amazingly says next to nothing about his own people's suffering at the hands of Israel? How could he accept so undignified and manipulated a role for himself, and how could he forget his self-dignity as the representative of a people that has been fighting heroically for its rights for over a century, just because the United States and Israel have told him he must? And when

Israel simply says that there will be a "provisional" Palestinian state, without any contrition for the horrendous amount of damage it has done, the uncountable war crimes, the sheer sadistic, systematic humiliation of every single Palestinian, man, woman, and child, I must confess to a complete lack of understanding as to why a leader or representative of that long-suffering people doesn't so much as take note of it. Has he entirely lost his sense of dignity?

Has he forgotten that he is not just an individual but also the bearer of his people's fate at an especially crucial moment? Is there anyone who was not bitterly disappointed at this total failure to rise to the occasion and stand with dignity—the dignity of his people's experience and cause—and testify to it with pride, without compromise, without ambiguity, without the half-embarrassed, half-apologetic tone that Palestinian leaders take when they are begging for a little kindness from some totally unworthy white father?

But that has been the behavior of Palestinian rulers since Oslo and indeed since Haj Amin, a combination of misplaced juvenile defiance and plaintive supplication. Why on earth do they always think it absolutely necessary to read scripts written for them by their enemies? The basic dignity of our life as Arabs in Palestine, throughout the Arab world, and here in America, is that we are our own people, with a heritage, a history, a tradition, and above all a language that is more than adequate to the task of representing our real aspirations, since those aspirations derive from the experience of dispossession and suffering that has been imposed on each Palestinian since 1948. Not one of our political spokespeople—the same is true of the Arabs since Abdel Nasser's time—ever speaks with self-respect and dignity of what we are, what we want, what we have done, and where we want to go.

Slowly, however, the situation is changing, and the old regime, made up of the Abu Mazens and Abu Ammars [Arafats] of this world, is passing and will gradually be replaced by a new set of emerging leaders all over the Arab world. The most promising is made up of the members of the Palestinian National Initiative; they are grassroots activists whose main activity is not pushing papers on a desk, or juggling bank accounts, or looking for journalists to pay attention to them, but who come from the ranks of the professionals, the working classes, the young intellectuals and activists, the teachers, doctors, lawyers—working people who have kept society going while also fending off daily Israeli attacks. Second, these are people committed to the kind of democracy and popular participation undreamed of by the Authority, whose idea of democracy is stability and security for itself. Lastly, they offer social services to the unemployed, health care to the uninsured and the poor, and proper secular education to a new generation of Palestinians who must be taught the realities of the modern world, not just the extraordinary worth of the old one. For such programs, the PNI stipulates that getting rid of the occupation is the only way forward and that in order to do that, a representative national unified leadership must be elected freely to replace the cronies, the outdated, and the ineffectiveness that have plagued Palestinian leaders for the past century.

Only if we respect ourselves as Arabs and Americans and understand the true dignity and justice of our struggle, only then can we appreciate why, almost despite ourselves, so many people all over the world, including Rachel Corrie and the two young people wounded with her from the International Solidarity Movement, Tom Hurndall and Brian Avery, have felt it possible to express their solidarity with us.

I conclude with one last irony. Isn't it astonishing that all the signs of popular solidarity that Palestine and the Arabs receive occur with no comparable sign of solidarity and dignity from ourselves—that others admire and respect us more than we do ourselves? Isn't it time we caught up with our own status and made certain that our representatives here and elsewhere realize, as a first step, that they are fighting for a just and noble cause, and that they have nothing to apologize for or be embarrassed about? On the contrary, they should be proud of what their people have done and proud also to represent them.

Al-Ahram, June 26–July 2, 2003
Al-Hayat, July 2, 2003

AFTERWORD

In rereading this collection of the last of my father's political essays, I am moved by the passion and commitment of his message, which is rooted firmly in the secular humanism he tirelessly espoused. His analyses leave the reader with the deep impression that he/she is dealing with a massive moral force who cannot simply have left us, just like that. Amazingly, my father would ask for my opinion upon the publication of each essay that makes up this volume, and I would be honored and flattered each time that he did. Of course, his work involved soliciting many opinions, which more often than not he valued greatly, but he never wavered in his core beliefs, one of which is the key theme in this book: that Palestinians are entitled to the same rights as any other people, and that nothing in the historical record could negate such a self-evident position. The principle of equality that he championed also applies uniformly in the rest of the Arab world, where autocracy, stagnation, and corruption disempower and disenfranchise its people day after day.

These works stand as a testament to an individual dedicated to documenting what was happening to the people of the world from which he came with a kind of eloquence and style rarely matched by the modern political commentator. My father brought to his writing a lifetime of erudition on topics as varied as literary criticism, opera, history, and, of course, politics. I felt sufficiently intimidated by the strength and power of his political writing not to consider making my own contribution to documenting the plight of the Palestinians, at least with the same rigor and consistency. He would not have been happy to hear me express such reservations, given that these pages are filled with exhortations to speak out and regain the moral high ground from the vast propaganda machines that have distorted the true picture of life in Palestine and the rest of the Arab world. It was perhaps this sentiment that held me back from writing about the experience of my wife and I being denied entry to the West Bank by Israeli border control officers in June 2003. Upon arrival at the border crossing terminal, we were separated and searched thoroughly, with me being subjected to the singular indignity of a four-hour interrogation and detention by a Shin Bet officer, who, as per the routine, photocopied and reviewed the contents of my wallet and passport, all in the name of "security." This treatment came behind locked doors with armed guards hovering around me, all the while my wife waited in a separate area of the border terminal without any information on my plight or well-being forthcoming. While our treatment was nothing compared to what many Palestinians endure, my father considered it to be of significance and urged me to document it in as public a manner as possible. While I pledged to my father that I would write about this experience, it is only after his death that I am able to fulfill my promise to him.

My father was, I think, the one prominent Palestinian who did not believe, as David Hirst writes, that the Palestinians are "doomed, through their own shortcomings as well as their enemy's superiority, always to lose, and subconsciously seem to know it."* He constantly strove to underscore that as a people, we were capable of much more than our leaders and the rest of the world supposed, and took heart from the tremendous courage the Palestinians themselves displayed and continue to display. As is evident from these pages, my father's two trips to South Africa, in 1991 and 2001, had a profound effect on how he felt the struggle should proceed. A serious public information campaign in the United States, Europe, Asia, Africa and, crucially, Israel, coupled with a program of mass civil disobedience in Palestine itself, were the only real methods to end the Israeli occupation and bring about a just solution to the conflict. The South African model, daring and unique as it was in the history of anti-colonialism movements, provided the way forward for Palestinians. Not that the leadership or the elite wanted to hear it, preferring instead to engage in secret negotiations and bandy about even the most basic and sacred of rights as bargaining chips. It therefore struck me as odd, even somewhat improper, that so many members of Palestinian and Arab officialdom came to pay their respects to our family upon my

---

*David Hirst, *The Gun and the Olive Branch: The Roots of Violence in the Middle East*, 3rd ed. (New York: Nation Books, 2003), p. 201.

father's passing. Perhaps they did not hear what he had to say about them, or just refused to listen and merely celebrated the fact that he was a "great figure."

But while the Palestinian and Arab leadership and intelligentsia have always been afflicted with the sense that they are fated to lose, and behaved accordingly, the people themselves do not suffer from such infirmities. It was that belief that impelled my father to write and speak as he did. I must confess that I was not always convinced in the viability of the South African model and did not think that we could really address and engage the Israeli people, who seemed to rely on impenetrable notions of both victimhood and superiority in dealing with us on all levels. "But Wadie," he would say, "has it ever been done before? Have we ever made an attempt to engage them and let them know that our dispossession was a result of their conquest?" His vision was one of two peoples living in one state, as there could be no military solution. In my father's view, however, the conflict could never be resolved through secret negotiations and backroom deals that depended solely on the generosity and goodwill of the stronger party, to wit, the Israelis. That is why I have no hesitation in saying that he would have denounced the so-called Geneva Accords, the Ayalon-Nusseibeh plan, or whatever type of secret and slapdash agreement that Palestinian elites reached with an Israeli counterpart without consulting the people beforehand.

It was not as if my father reveled in being a great sage and predicting the failure of the Oslo Accords and the self-styled "peace process." He was as brokenhearted as the rest of us that the Palestinians' lot continued to deteriorate. While many people remarked to me that they enjoyed his writing, they did not see in it much of a blueprint for the future in what he said. Of course they were simply incorrect. My father did have an idea for resolving the conflict, but both the Palestinians and Israelis did not want to submit to the reality that such a solution would require a great deal of time and effort, and ultimately demand of all parties involved that they reconcile themselves to the presence of the other. I often wanted to ask him why he did not attempt to lead the movement he envisioned, since he struck me as the one person who was capable of engendering the requisite support in many diverse circles the world over. The reason for my hesitation was that his illness, which ultimately did him in, did not allow him physically to play the role of a full-time political activist and leader, and I knew that to ask was to risk bringing him down, though momentarily. While he only writes about his illness intermittently and sparingly in this book, the sense of urgency that it generated clearly informed and instructed his message.

While the loss of my father's voice and presence is still too much to bear, even now, his writings remain as a testament to the historic victory that an oppressed people might achieve. The amazing memory that I am left with is his dedication to the idea of speaking out and staying informed, no matter how sick or infirm he was. During our innumerable trips to the hospital in his last few days, when he was too weak and tired to do it himself, he would sometimes ask me to read him the paper, patiently listening to my hasty and unsolicited editorializing. Indeed, it still pains me to remember that in his last full day of consciousness and alertness, prior to succumbing to his illness, my father was overcome by emotion because he felt that he had not done enough for the Palestinians. All present at this extraordinary scene were dumbfounded: if Edward Said had not done enough for Palestine, then what have we done? That will have to be answered by the present and coming generations, but our overwhelming sense of loss is matched by our immense affection and gratitude for his trailblazing example.

Wadie E. Said
March 2004

Index

A Note on the Author

Edward W. Said was University Professor of English and Comparative Literature at Columbia University. He was the author of more than twenty books, including *Orientalism* and *Culture and Imperialism,* and his essays and reviews appeared in newspapers and periodicals throughout the world. Edward Said died in September 2003.